7
UNIC🦄RN
DRIVE

BY DANI POLAJNAR

FROM STARTUP TO A BILLION DOLLAR SALE IN 7 YEARS

THE ADVENTURE OF IZA AND SAMO LOGIN

LOGIN5 APHRODITE

7 Unicorn Drive
From Startup to a Billion Dollar Sale in 7 Years
- The Adventure of Iza and Samo Login

Author: Dani Polajnar
Translation: Noah Charney
Proofreading: Josh Rocchio
Graphic Design: Rdeča Oranža d.o.o.
Unicorn Design: Andrii Kravchenko
Publisher: Login5 Aphrodite Limited

—————————————∞

ISBN 978-9925-7731-3-8

—————————————∞

Table
of Contents

7 UNICORN DRIVE

Part One

CHAPTER ONE

Farewell to the Penguins

Deception Island, Antarctica, 11 January 2017

"Five billion," she thought. "Five freakin' billion..."

"Three...two...one...go!" The command echoed throughout the space, bouncing from wall to wall. From the darkness a silver, remote-controlled airship emerged, gliding several meters off the ground and just above the participants' heads. Drums thrummed as it pushed aside the thick fog and flew towards the enormous animated target on the jumbo LCD screen that hung from the ceiling of the sports arena. The balloon, a five-meter-long zeppelin shaped like a cigar, was bound straight for the bullseye. Any second now it would crash into the screen and the liquid crystals within would tumble down like snow upon the enthusiastic crowd, necks craned in rapt attention. When the tip of the airship touched the target on the screen, it did indeed explode, but only into an animation of shards of splintering glass. The onlookers applauded as five animated animals emerged from behind the "shattered" glass: three kittens and two dogs. Below them, a caption on the screen read "5,000,000,000 downloads of Talking Tom & Friends apps!"

The emotion in the room swept from face to face in a tangible wave, as the two hundred participants greeted the news about this latest milestone. The drumming from an ensemble in military uniforms, headphones over their ears, increased, as they pounded away in a heartbeat crescendo, shaking the room with the reverberation of the powerful sound system. Colored lights flashed and spun through the man-made fog, deepening the club-like euphoria inside the arena. The New Year's team-building event had reached its peak.

A door burst open and in rolled a cart carrying a colossal cake, to which an airship made of sugar was harnessed. Seven bubbling volcanoes surrounded it, shining lava-like light on the number five billion, written out in sugar.

Samo looked over at Iza, who smiled and bathed in the positive vibes that emanated through the arena. Even he had to admit that he was satisfied. Standing side by side, as they always had, they looked out over the fiery cake, which was slowly wheeled towards them, their colleagues on the arena floor parting like the Red Sea before it.

Iza picked up the microphone awkwardly. The lights stopped spinning. The drums went silent.

"This is for you, dear colleagues. We reached one heck of a milestone and today's team building is a celebration of our success. Today you split up into mixed teams and built thirty aircraft. We raced them in this arena and the winner revealed this astounding number of downloads of our apps. This is a testament to teamwork at the highest possible level. It's what we saw every day in our office this year. We know very well that this sort of success doesn't just happen on its own. It wasn't easy, but it was great fun. Teamwork. Have fun. No limits. Three of our core values that have proven to be alive and well this year. Bravo. Well done, all of you. You are the very best. We look forward to more of the same!"

The drums resumed, the lights shifted, cutting lasers through the fog, while the volcanoes began to dim their glow. Iza and Samo took a single long knife in their joined hands and gently cut the first slice of the monolithic vegan strawberry cake, offering it to their closest colleague. The MC took up the mic and shouted, "Let the party begin!"

Iza turned towards Samo and whispered in his ear, "You know that this is probably our last team-building event with them, right?"

He nodded. She couldn't hear his reply through the cascade of music and cacophony of exuberant voices. With mixed emotions, she looked at the cake before her. The picture in her mind's eye blurred. The cake's creamy topping slowly morphed into ice. The fog in the arena melted into steam from the heater in the cozy, elegant shipboard cabin. Iza shook herself out of her reverie, the daydream memory of that last team-building event.

She was staring at a glacier, a half-smile on her face. She blinked in the dazzling daylight of the sun reflecting off the mirrors of ice there, in Antarctica. That had been an incredible time in their lives. Iza sipped her steaming cup of green tea and slowly turned her gaze away from the glacier, with its endless ramparts of ice. She adjusted her large ring with its turquoise stone and crossed the lavishly furnished cabin to Samo, who was adjusting a giant lens on his camera.

"We did a lot, Samo. We really did. We focused wholly on our goals and our hard work paid off."

"Yes," he replied. "But this is just the beginning. The whole odyssey to date has just been the first step on our path. Now we can really spark some positive change. Look at these palaces of ice outside. If we don't get to work, if we don't continue on to the next step of our plan the right way, and soon, then this may be the last time we see all of this. Our planet's years are numbered. But we can do our part to fight against that..."

Iza nodded and looked again out at the horizon. A flat sheet of ice, white and smooth like bed linen, stretched out before her. A colony of gentoo penguins sat quietly upon it.

"Do you think we could've done all this if we hadn't been so connected, the two of us as a couple? If we hadn't been so demanding of ourselves? And so humble before the Universe?"

"I don't know. It was probably all those things together that made it work. That will continue to make it work. Above all, our basic intentions were good. They still are. Now's the time to start implementing everything we've been planning for so long."

He zipped up his red down jacket, picked up a tripod, and opened the cabin door. "I'm going outside for a bit. I'll try to get some photos of these penguins. While they're still around..."

The door slammed shut behind him. Iza continued to stare. "Everything we went through to get here," she thought, "and everything that awaits us."

The silent penguins slowly turned their heads to stare at the blue and white ship as it sailed past their receding home. Just as the ship slipped out of sight, the penguins began to squawk and shake their wings, as if waving goodbye, or perhaps in a hopeful gesture not to forget them.

Samo and Iza would not.

CHAPTER TWO

Birth of the Unicorn

Ljubljana, Slovenia, 14 July 2009

"100 million in profit? In five years? You've gotta be kidding." Andrej tilted his head, scanning Samo's face for sarcasm.

"I'm perfectly serious," Samo replied. "100 million. After taxes." He let this sink in for a few seconds, before adding, "and we can do it with this team. With all of you seated with me at this table. That's why I wanted each and every one of you. Now, are you ready for the master plan?"

About an hour earlier, they'd arrived at an old restaurant just outside the city center. Three young men, all coworkers at an IT firm, Delta Search, were waiting impatiently. They'd driven together from work, leaving early, to be sure they wouldn't be late for the meeting. The sun felt good on their faces. While their "uniforms" were similar – sneakers, shorts, and colorful t-shirts – their thoughts drifted in different directions. None really knew what to expect, but the general vibe in the air was that, whatever was going down, it was going to be new and exciting, even if almost certainly exhausting.

Luka wiggled and fiddled, thinking ahead to the meeting, and complained, "How could Samo have chosen this old clunker of a restaurant for such an important meeting? We should've met somewhere in the city center..."

Andrej smiled. "Feeling nervous, are we? You know Samo. Why go all the way downtown when there's a restaurant so close? It has chairs, it has beer. What else do you need? It's not like we're attending a wedding."

"Totally," Peter added, flicking his old chewing gum into the trashcan and checking his watch. "It's already ten past five. They should be here by now."

These three comprised just half of the team that Samo had invited as elite members of whatever the heck his new project was. Samo had sold his ownership share in Delta Search and knew he wouldn't be lingering there much longer. Some force within him was pushing him onward. So he'd chosen the best among his colleagues and asked them to this meeting, to see if they were up for a change and up for a challenge that would probe the boundaries of the possible. He believed in his vision wholly. It wasn't exactly clear to him, well, what this new enterprise was going to do and how. He just knew he had to do it. And he knew why.

Samo had taken his time watching his coworkers at the office as they went about their tasks. He watched them bite into complex computer problems, some working late into the evening, on weekends, and even during vacations. Whatever was necessary. They were committed to their projects and work was an important part of their lives. He was no psychologist, but he knew the profile he was looking for. Of course, his teammates had to excel in software application development, problem solving, and product management. That was a given. But the most important characteristic for him was passion and commitment to work. People who, once they believed in an idea, would know how to glean the most out of it. But a good team had to be balanced, stocked with the right sort of energy and complementary skills. Many of his coworkers excelled at the software side of the things, but their passion was lacking. That's what he was looking for. He needed people in whom he believed. Which led to six very different characters making the list.

When he'd drawn up the final cut, a week ago, he'd invited them each, one at a time, for a brief chat, introducing them to the basic framework of this new business venture of his. They knew Samo as a man of above-average capabilities and an incredibly analytical mind. He'd shown this many a time. From his first day at Delta Search, he'd performed all that was asked of him quickly, accurately, and with aplomb. He'd climbed the rungs of the career ladder quickly and became first the head of R&D, then a partner in the firm. Whatever task was set before him, he dove into it, studying it to the last detail, whether at work or during his free hours at home. He was a ninja of task and time organization, and anything he tackled would be completed with results that exceeded expectations.

And so it was with the first steps of this, his new project. Though no one else had been aware, for weeks now he'd been covertly testing his colleagues' competencies and dedication, until he focused in on his foreseen dream team. While he honed in on the Final Six, in the evenings at home he mapped out a plan for the initial investment capital, which he'd raise through the sale of his share in Delta Search. His particular interest was in the potential of the mobile app market. It seemed ripe with opportunity, the ideal focus for his new company.

Samo had a way of focusing that was almost preternatural, like the best strikers in soccer – eyes on the goal – and no detail would escape his notice on his path to it. His mind seemed to take routes that simply didn't occur to others. When he saw a pile of puzzle pieces, he often put them together into something new and unique. Though soft-spoken, he had that rare charisma of absolute confidence. His six chosen teammates knew this and so they required no convincing to sign on to whatever he envisioned. "If Samo thinks this will work," they'd each thought to themselves, and then articulated when they got together, "then it'll work. Whatever the heck it is." Each of them agreed to his proposal individually, but this would be their first meeting as a group.

Now, a week later, at this old restaurant not quite in the city center, a few minutes past five in the afternoon.

Andrej, Luka, and Peter stood, stretched, and walked towards the restaurant's entrance, but were stopped by the leonine roar of a sports car as it rounded the bend, then slowly pulled up in front of them. It was a brand new, dark green Lotus Elise.

Out stepped Samo. "What's happening, boys?" He greeted them with a half-smile and adjusted his sunglasses.

The three colleagues were stunned and just stood there, glued to the spot.

"Where," began Peter, eyeing the car, "did you get that?"

He swung his Delta Search name tag, which dangled off of a blue lanyard, over his shoulder so that he could lean down to get a good look at the car's dashboard. Peter wasn't sure what to look for in admiring this work of art on wheels. He didn't even have a driver's license, much less a car.

"A going-away present to myself," Samo replied, adjusting the waistband of his worn-out jeans. Samo was already successful enough, sure, but what surprised his colleagues was that he would indulge himself like this. A few years ago, he'd been driving an old Fiat Punto. When Samo went to the supermarket with his wife, he'd buy only the bare essentials. When he treated himself to something, it was usually because his wife insisted he do so. The guys didn't look at this purchase with envy, because they felt it was about time that he treated himself to something nice. Something that would feed his soul. It signaled to them that he was ready to be the front man in this new venture, and only solidified their decision to step with him into an uncertain future.

"My wife's been saying for ages that you should treat yourself to a gift to signify all your victories. Small or large, as long as it means something to you. We should know how to reward ourselves. The sale of my stake in Delta Search marks a small victory, a step towards much greater ones. She insisted. So, I bought this."

Luka, eyes wide, opened the door and sat enthusiastically behind the wheel. "Good thing you're so slim and short, I can barely fit in here."

Samo smiled and scratched his thick, dark brown hair. "Yeah, but those qualities don't help me on the basketball court. Everything is good for something." He tapped his stomach. "And my gut isn't too big to fit behind the steering wheel. At least not this week." He was 38 and his belly was slowly filling out his blue polo shirt.

While they were admiring the car, the other three team members arrived directly from Delta Search, followed by Iza, Samo's wife. She was going to be in charge of shared services and administration for their new endeavor. Of the whole group, she was the only one not previously employed at Delta Search, as she had run her own consulting company.

"Sorry I'm a little late. An important meeting dragged on."

Iza often said that she already had her dream job. That's why she didn't want to commit to this new startup full-time, but would be in for only a couple hours a day. She was only doing it because she knew why Samo had wanted to take on such a project. If it had just been about business and money, she surely wouldn't have gotten involved.

They entered the restaurant, walking beneath a wooden trellis, past the yellow façade and out into a garden terrace, which was decorated with wooden barrels and small cypresses. The summer heat wove around the dirty canvas umbrella above their table, round and metallic, covered with a white linen tablecloth, as the eight of them sat together for the first time. The scent of a deep fryer wafted over, and they couldn't help feeling a bit of tension and anticipation, cut comically by the polka music that spun from an invisible radio.

Seeking to break the ice, Iza spoke first. "So, how's everyone doing? Busy day at the office?"

Vague but affirmative murmurs followed. It was a table full of introverts who weren't exactly experts at mindless chit chat, but that wasn't why they were here. They wanted to cut to the chase. Samo leaned forward.

"Right, guys. I've already briefly presented my idea to you. Today I'd like to discuss it in more detail. The bottom line is..."

"What'll it be, fellas?" A waiter interrupted to take their drink orders. Samo turned to look at him. Really? Right now? He'd been thinking for a week how to start this conversation, carefully crafting the first words of his speech, and...well, so much for the moment. He breathed deeply.

"A Guinness, please." The others chuckled at the scene, knowing how much it bothered Samo to be interrupted during something important. Iza laughed too. She thought about commenting, to tease her husband, but decided it was best to refrain, at least for now. They all ordered drinks. When the waiter retreated, Samo resumed.

"I wanted to say that it must be immediately clear to everyone that the essence of this project is not just about money. The point is why you want money. It's no secret that our planet is rushing towards an abyss with its current path of wanton CO_2 emissions, plastic and chemical pollution, dwindling sources of available drinking water...

Something will have to be done, otherwise the end of humanity as we know it could come during our lifetimes. It is my sincere wish to help shift things for the better. That's my personal mission. But it's difficult to bring about large-scale change without money. Lots of money. And so I'd like to make enough to make a difference. So much that we can really do something with it. I want to use this money to help get the planet back on the right track."

While this speech might have surprised a passer-by, those gathered already knew Samo's overall plan. They nodded quietly and, for the most part, agreed with him. It was obvious to everyone that the environmental issues were very serious, and the planet could not go on like this. But a noble ecological crusade was not sufficient to make everyone leave good jobs and leap with Samo into the unknown. They were interested in the shorter-term financial benefits, of course, but their interest was mostly in trying to achieve something completely new. As self-proclaimed geek programmers, they were drawn to the idea of elevating their craft beyond what had been done to date, of ploughing the furrow of the mobile app market and taking it to a new level. They all had the firm belief that Samo was blessed with a Midas touch – that everything he aimed his laser focus at would end up successful. Their belief in him was so strong that it superseded the immediate financial gains and the fact that, while they all felt that doing something for the planet was a good idea, none were passionate about it the way Samo and Iza were. The ability to, relatively quickly, amass enough of a fortune to really change the world for the better seemed rather far-fetched at that point, seated around a table beneath a dirty canvas umbrella, nursing a beer and waiting to be told what, exactly, this new venture would consist of.

Samo understood all this. He didn't need them to take on his personal worldview. He only needed the general acceptance of his team members, and their understanding of what he was in it for. The core values had to be shared. The rest was down to working together as a cooperative team with a passion for the project. Samo was certain that this team had all he could wish for. They'd already proven themselves on the battlefield, so to speak, at Delta Search.

"Our ultimate goal is very simple," he continued. "To set up a highly profitable, fast-growing company where we will do interesting things that offer us a good challenge. In my opinion, developing mobile apps is the way forward. What sort of apps, precisely, I don't know yet. But I do know this: we're going to make $100 million in profit in the next five years. But I also know this: after those five years, and a maximum of two additional years of earnout, we will sell the company or close it. That is all."

There was silence around the table for what felt like minutes. Then Andrej scratched his receding hairline and leaned in. "Do you really think that's possible?" Tomi and Patrik had the same questions on the tip of their tongues, and so they nodded along with Andrej, waiting for the reply.

"Of course," Samo replied, now deadly serious. "100 million. In the mobile app industry, it's possible. But no harm done if we earn even more. Maybe we'll even wind up as a unicorn? Why shouldn't we?" He smiled slyly. "Each of you invests an initial share of startup capital, Iza and I will cover the rest."

More silence followed. Most of the guys around the table dropped their gazes to the floor and suddenly became very interested in how the garden terrace was paved. But Iza kept her eyes glued on their faces, studying them intently. She didn't really know them, and she was trying to analyze whether these were the faces of a team that could achieve their shoot-for-the-stars ambitions. She believed in Samo whole-heartedly, of course. But these boys? She hoped they were the real deal, but she imagined they would need a good deal of mentoring and firm leadership.

"So, what do you say?" she finally said, shattering the awkward silence.

Frenk jumped in. "Okay, it sounds great. Even if we fall short of 100 million. 1 million sounds pretty good, too." He was a junior developer at Delta Search, and his comments did not come without a splash of sarcasm. He was the most rational member of the team, the one who could be relied upon to pay closest attention to details. For instance, he was the only one at the meeting to have noticed that the collar of Samo's polo shirt was crumpled on one side. Apart from Iza, of course. For Frenk, every question had to have a clear answer.

"But," he continued, "how do you plan to pull it off? You surely don't expect us to leave perfectly good jobs and dive into a project without a good idea of what sort of waters we're jumping into? This is Slovenia, not Silicon Valley. We're not used to such fairy tales with quick, happy endings here on the sunny side of the Alps. That's the American dream."

Samo was calm in his reply, firm in his conviction. "We know what we're going to do. We know we'll be developing mobile apps. That, in my opinion, is our future. We know that this team has the highest potential. The market isn't fully saturated yet, and we will find the right niche. We must find the right niche in order to make a splash. I don't know yet exactly how and with what sort of an app. We have to comb for the right opportunity. But in the app world, it doesn't matter if you're in Silicon Valley in America or the Tuhinj Valley in Slovenia or in a crater on the Moon. Location is irrelevant to mindset. All you need are the right people and an internet connection. We have both."

He looked over at his wife, then continued. "Of course, we must have the Universe on our side, too. Iza will see to that."

Samo smiled, but Andrej rolled his eyes. He knew that the Logins were into energies and vibrations and star alignments and that sort of, as he considered it, "nonsense". But that didn't bother him. People could believe what they liked, he didn't care. He wasn't about to let it affect him, so he kept his head down and let New

Age talk float off into the ether. Everyone was entitled to their own opinion. At a dinner party not long before, the guests were making fun of alternative philosophies, and he'd mentioned that the Logins were way into such things. At the time he thought, in their defense, "So what?" The Logins were more successful than the rest of them and, who knew, maybe it didn't hurt to have the stars on your side, if you went in for that sort of stuff?

It was quiet again. Then Luka spoke. "Guys, I have something to share. Very recently I dreamed that this was going to happen. I had a dream that Samo stopped me in the office and asked me to join a new project. I dreamed that we sat here together, as in this exact restaurant, just as we're sitting here today. Really. I know it's weird, but I'm serious. So I know, for me, this is the right direction, and I'm all in. We just need to have the right collective energy and the stars will align."

Andrej rolled his eyes again and looked away. "Energy alone won't earn you 100 million," he thought to himself. He believed in Samo and his business sense. That had been proven time and again through scores of successful projects and big earnings. This idea felt underdeveloped and overly ambitious. 100 million profit in five years? And no specific plan? Really?

A heated debate erupted around the table over the next few minutes. It wasn't about vision and mission, but about how to map out the early days of the new business. The dialogue helped unify the team members and solidify their belief in its success. It was the definition of synergy. Those around the table might have varied beliefs, just as they had varied skill sets, but they were there to help each other and build a strong team upon each other's shoulders. That was the moment when all of them saw that, whether or not they made 100 million, this was a team that clicked.

They agreed to give their notices at Delta Search so that their final days working there would coincide as closely as possible to Samo's.

Since he had the highest position in the company, as Head of R&D, he also had the longest notice period. As per their contracts, each one had to complete their active tasks for their soon-to-be previous employer to the best of their abilities in order to make their departure as easy as possible. This way everyone would be ready to begin work at the new startup on 1 January 2010. So they still had some time.

Talk then shifted to stakes in the company. They sat at the table for hours, juggling ideas and arguments with constructive passion, dividing the stakes and roles in the new company according to abilities and seniority. Samo insisted on a majority ownership, because he wanted full control over the company. He also wanted to reserve 10% ownership for potential new employees, in the forecast event of success and rapid growth. That meant that the seven others around the table would receive shares between 2% and 16%.

The smallest shares went to Iza and Peter. Iza planned to work for the new company only at a quarter time, and Peter would work at half-time, as he had independent projects he wished to complete. The total initial capital was mapped out for the new company: 8000 dollars. This was the amount required by Slovenian law to start a new firm.

Peter shook his head. If they ever actually saw a profit of 100 million, then the few hundred dollars they were being asked to invest was microscopic. You'd think you'd need to invest millions to make 100 million. If he needed to, he'd borrow something from his parents. Even if the profit ended up "only" being 1 million, this was the deal of a lifetime.

The others had similar thoughts pinging around their heads. There was some uncertainty, a certain vagueness about the start of this enterprise. But the idea of something new and promising pushed them forward. Nothing ventured, nothing gained. What everyone responded to was the electricity in the air above their table, charged ions whizzing around throughout their dialogue. They could hardly wait to start working together.

Before go-time on January 1, they would meet regularly and share ideas, honing their plans. It was late evening by the time they stood up on aching legs, stretched, shook hands, and set out on their separate ways. The six teammates drove back to Delta Search – three in Tomi's car, three in Andrej's – to pick up their belongings, leaving Samo and Iza alone in the restaurant's parking lot. They stood beside their cars, bathed in the warm, orange light of a streetlamp.

"So...that's it?" Iza asked.

"Yup. That's it." Samo was visibly relieved. Iza smiled and blew him a kiss. She knew how important today's meeting had been to him. She watched him sit, contentedly, in his new Lotus and fasten his seatbelt. First goal? Achieved. "He'd assembled a good team," she thought, "and distributed shares in the company fairly, keeping enough for himself to be able to actualize his calling when the project turned successful." She had no doubt that it would. Their dreams of a better world.

He adjusted his rearview mirror, pressed the gas pedal, and pulled out of the parking lot onto the empty road home. Iza drove behind him in her red Alfa Romeo. They would follow each other anywhere and everywhere. Their dreams were shared, their life was shared. And they always would be.

CHAPTER THREE

A Day in the Bay

San Francisco, California, 15 May 2014

"Venti caramel macchiato, please," he said to the barista at the Starbucks across from his office, without looking up at her, as he was playing with the fastener on a green folder. "The name's…"

"I know," the barista interrupted playfully. "Danny Keaton. You order the same thing every morning. Then you sit in the corner and browse your phone. Did I get it right?"

"You got it, hon. Right as usual. Since my birthday party last week, I believe everything you say. Knowing your regular guests is why we regular guests like coming here."

"It works, yes. But just because you all like partying with me doesn't mean you all like me. So, you turned 26 last week. Wasn't exactly a lifetime ago. I certainly haven't forgotten the post-party hangover."

"Yeah, it was a pretty good time. But next time watch out. My Bay Area Biz colleagues can be sharks. Handsome young men. You got a glimpse of it last time. Watch your back when they're around!"

"Don't worry about me. I eat journalists like you for breakfast. You only talked about business stories the whole time. Honestly, I wouldn't give them the time of day." She winked and inflated a large, pink gum bubble in his direction.

"I'm no traditional journalist. I'm a copywriter. Well, officially a junior copywriter, but that'll change soon. You'll see."

"Yeah, you'll sure show me," she replied, smiling. "But first, show me $4.75."

He put a fiver down and left her the change. Then, as he did every morning, he sat in the chair in the corner that overlooked the busy street. Each day the same view, but it always differed. Like the old saying that you can never step in the same river twice. He liked going to the same spot. It gave him a sense of organization and goal-orientation. Every morning he said goodbye to his wife and drove his aging blue Mazda Miata to work. He parked in the same spot in front of the office building in downtown San Francisco. Always, he made sure that the distance between his front and rear bumpers and the cars around him was as close to equal as possible, short of using a ruler. But he also liked that the view out the window, while ostensibly of the same road, was always morphing. He was open to the changes that life might bring him. So long as the changes made rational sense, of course.

He was in casual Friday mode – worn jeans and a blue UC San Francisco hoodie, a relic of his MBA two years back – for his day at Bay Area Biz, the local newspaper for which he wrote a weekly column called "Best in Print". He sipped his coffee and toyed mindlessly with the friendship bracelet his wife, Nancy, had woven for his birthday.

He set his phone down, finished his coffee, waved to the barista, and stepped out into the warm breeze of the spring morning. He tucked the green folder under his arm and crossed the street, entering the glass building. Up in the elevator to the eleventh floor. The elevator stopped, dinged, and the doors opened onto the newspaper's editorial office, with a sweeping view of the bay in the background. The focal point of his office was a picture window behind a wide white desk. His bookshelves weighed down with blockbusters by Stephen Covey, Jim Collins, Simon Sinek, Patrick Lencioni, and other best-selling authors on business, leadership, entrepreneurship, and management. Business books were his work and his pastime. He gulped down stories on contemporary economics and recycled them, in abbreviated versions, in his newspaper articles. It was a niche specialty and he was good at it. "Fifty good columns a year," as he'd been repeatedly told by his editor-in-chief, Clyde Macmillan, at their weekly team meetings.

He lay the green folder on his desk, opened it, and removed a copy of his latest column, finished the night before. It followed the same formula: a summation of the best new business books on the American market, annotated with his comments on them. He sat heavily in his chair and swiveled it around to look out the window. But he looked past the view of the bay. Instead, in his mind's eye, he saw his future house, his daily daydream: a big one in Pacific Heights, a sailboat anchored out back and painted in Marina Green, both hosts to his carefree life with Nancy and the family they'd planned and planned and planned. Aside from Nancy, he didn't have any of it, not yet, anyway. But what he did have, as he always did, was a carefully orchestrated plan, which he kept in an app on his iPhone, and which he'd glance at several times a day, for reassurance and to keep his eyes on the prize.

"Where are you, Junior? We're waiting." A call from the editorial boardroom snapped him out of his reverie. He grabbed the folder and hurried across the hall.

"Here I am."

Every Friday at 9 am, when all the members of the press team met in the large corner boardroom overlooking Columbus Avenue, they'd run through the weekly plan. These meetings didn't take long and they centered on the newspaper's next steps. And every such meeting ended the same way. Clyde, in his sempiternal brown suit and a red tie, which was tied with too fat a knot, resulting in it riding way too high up his belly, would limp back and forth and up and down the boardroom, repeating each team member's personal annual goals, aloud, before everyone.

"Jim. Ten cover stories about IT blue chips. Shawn. Fifteen interviews with celebrities. Danny. Fifty good columns on business books." And so on. The veteran reporters rolled their eyes at this tradition, and Clyde saw this – he saw every detail in his domain – but he just smiled at them and added, "Gentlemen, you know what the most successful directors in the world say: the boss has to repeat key points, ad infinitum, to etch it all deeply into your little brains." With this, he would end the meeting, smile, and then limp his way over to his own office, leaving the door open. His co-workers would watch him talk on the phone with business partners for hours on end, still using a traditional desk phone with a corkscrew cord, tucked under his chin like a violin, while he wiggled in his swivel chair, looked at the sea through his window, and played with an hourglass that he kept on his desk.

They admired him, particularly his tidiness, which was not at all the cliché of a newspaper editor. The only messy bit was a pile of crumpled papers by the window – his failed "free throws" in the direction of his trash can.

His well-meaning leather chair creaked beneath his corpulence – at least thirty pounds overweight on a good day – but he didn't really mind. He was in his fifties and couldn't be bothered with such trivialities as physical health. Next to the computer on his desk, a small statue of a Navajo tribesman stood watch. It was a talisman for good luck that he'd brought from his home in New Mexico when he'd first moved to San Francisco as a journalism student, with just a suitcase and a whole lot of drive. Clyde was a wizened, seasoned, old-school journalist, a vastly experienced editor with good connections throughout the West Coast's business world. He was particularly tuned in to the tech companies in Palo Alto. This allowed him, and this newspaper, to be the first to report breaking news, which led to the paper selling like Caramel Macchiatos. He knew the juicy tales, too, of entrepreneurs' private lives, but he never went public with gossip. This meant he was trusted, and he also led by example. Danny appreciated this and him, both as a boss and as a good man. Clyde reciprocated, and worked with Danny more closely than with other members of his team, giving him a bit more leeway, and a modicum of paternal affection.

They often spoke about the modern business world and what the future might hold. Clyde was eternally optimistic. His enthusiasm and positive thinking were infectious, spreading across the office floor and lifting up even the most curmudgeonly of colleagues. That's why Danny so enjoyed his company. Positivity and a good, thoughtful debate brought out the best in him. Clyde was his ideal conversation partner. They had a lot in common, both workaholics, typing away well past seven in the evening, when the rest of the staff had long since left. During those quiet evening hours, they would look up from their respective offices, then adjourn to the building's terrace, where they'd enjoy a gin and tonic and chat for hours more, as the sun set over the bay, silhouetting the distant sailboats, as their debate ranged from politics and economics to history and the meaning of life, the universe, and everything. Danny wasn't much concerned with the way the world was headed. He honestly didn't give it much thought. But he drank in Clyde's words, whatever the topic, with business and money enlivening him the most. Neither of them was shy about sharing their opinions and they seemed so intellectually connected that a third party would have had trouble following their conversations. So, when colleagues spotted the two of them engrossed in these chats, they tended to avoid joining them. And that was fine for them both.

Danny had confided in Clyde, on several occasions, his life goal: to make it big as quickly as possible, which meant enough money that he could be carefree for the rest of his life. Clyde always rebutted that money wasn't everything, but this ricocheted right off Danny's ears. He was stubborn and determined that, one day, a lifetime opportunity would come knocking. Danny didn't fantasize about running a big company or getting lucky in the stock or crypto markets. His focus was on writing books of the sort he reviewed each week. The sort that bloomed with potential in the business world. But, in order to stand out, he knew very well from his own evaluations of what the book world was offering, he needed some unique hook. An unusual story that would catapult him into the stratosphere of business writing, opening the door up for big lecture tours and glowing write-ups from other journalists like him.

Chats with Clyde inevitably circled back to this same theme. He'd been on the lookout for just such a story ever since he'd joined the newspaper, two years back. He'd thought he'd found his white whale a few times, but larger newspapers or other writers had beaten him to the scoop, every time. Their connections to the big IT companies and startup accelerators trumped his own. Clyde tried to slip him a hint when he could, when his private contacts caught wind of something, but Danny had been too late every time so far. And so he dithered in his realm of book reviews and had yet to land the big, front-page feature story that could be developed into a best-selling book and make his name.

"I don't know, Clyde," Danny said on the terrace one late afternoon. "It seems to me that history keeps repeating itself. Every time I'm about to break a story, I read about it in another paper before I've finished the first full draft. I trawl the internet daily, but I haven't found any proper lead that someone else hasn't written about already. I'm not sure if I'm going about this the right way. Maybe I should be focusing elsewhere..."

"Don't worry, son," Clyde replied. "You're still young, with your whole career ahead of you. Keep your eyes peeled and you'll find it sooner or later. Maybe a different approach would be good? If you're always looking at the same sites and same forums, typing in the same keywords, asking the same people, then you can't expect anything other than what you've already found. Remember, if it's already online, then it means someone has already written about it. Try focusing on other things, asking other people. Open your mind. Step off the beaten paths and shift your current patterns, and you'll see what else opens up to you. Failure shouldn't throw you off. Keep on keeping on and don't look straight into your problems, but around them. Problems are like the sun, goes the saying: if you look straight at it, you'll see nothing because it'll blind you. But if you push forward, keeping your head down, it'll light your way. A friend of mine teaches driver's ed. He says the same thing when a group of future motorcyclists is in his class. If you see an obstacle on the road, never stare at it. That's a setup for an accident. You keep it in your peripheral vision but look ahead, to the solution, the road around it."

Danny nodded silently, drained his gin and tonic, and placed the glass, now just half-melted ice cubes, onto the table on the terrace. He would be focused, keep his eyes peeled, and he would find the opportunity he so badly needed. The setting sun was an orange fireball smoldering in the distance behind the Golden Gate Bridge. He would try not to look directly at it.

CHAPTER FOUR

Teamwork Makes the Dream Work

Kranj, Slovenia, 21 August 2009

"Have fun, ladies. And be sure to read that text for next time."

"Thanks, Iza. It was great." The other participants of the workshop enthusiastically concurred. "Thank you again for your warmth and wisdom. Until next week!"

The door gently closed behind the last participants, making the bells that hung above them jingle pleasantly. The room was still powdered with the scent of patchouli that was ashing beside the exit. In a corner stood a golden Pyramid of Horus, a line of small candles flickering beneath it and a glass cabinet above, filled with crystals that projected their magical energies into the space. Iza adjusted the cushions on the eight wooden folding chairs and arranged them in a perfect circle.

She was dressed in a simple but elegant, long, white dress. A silver necklace with a large, white pearl pendant adorned her neck. Whenever she appeared in public, she inevitably looked perfect, and today was no exception. She had striking, red, curly, shoulder-length hair, and eye-catching iridescent fingernails offsetting a large ring topped with a turquoise stone. She radiated self-confidence and understated glamor. Those around her had often described feeling a sense of feminine grandeur that few radiated and that was difficult to articulate.

Iza was already tired. The theta healing workshop she'd just run had taken a good deal of her energy. But this was to be expected. She loved doing it. Ever since she'd opened her Kali Center, which hosted seminars on spirituality, her life had felt fuller. She was tired, she could admit, but it didn't bother her that evening. Tonight was special. A different group would be arriving within the hour and they were not the sort who regularly attended such seminars.

She picked up her phone off a shelf by the window and switched off silent mode. Under "Favorite" contacts she pressed "Hubby" and waited for it to start ringing.

"Hey," Samo answered.

"Where are you?" Iza asked.

"We just left the office. We'll be with you in a half an hour. Okay?"

"Great. I'm ready and waiting."

"Cool. See you."

She hung up the phone, plugged it into a small speaker on the shelf, and pressed play. Gentle, meditative music streamed into the room. She settled cozily on a soft couch in the bay window, where her clients usually sat. "I still have some time," she thought. "Just right for a quick jump into theta." She closed her eyes and swam into a state of meditations, breathing slowly and deeply. This is what she loved doing. She believed that, in this state, she could communicate with the Universe and tell it all her desires and requests. Manifestation was one of her favorite techniques and she was certain that it always worked, as long as it was used in the right way and with the right purpose.

"Thank you for making this workshop a success. For helping the boys understand and internalize the content, and then use it in their work. Our project is moving forward as envisioned. One hundred million, seven years, a better world. We are committed. We work hard. We believe in our common goal, a goal that is ethical..." She whispered to herself in a relaxed manner, as she willed her intentions to sail up to the Universe.

Twenty minutes passed quickly. Slowly, she opened her eyes. She stood up and prepared the final details for the upcoming workshop. She did not yet know the group well – she'd only been with them once. A month or so prior, at the old restaurant in Ljubljana. But she'd certainly heard a lot about them. Samo had described each one of the team members to her, at great length, over many evenings, explaining why he had invited each one to join them. It sometimes seemed to her that Samo spoke so much about them more to convince himself than for the importance of her knowing all the details. Whatever the case, she understood that this was an interesting and capable team of very different characters. Despite believing in her mission and the power of alternative approaches, she did wonder how the team would react to this space, with its crystals, mandalas, and angel cards. "Maybe it would be better to tone this space down a bit, at least for the first meeting."

She aired out the room, switched on the white neon lights, and awkwardly hefted a cumbersome, three-legged flipchart up the stairs from the basement. She set it in front of the Pyramid of Horus, masking its presence, at least from the entrance. She then took colored index cards and markers from a drawer, figuring they would need them. Three packs of angel cards were spread out on a coffee table in the middle of the room. She scooped them up and tucked them away in the drawer. After that, she filled eight glasses of water from a jug with crystals inside and sipped from one of them. Right then she noticed the six headlight beams piercing the bay window from the parking lot outside. A moment later the bells above the door rang and in walked Samo, followed by six of his Delta Search colleagues.

"Welcome to my humble Kali Center," Iza said with a smile and open arms. The turquoise stone on her ring seemed to phosphoresce in the neon light. "Make yourself at home."

The boys looked around the room shyly, locked eyes on the chairs, and took their seats.

"What's happening? Early Halloween party?" Andrej joked. The others half-laughed, but Iza did not. Samo was also straight-faced, so no one else commented and they ignored Andrej's attempt at humor. They knew him by now. Hyper-rational, he dismissed anything that required a belief in anything other than empirical evidence. "It's a load of rubbish, if you ask me," he had said more than once, when chat had shifted to the topic of spirituality. He would follow this up with the hopeful addition, "and you all know that's how I feel." He was a programming geek from head to toe. If you looked up "technical engineer" in the dictionary, you'd find his photo. He and Samo were the oldest and most experienced members of the team. He had been the first one invited by Samo and he would hold the second-highest amount of shares in the new startup. His knowledge, accuracy, and critical eye were all much appreciated and had provided a leg up for several joint projects at Delta Search. Before their new venture, when he and Samo were sitting alone together at the Delta Search office one late afternoon, programming, Samo had turned to him and started, "Since Delta Search was sold, I no longer see a future here. I've been considering a new startup. I'd like you to be in on it with me. To be honest, I can't imagine pulling it off without you. What do you think?"

For Andrej, that was already enough for him to go all in. He looked upon Samo as the Greek god of programming, as he'd often say to others over after-work drinks. To hear that Samo wouldn't feel confident moving forward without him meant the world. The pact was sealed at that very moment.

Iza got the meeting started by slowly approaching the flipchart and seizing a thick, black, felt-tipped pen. She spun on her heels to face the assembly, which was still chattering away. She slowly smiled, turned to face the paper, and began to draw a large, inverted triangle with a circle inside it. The voices subsided and she felt seven pairs of eyes on her back, watching with interest. Then she took up red, then blue, then green pens, in turn. She colored in the upper right section of the triangle red, the upper left blue, and the bottom corner green. Only the circle in the middle remained white. She sat in the nearest chair and looked at each member of the team, one after the other, slowly and in silence. It was a little awkward for everyone.

"A proverb I'm fond of says," she began in a measured voice, "'if you want to go quickly, then go alone. If you want to go far, then travel together.' As Samo has already outlined for you, we wish to go far. We have seven years. We know what our goal is, but we don't yet know exactly how we're going to achieve it. We only know that the path is steep and clouded by fog. To achieve a significant goal, we must build a strong house and a strong house begins with a solid foundation. We also know that nothing great has ever been done by a single person alone – there is always a team in support. That's why gathering a good team has been our number one priority."

The group nodded, all aware that, without teamwork, no project of complexity could succeed. They'd experienced this first-hand at Delta Search, where they'd grown accustomed to working hard together whenever confronted with a difficult task.

"I'm not just talking about the fact that we need to gel into a good group of colleagues," Iza continued. "I'm referring to the very highest level of mutual respect and trust. When I say trust, I don't mean that we simply trust each other to keep our promises and finish our assignments on time. That's a given. For a true team, trust means more. We want and even expect our colleagues to call us out if we ever stray from the collective good and thus endanger our enterprise. If our common goal is the same as our individual goal, then we will never harm each other en route to it, because to do so would be harming ourselves."

She paused for the words to settle like fairy dust upon the listeners, who were hanging on her words.

"Trust is built through honesty, by praising one another's strengths but also by pointing out our weaknesses, by asking for help when we need it. That takes courage. If we open up and lay bare our weaknesses to each other, of course we do run the risk that someone might sting us where it hurts the most. We're pointing out the chinks in our own armor. So, we have to trust each other that this will not happen. For the good of the team, we must shed that armor. The sooner we do so, the better for us all."

They'd never heard anything like this. This resonated and it made perfect sense, but it was something new to all of them. They were visibly discomfited. Iza looked at Samo, who also felt the insecurity in the air. He commented, in his own style that was complementary to Iza's, "Don't be frightened. No one will have to share stories about your first kiss or when you got caught sneaking a peak at a Playboy." The shot of humor helped clear the air and the group laughed. Iza did, too, but then jumped right back in.

"We only need to know what motivates us and what holds us back. Why does one of us communicate one way, another one of us another? Why is one person more precise, another sloppier? Why are you compassionate while I am tough? When faced with conflict, why does one person react this way and you differently? We are all different people and that is as it should be. Diversity is beneficial to a team. But it is important that we recognize those differences and respect them. That's why psychologists have developed personality tests that illustrate these differences. We will take one such test today. Are you curious what type of personality you are?"

The group was all interested in analytics, so this concept was appealing and it pulled them together. This was made manifest by each of them leaning forward slightly in their chairs in anticipation, which Iza and Samo duly noted. Andrej, the skeptic, seemed most enthusiastic of all, which pleasantly surprised them.

"The questionnaire we'll fill out today is called SDI, the Strength Deployment Inventory. I'll admit, I don't know exactly what the name means, but I know that the test works!"

They all laughed again. Iza had this all choreographed. She'd completed an intensive certificate program for teaching just this methodology years ago, but she knew that humor and self-deprecation helped smooth the path.

"Before we dive in, we need a bit of background. See that triangle? SDI roughly divides people into four main groups. Red are action-focused with the greatest emphasis on performance. Blue we might call people people, with a focus on interpersonal relationships. Green are process-oriented analysts. In the middle of this triangle is a hub, a circle in which sit those of us who have a little of all three groups within us. When we finish the questionnaire, each of us will have a dot on the triangle and we will see what our team looks like. Are you in?"

They all nodded in earnest and Iza passed out printed questionnaires. They took out pens and began to fill in the blanks next to the written statements.

The workshop concluded with a hot debate on team roles, personality profiles, and the importance of interpersonal relationships. It was a great success from Iza's perspective. She saw how motivated the team was and decided to implement similar questionnaires to spark future debates down the line. It was late when they stopped for the night, and everyone was tired but also buzzing about the new project.

———————————∞ ∞———————————

Iza and Samo lived in a house not far from Kali Center. As soon as they walked in the door, Iza sat down at the dining room table and lay the completed questionnaires upon it. She pulled a pen out of her purse, flipped open her laptop, and went through the team members' responses.

"Samo, I can't wait any longer. I'm so curious about what sort of team we've gathered. Can you check on the kids, see if they're already asleep?"

"Sure." Samo creaked his way up the wooden stairs. He was back a few moments later. "They're both sleeping like angels. And look, they even made us dinner. How about that?"

He pointed towards the stovetop, where a pan of vegetable risotto awaited them.

"Super, super. Well, they are already teenagers. We must have raised them well. I'm proud of how independent they are." Iza was typing away as she spoke. "Since we were otherwise busy all day today, tomorrow we should go on an outing together as soon as you get out of work. Maybe a short hike on one of the nearby hills? If they're up for coming along, of course. What do you say?"

Samo mentally scanned his schedule. "I think it'll work. I'll slip out a bit early if I can."

He turned to the stovetop and lifted the silver teapot. "Tea?"

"Please. With pleasure."

Soon it boiled and he poured the water over home-dried chamomile, as the herbaceous aroma wafted through the kitchen. He handed a cup to Iza and took his own in his hands, as he sat on the wooden kitchen counter, his legs dangling above the floor. He watched his wife, immersed and fascinated, as she reviewed and analyzed the team's data. Slowly sipping from the steaming yellow cup, he awaited the verdict. His mind meandered over their years together and how much he still admired her. They'd been a couple since they were teenagers and yet their relationship was still so vibrant. They were so ideally compatible. This was the source of their profound respect for one another. He was so happy that he'd found her. "I should remind myself of this more often," he thought to himself, "and take more time to appreciate our life together." Statistically speaking, the chances of two people meeting and falling in love, two people so ideally suited to one another, had a probability approaching zero-point-zero... "Stop thinking so analytically, already," he scolded himself. "You can't translate interpersonal relationships into cold numbers! Or can you..."

She felt his gaze upon her, so she turned to him, returned his stare lovingly, smiled warmly and asked, "What?"

"Nothing, nothing," he replied, a bit embarrassed. "So what did you discover?"

She shook her head, turned back to the laptop and took a deep breath.

"It's exactly as I feared. Almost exclusively green."

"Really?" Samo cynically replied. "What did you expect? We're programmers, after all."

"I know, but all the same... Only two of us have no green traits, and one is a hub. It will be...interesting to lead a team like this. A good thing you're green-red..."

"Don't worry. We have a clear goal and that is why we need good programmers. And programmers are usually green. Silicon Valley works well enough, and it's mostly green there, isn't it? We'll add the right additional people when needed. What's most important is that we are fully committed to the idea. This will help us most to get the ball rolling. I chose them based on their personalities and how they've already proved their mettle in past projects. We'll sort out the rest. First we've got to properly begin and then we'll adjust as necessary."

Iza had seen this coming from the start. A group of programmers glued to their computers all day could cover one dimension well, but she'd have to take on the brunt of, well, everything else. "This agreement of ours, that I'll be in the office just 25% of the time, is probably only going to work for the short term... Well, we'll see. When shall we hold the next workshop?"

"Thursday afternoon," he replied. "And then we'll have to also begin talking business. We need to get this party started as quickly as possible."

Iza sensed Samo's enthusiasm as well as his impatience. "Don't be in too much of a hurry," she said. "You know very well that everything depends on how we lay the foundations for our team." She'd seen many a team get stuck into difficult projects too quickly and get stuck, giving up before they'd reached their true potential. "We should be fast but not too fast. If we want to climb great summits, we need to plumb great depths first."

She waited on her goal-oriented husband's reaction. Samo was weighing her words while he played with the cup in his hands and looked at the floor. He knew she was right, but said nothing.

"Good," she thought to herself, "I'll take that as a yes."

Samo lay his phone down on the nightstand, pulled a soft blanket up to his neck, and stared blankly at the ceiling.

"What if it doesn't work?"

Iza slowly lowered the book she'd been reading and turned to face him. "What if it doesn't work?" she mirrored.

"This story of ours... What if it's not the right path? Maybe we should all stay a little longer at Delta Search, earn what we can there, and use that money to help the world. That's not as far out there..."

The idea of a new company alternately made Samo feel a rush of self-confidence and a freefall of self-doubt. It was as if he were standing upon a set of scales, one foot on each side, now tilting this way, now the other. He knew he had to do something but this was truly a giant leap for him. Every ounce of support and understanding was welcome.

"Ah, Samo, I know it's hard for you. After ten years at Delta Search... I can imagine. You built that search engine from the ground up. It's your baby. I know it's not easy to let it go and jump headlong towards unfamiliar terrain. But I am certain that this is the right time. For you, Delta Search is history. The new team needs your full focus. No baggage. No chains around your ankles to keep you from sprinting forward. Of course you are afraid of failure. Of course you have doubts. That's perfectly normal as we chart unexplored territory. If this had all been thoroughly plowed already, then there would be no niche for us to find. Imagine what it was like for explorers in Africa centuries ago. Do you think they were unafraid?"

"I know... Well, it's not really the same. It's just business, after all."

"Wild business. With good intentions. We both know it's right. And only when you know that it is right, can you follow your inner calling."

"That's true..." He felt the power surge back into his mission again, the magnetic draw he'd felt for so long to work on a new project. The feeling increased and receded, like the tide, but it was always there.

"We are all looking for rational confirmation that we're headed in the right direction," Iza continued. "But we're not going to find it, not yet, anyway. Unknown routes cannot be found on the map..."

He nodded. She hadn't said anything that was new to him, but it was all things that he knew he needed to hear. Precisely what he needed.

"Look, you have a clear intention. You're motivated. You're capable. You've already gathered a great team. You have start-up capital. What else do you want? How about a good woman who will support you uncompromisingly on your way? Oh, right, you have that, too..."

She slapped him playfully on the shoulder. "You really are a lucky guy."

"Well, yeah, okay, but..."

"But nothing! The team needs you now more than ever. With all the work done so far, with proving how successful you were in past projects, by being honest and a good boss, you've earned their complete trust. Now they need you to lead them into the unknown. Without hesitation." Iza was surprised by her own words. She internalized a surprising feeling and found herself intrigued by her own response. She hadn't realized that she was so convinced of the correctness of their decision, and she nodded to herself in approval. Then she picked up the book from her lap.

"I read an interesting passage. This book by Adizes describes how organizations grow in stages. We're currently in the first phase of growth. Hang on, where was it... Ah, okay, listen to what he says about leadership. 'Founders necessarily manage their newborn companies in a kind of heroic or authoritarian way. Without a strong-willed leader, an infant company may die.'" She waited a few seconds for the words to settle. "Well, what are we going to do now? Will you be our hero and lead us boldly forward, or will we begin our quest in doubt and uncertainty?"

Samo sighed deeply and looked at Iza with as straight a face as he could muster. "Okay. I'll be your heroic leader. The new team will be my fearless army. You'll be our nurse. What do you say?" His straight face broke out into a sparkling laugh.

"Oh, go take a long walk off a short pier," Iza said, trying to hide her smile. She shut her book and switched off her reading light. Then she took his hand gently into hers. "I'm certain that everything's going to go well."

Over the coming weeks they met, talked, and got to know each other over the course of several more group meetings. It helped in setting the foundations for building a strong team. Samo and Iza made it clear to all that having a connected, dedicated, strong team was the basis for anything they might accomplish down the line. The team understood and agreed with this. No one doubted that they were capable of doing big things. But the path to one hundred million in seven years, starting from zero, remained obscure. No matter, they thought. If Samo says it's possible, then it's possible. Outwardly, Samo never indicated the slightest doubt. His focus, dedication, and passion were viral. The team gladly followed his lead. They were always critical of the details, but whole-heartedly embraced the vision. That's what fanned the flames of the enterprise.

The more they got to know one another, the more Iza trusted the group, and vice-versa. But it didn't take long for the group to realize that the path she would be guiding them along would not be, well, traditional. Her interest in mysticism had already enhanced their enthusiasm for the project and, most importantly, hadn't scared anyone off. As a result, she no longer hid away the crystals, the pyramids, the posters, the angel cards. She even worked them into some of their team-building exercises. After a workshop concluded, they often lingered to chat about concepts like the power of crystals, spirituality, manifestations, and the like. Iza was at home in this realm, but for the others it was new and, once they got over the initial cynicism, very interesting. It certainly couldn't hurt, they rationalized. They also couldn't prove that it did not work, so why not give it a try? Only Andrej remained reserved on the subject.

They also began to pivot towards discussions of the business. It was clear that they wanted to focus on mobile application development. But which apps? And how the heck were they going to transform this general notion into one hundred million in seven years?

CHAPTER FIVE

Eureka in Pescadero

San Mateo, California, 16 May 2014

"Howdy, neighbor!" the rotund man shouted from across the street.

"Howdy yourself!" Danny replied automatically from the driver's seat of his convertible.

As he did every night, he parked his Mazda with meticulous precision between the two lines that marked his spot. Out he stepped onto the sidewalk then the few paces further to the front porch of his old house in San Mateo. He and Nancy had moved out of their rented apartment a year ago, when he inherited the house from his late parents. He didn't go inside straight away. Instead he sat on an antique wooden swing, supported by squeaking chains, and thought. Nancy had seen him through the window when he arrived. She put down her book and popped her head outside the door.

"Hey honey!"

"Hey…"

She heard the discouragement in his voice. "Have a nice day?"

"Meh. I've had worse." Danny let his briefcase slump against the railing and swayed screeching on the swing.

"Worse, huh? Anything wrong?"

"Nothing's wrong. But nothing's right, either. Everything is the same. I think I've had enough of the same old same old."

Nancy paused at the threshold, unsure, then she said, "Let me bring you a beer and we'll talk, okay?" Without waiting for his answer, she grabbed a couple of cold ones from the fridge, popped them open, switched off the kitchen light, and returned to the porch. She sat on the edge of the porch beside Danny, handed him a beer, and leaned her chin on his knee.

"Well, we've gotta get you back on the positivity track. Don't you know that cute girls like me fall in love with boys who are bursting with positive energy?" She was trying to cheer him up, at least a little. "Tell me about it. What's bugging you?"

Danny looked down at her and offered a sour smile, which was all he could muster. "I'm not that happy with the way things are going at the moment. I want to feel like I'm moving forward. Right now I'm stuck. It's hard to put into words... It's like I've been doing the same thing every day for two years now without the slightest indication that something will change, that progress is being made. I had a long chat with Clyde yesterday... I'm pretty sure he understands me, where I'm coming from, but still, nothing really happens. I think I deserve more from life."

"What exactly do you want so badly? More of what? More money?" Nancy spoke in a soft, almost sad tone. "You have everything you need. You have a roof over your head, a good job, a good...well, a car, anyway." She turned her half-smiling face at an angle. "And we love each other, right? You know how many people want all this, but don't have it?"

"Yeah, I know. But I'm still missing something. I need some new opportunity, whether it's a promotion or about my salary, I don't even know. The house is old and will have to be renovated, top to bottom. The car will soon be in its teens. I guess that's all we've got now. Where are we going to get the money for all that? As it is now, we can't really plan on raising a family..." He took a long pull on his beer. "And this job has grown monotonous. I mean, I like what I do, it's just that every day is just like the one before. Clyde is a great boss, but somehow it's not enough for me anymore. I want to move on, to feel like I'm moving. I guess I need some breakthrough that would launch me in a new direction, that'd feel like real progress, in interest or income. A major shift. But that just doesn't happen. Everything I think to try has been done by someone else first..."

Nancy knew Danny well enough. When he was in one of these funks, there was no point trying to un-funk him. It happened often enough. She felt like he didn't realize how good they had it. He had a habit of chasing things that, when he caught them, made him no happier than he was before. But she tried to be understanding. He had to follow a path that felt like it was his. If something was wrong, he'd have to change it. But now wasn't the time. Not now.

"You know what," she began, "how about we go to bed a little earlier today and set off for a nice trip tomorrow morning? It's Friday, the weekend is ahead of us. Weather's supposed to be great. What if we go for a long walk on Pescadero Beach? It's been ages since you took me out. We always love it there and now's the ideal time." She smiled. "And if you don't want to take me out, then I'll take you out. We could collect shells, like we used to. And there's that specialty coffee shop near the beach you like so much. Whaddya say? Road trip!" She stood, slid onto his lap and the old swing groaned under their combined weight. She kissed him gently on the forehead, rubbed her nose against his, and looked deeply into his eyes. "What's the deal, old man? Am I getting any action?"

Danny breathed in a deep swallow of warm night air. He was being pressed a bit, which he normally didn't like, but on the other hand a kick in the butt was welcome, to help him shift out of his inertia and not waste a weekend wallowing. "I'm in, let's do it. Just don't break father's swing..."

———————————— ∞ ∞ ————————————

Their rotund, nosy neighbor watched, while pretending to focus on watering his lawn, as they rose early that morning, quickly drank a cup of coffee, and ate Nancy's chocolate muffins on the porch. They made a few sandwiches, filled water bottles, and drove west. It was an hour's ride through a winding road that split the hills above Silicon Valley. The sun bounced off the Pacific, glimmering in the distance as they began their descent towards the coast. It looked as though they might drive straight into the ocean off a cliff when Danny turned left onto Cabrillo Highway. They pulled over in a small parking lot beside Pescadero Beach. They'd been here a few times before and Danny always liked to park in the same spot. He'd parked in the same place a year ago, when he'd asked Nancy to marry him on a nearby cliff. They wound their way down a narrow path that met a long set of stairs down to a sandy beach. Every time they came here, it was different. The waves carried things away and brought ochre sand in its place, sometimes piling it into dunes, other times stripping the shore to bare, skeletal rock.

They had fond memories of this beach and Nancy was happy she'd been able to convince Danny to make the trip. They slipped off their shoes and walked at leisure the length of the beach, hand in hand. In the distance, they spied jagged cliffs, sea foam smashing against their hulls while an army of seagulls landed and flew off from ocean rocks. The soft, warm sand squished between their toes as they walked.

"A yoga instructor told us to walk on the ground as if the Earth were kissing your soles," Nancy said. "Can you walk across the earth like that? It's amazing how soothing it is. We give ourselves far too little to mindfulness, considering how well it reduces stress. Don't you think?"

"Totally. Get rid of your socks, and problems disappear. Easy as pie," Danny replied, sarcastically. He liked being here with his love and, to be honest, walking on the sand really did feel good for him, at least it usually did. But they'd been walking for an hour and he still couldn't relax, let alone feel at one with the moment. He was still a bundle of nerves, thinking about his job even as he tried not to. His job and money. "I'll be able to relax once I find a great story."

Nancy frowned and replied sharply, "Oh, come on. Decompress a little. Worry about that on Monday. Now just breathe and be here with me. Okay?"

The cold, firm tone of her voice sobered Danny up a little. He could tell she was serious. Also, he remembered the reason they were here today, which was not to give him time to grumble about his career.

"Okay. I'll try," he replied, with some remorse.

They walked on but, despite his efforts, he couldn't push his intruding thoughts away. They were swarming him. Nancy leapt onto piles of sand, made towers out of smooth stones, and teasingly sprayed him with seawater, while he thought about what exciting business story might lead him on a better path.

As a boy, his father had taken him to Palo Alto several times, where they would stop in front of a small garage beside a house on Addison Avenue. "You see that little green garage over there, son? Well, this is where it all began. Here two friends, Bill and David, founded Hewlett Packard a long time ago. As soon as they finished their studies at Stanford, which is a few clicks in that direction, they got to creating right here. Do you know how they decided on the name of their company? Well, it's their last names, but they couldn't decide which one should come first, so they flipped a coin. That's why it's not called Packard Hewlett. The company grew and grew. Today it's one of the biggest IT companies on the planet. Other, similar companies have grown in its wake. You've probably heard of Xerox, Apple, Intel, Oracle, Cisco… All of them are big IT companies in our neighborhood, by the Gulf. That's why it's called Silicon Valley. It was born in this green garage, right here. A small story at first that has grown into countless astronomical success stories. When you grow up, there will be even more such stories. You'll see. The future will be built here…"

Danny recalled these afternoon outings with warmth, driving from Palo Alto to San Jose with his father. From that moment on, he'd been drawn to tech stories.

"Daniel-san, Earth to Daniel-san," Nancy said, waking him from his reverie. "Where did you drift off to? Down to Earth, big guy. Enough of this daily meditation. What if we hit up that coffee shop, then head on home?"

They trekked the stairs to the top of the cliff, hugged in triumph, and marveled at the beautiful view once again, before they drove off. They always liked to stop for coffee in the small town of Pescadero. The joint was a combination antiques shop, grocery store, and cafe. They liked the odd retro atmosphere and equally odd music that was played, each visit transporting them to a faraway place and time.

"That's it," said Danny. "A different, unusual story every time but always in the same environment. That's what I'm looking for in the business world…"

They ordered at the bar and brought their coffees, in black cups, out to a small terrace by the road. They sat on rough wooden chairs behind a square table. A woman and her daughter were at the neighboring table, each browsing their phone.

"That was a nice little morning, wasn't it?" Nancy said, as if trying to convince them both. "Well, at least I liked it."

"It was lovely for me, too," he replied, "and sorry for my mental wanderings. This is really gnawing at me. I've got to do something about it." He sipped his coffee, bitter and black.

Nancy pretended not to hear. "I'd love to have a cottage somewhere along the coast, so I could walk on the beach every day. If we have children, it would be a nicer place for them to grow up here. Hmm..."

This didn't sit well within Danny's mind. What kind of house on the beach? Is she kidding, he thought? We can't even sort out our house in San Mateo. A weekend beach house? Only in our dreams. His thoughts boiled, but he said nothing, looking away so his wife wouldn't see that he had wandered off in thought.

"I'll just run to the restroom," she said, and ducked back inside the cafe. It was good timing for Danny, who had a moment to himself. He looked around the terrace. The mother at the table beside them had gone inside and left her daughter there, alone with her phone. Then the daughter started laughing heartily while typing at the pale glow of the screen. She rocked back and forth and was clearly having a blast. Danny watched her for a while, took another sip of coffee, and breathed in the fresh sea air. He turned on his phone and quickly, out of habit, scanned his emails. Nothing new. He turned it off and looked mindlessly over to the girl at the next table. She was still laughing. It was easy to envy her childish playfulness, how carefree she could afford to be at that age. He couldn't resist his own curiosity.

"Hey there, can I ask you a question? What are you playing on your phone that's so much fun?"

"Oh, it's just a game," she replied curtly, before she laughed aloud again. It was such a heartfelt laugh that it made Danny smile, despite his general mood.

"What's the game?"

"A new one I just installed. Everyone at school is playing it. It's really fun..."

"Cool. What's it about?"

The girl was so involved in the game that she only half-heard his question. "Um, so you have to rescue this bunny trapped in a castle. It's called Rabbit Trap Quest. He's so cute and looks so sad in this cold room... I mean, look at him." She turned her phone so Danny could see the screen. There was a sad but cute white bunny wearing a pink necklace, trapped within gray castle walls.

"He is cute. And so sad. I hope you can save him. What did you say the game was called?"

"Rabbit Trap Quest. RTQ for short. Download it and try it," she replied, though her focus was firmly on saving rabbits.

Rabbit Trap Quest? That wasn't one Danny had heard of. He used to spend time reviewing what was new in the mobile app market, and had his finger on the pulse of dozens of new games coming out every week. Why not check out this one? He picked up his phone, opened Google Play, and typed in "rabbit trap". He found it and the game loaded quickly. An evil fox appeared before him, mocking with the words, "So you wanna save the rabbit? Ha ha ha!" Danny smiled and began.

The game had him hooked immediately and time flew by. He turned it off, but then quickly returned to it. The fox appeared again above the credit RTQ by Y-PLAY. Y-PLAY? He'd never heard of it. He turned off the game and Googled the company's name. As he flipped through their website, he found that they'd only been on the market for a year and had seen incredible growth during that time. It was a small startup from Oregon that had racked up crazy numbers in record time. He looked for more information, but found nothing beyond the company's own website. Nothing. His heart started beating faster and his eyes widened. He scrolled through page after page of search results, but nothing proper had been written about it yet. No serious articles, no interviews with execs, just some general reports and comparisons between competitors in the market and some fan forums. How was this possible?

Just then, Nancy returned to the terrace and saw her husband nervously pacing, his face locked into his phone. "Danny, is everything okay?"

"I think I just found my story!"

∞ ∞

On Sunday morning, Nancy visited her mother and Danny spent most of the day at his computer. He reviewed all the databases and records he could find on Y-PLAY. The less he found, the happier he grew. The analytics platforms reported that Rabbit Trap Quest had been advancing rapidly in recent months and was among the most-downloaded games on all platforms. He sent off some emails to a few addresses he found on their site, asking for additional information and for an interview, hoping to get an answer the next day.

He got up early Monday after having taken forever to fall asleep the night before. He kissed Nancy's forehead as she slept on, threw his laptop into his briefcase, and drove quickly to his office on the unusually empty, early morning roads. He even skipped his quotidian morning coffee at Starbucks. He didn't want to waste a minute, so he settled for the office coffee machine. When Clyde walked through the door, shortly after nine, Danny called to him. "Morning, Clyde! Come a little closer, would you?"

"You're already here?" the editor responded, stopping in the hallway with surprise. "What's up?"

"Ever heard of Y-PLAY Games?" He tried to mask his enthusiasm.

"Rings a bell. A little startup near Seattle, right? Don't know much more, why?"

"They're from Portland. Mobile game developers. And no one is writing anything about them. Their latest download figures are, quite frankly, staggering. They make Rabbit Trap Quest, that bunny game that..."

"Oh yeah, I've heard of it. My granddaughter spent the whole weekend looking for traps and throwing carrots. So that's them." Clyde recalled a pleasant Saturday visit where, on his patio, his granddaughter had showed off her accomplishments in the new game du jour.

"Yes, that's them. And they don't have any media coverage yet. Look at this."

Clyde approached Danny's laptop and looked at the graphs of app downloads. "Uh, interesting," Clyde said, "have you gotten in touch with them yet?"

"I sent a few emails but I don't have other contacts there. Nothing yet. Well, I'm not surprised, as it was the weekend."

"Great, well, if you get this exclusive, we'll run it on page three, okay? I can call around a bit and try to get a direct contact number."

Danny glowed. This was what he'd been looking for. Now to work. He'd prepare well, get a good interview, and rack up a win. He wanted to call Nancy, but changed his mind. He didn't think he should interrupt her at the beginning of her work day. Instead, he settled for a short text.

"I guess I got it. 😊 Love u!"

∞ ∞

It was Tuesday morning, thirty minutes before the work day officially began, and the Bay Area Biz offices were thrumming. By the time Danny arrived, it was already bustling. He set down his bag on his cluttered desk and heard the call from across the hall. "Danny, is that you? Come here for a sec." Clyde had the habit of summoning his staff through calls across halls. He always had the door to his corner office open, and Danny strode in and stood before Clyde's desk. Clyde leaned back in his cushioned, oversized office chair. He scrunched a piece of paper in his hands and, as was his habit, tossed it towards the wastebasket in the corner. And didn't make the shot. He puffed out his cheeks and slowly exhaled, his lips wobbling in the wake.

"You see TechGrunge magazine today?"

"Not yet, why?"

Clyde sat up straighter, grabbed his computer screen, and turned it toward Danny without a word. The lead story, in a bold headline, read "Y-PLAY Games Smashing Mobile Game Market."

The blood flushed out of Danny's face. It looked as if his veins had frozen solid. He slumped into a conference chair in the middle of the room, staring blankly at the screen before him. Clyde watched in silence, gave him some time, then added, in a calming voice, "TechGrunge obviously got an exclusive just before we could. That's why no one replied from Y-PLAY. Sorry, they beat us to it…"

CHAPTER SIX

Nomen Est Omen

Kranj, Slovenia, 16 September 2009

Iza stood behind a glass vitrine, arranging the bookshelf while keeping an eye on Samo. He sat on a bean bag and spun a pencil around his fingers in thought. Without focus, he stared at a large, multi-colored picture of a fairy that adorned one of the walls at Kali Center. A small, purple notebook sat in his lap, its covers bent and dog-eared with use. He slowly lowered his gaze to the notebook and scribbled on the paper, which was already covered in his scrawlings. Most of the words were crossed out.

For some time now, he'd been looking for the perfect word to describe their new idea, their team. The name of the new company. He was after a word that embodied their path, what was awaiting them in the future. It had to be just right and it had to feel just right to all the co-founders. They'd discussed it at some of the meetings, but someone inevitably found something wrong with each suggestion. They needed something that everyone believed in, but the ideas were all over the map and there was doubt in the air about whether they'd ever agree on one. They didn't even have a strong idea about what the name should represent. Samo had gotten in the habit of brainstorming ideas and jotting them down in his purple notebook. But before proposing anything to the team, he always checked online to see whether a matching domain name was available. But all his best ideas to date had already been taken. Disappointed with each dead-end, he crossed out the words that were no longer in the running. There had been three he'd loved, but each one had been relegated to the scratch pile.

Iza approached and put her hand on his shoulder. "Still working on a name, huh? Maybe we should be a little less democratic in our process and just pick something already?"

Samo dropped his crossed leg to the floor and leaned forward, elbows on knees. "I don't think so. If we all want to believe in an idea as much as possible, then it must be our idea collectively. The guys have good ideas, we just have to find the right one. And by the right one, I also mean one that isn't already a registered domain name. Let's spend some more time on this today at the start of the workshop. Something's gotta give. We hurry past it at every meeting, but we should dedicate more time today. That's the start."

Iza looked out the window in thought. "Well, don't forget the numerological side of things. It has to be positive. That only makes the task more difficult." She strongly believed in the vibration of numbers and the importance of numerology in achieving goals. It wasn't just numbers, but words, too. The invisible energies and mysteries of the Universe strongly influenced all of her decisions, and this was manifest in names, dates, numbers, and more. Samo understood this about Iza and supported it, so numerology played a role in all aspects of the new company.

"I know. The name has to be just right and we'll keep searching until..." Before Samo could finish his sentence, the door opened.

"Outfit."

It was Andrej who had spoken, loudly and with confidence, as he entered, followed by Luka, stepping into the incense-scented room.

"What?" Iza asked in surprise.

Andrej repeated, proudly and enthusiastically. "Outfit. Our new name."

"Outfit?" she mouthed. "What does that mean?"

"An outfit is like a group of people acting as a team. They use it to describe units in the army," Andrej elucidated. He spoke the best English of all the team members. "We're venturing into unknown waters, just like a military unit. We know what the goal is, but we don't know what the circumstances will be and how exactly to reach the goal. We can be an outfit. Isn't that cool?"

Iza raised her eyebrows. "I like it. I mean, I don't see myself as a soldier. Not even if you put a rifle in my hand. That feels very foreign to me... That said, it does embody the team spirit we need. Outfit. Okay, sounds good. Samo, what do you say?"

There was no reply because he hadn't heard the question. He was already balancing his laptop on his knees, typing impatiently. "The domain name is free!" His eyes looked up towards the others in the room, just as the entrance bell jingled and the rest of the team joined them.

"Team," he practically shouted, unable to control his excitement, "get your asses in here. Andrej just floated a new company name. Outfit. Like a team of soldiers embarking on a perilous mission. What do you say?"

"Well, hello to you, too, Samo. Have a nice day?" Frenk, unshaven, smiled. "Outfit? Soldiers... Uh, well, sure, we can go into action. Either we triumph at the front or die in glory!"

Everyone laughed and began to chat about the new idea and the names' various connotations. It seemed to suit everyone, finally.

"Guys, stop!" Iza shouted over the enthusiastic din. She stood by the glass case, holding open a book on numerology to which she'd referred several times already in their workshops. Those assembled turned and stared at her, and she looked back at them, heavy book in hand, like a school teacher, her reading glasses slipping down her nose. "That won't work. Numerologically, the word 'outfit' represents the number thirty. This is not a good number for us. It will certainly not aid us on our journey. We need a really good number. Unfortunately, this isn't it. The closest good number for us is thirty-seven..."

The room hushed with disappointment until Andrej chimed in. "Then there's no problem at all. Let's just add the number seven to the name. Outfit7. Then the stars align, right?"

"Yes, that would be thirty-seven, then." Iza flipped a few more pages, found a passage, and read aloud: "The number thirty-seven represents kindness and compassion for all living beings, success and respect, a large and diverse circle of friends and acquaintances (old, young, educated, uneducated, wealthy, poor...), sincere friendship, protection. This is a lucky number that is totally different from others, in that it brings success and happiness." Iza smiled broadly. "Wow, isn't that exactly what we want?"

"It couldn't get any better," Luka added. "It describes our mission and success at the same time. Who wouldn't want a large circle of dedicated people, when we're talking about creating mobile apps? After all, our success will only be measured by how many 'shares', 'likes', and downloads our 'friends' make. I think it's the bee's knees. The name and what it means. Outfit7. Awesome!"

Patrik coughed to get everyone's attention. "My dear colleagues, considering that you are all technicians, I assume it will be important to you... What does Outfit7 mean to us? Aren't there eight of us?"

Iza turned towards the fairy in the painting on the wall and her broad smile grew even wider. "There are seven of you gentlemen. I'm separate but linked. Like in the fairytale. I'm Snow White and you're...the Seven Dwarfs. When I was little, I always wanted to be Snow White. Looks like my dream has come true." She turned toward the others with a look packed with positive energy, as she scanned the room.

Samo opened his laptop to check the domain name. "That's also free," he said. He closed it and adjusted his glasses. "Well, this is obviously it. Come on, hands up for everyone who's voting for our name to be Outfit7." Seven hands shot into the air, followed by his.

"Agreed," said Samo. "We are Outfit7. Plus Snow White." He winked at Iza, who sat beside the rest of the team. "This calls for a round of beers after the workshop at the bar across the street. You in? Andrej's buying, since he was the one with the great idea."

They all nodded approvingly and pointed at Andrej, already fantasizing about their frothy beers.

"Just kidding, Andrej, don't look so serious. I'm happy to treat you all. But we still have work to do before happy hour." He walked over to the flipchart on its stand. "So, where did we leave off last time? We've already written down some good ideas for apps. I checked them online. I'm afraid that none will work for us. All of them exist already, in one form or another. Well, all of them except for one…"

CHAPTER SEVEN

The Man Who Knew Them All

San Francisco, California, 3 November 2014

"Yesterday, I had an interesting dinner in Palo Alto," said Clyde when Danny had awkwardly entered his office. "But more on that later."

Danny noticed an unusual spark in his editors' eyes that day. Something was cooking. It was obvious that Clyde could hardly wait to tell him. He sat in the chair across from Clyde and his editorial desk, a worn green folder resting on his knees, waiting quietly. This was Danny's third annual interview. They were held between each journalist and the Editor-in-Chief of Bay Area Biz. Danny liked to talk about progress, about orientation, about linking everything with the company's values and mission. Clyde was a true master of such conversations. He was great at giving his journalists extra impetus and understanding about the essence of everything they did, and how that translated into their daily work. Danny was no exception, feeling recharged and with renewed purpose after such meetings. But today was different. His enthusiasm was deflated. If asked, he'd have rather postponed it for another day. But Clyde had stoked his curiosity. So he waited, didn't press, and let Clyde guide the conversation.

Clyde stood by the wastebasket, which was surrounded by crumpled papers that had not made it inside. They remained that way until the weekly visit from the cleaning lady. Clyde stared out the window at the bay, then removed his brown blazer and hung it over the back of his shabby, cushioned office chair. He straightened his red tie, placed his hands on his desk and leaned forward, making eye contact with Danny.

"I've been watching you," he began sternly. "For quite some time. Half a year has passed and you're all black and blue. You're doing well, but I think you're avoiding us a bit. This behavior has to stop. What happened months ago is ancient history. You've written some very good columns lately. So what's the problem? Your energy is elsewhere. Wake up from your zombie state, son."

Danny looked his editor straight in the eyes, but didn't know exactly how to reply. He had not found a recipe for moving forward. His optimism had plummeted of late, that was true. He did his job well enough. Everyone was satisfied with his work. But he wasn't satisfied with himself.

Clyde continued. "It seems to me that you don't know yourself what the problem is, why you feel this way. There's nothing actually wrong, but you're acting as if the sky has fallen."

"I know, Clyde. I'm not sure what to do. I'm going through a weird phase..."

The editor sighed and continued firmly. "You need to stop feeling sorry for yourself. Look, I've got something for you. But you have to take it seriously, with positivity, and do your best. But with you moaning around here like a half-empty tire that might be a long shot..." He tilted his head and smiled slightly, just enough for Danny to notice.

Danny's eyes widened a little. He put his green folder on the table, crossed his legs, and prepared to receive the brief. It was clear that Clyde had something special in mind.

"Yes, boss. I'm working on it. Like I said, Nancy and I are going to the coast for a long weekend, the first in a long while. I'll recharge. That's the plan."

"See that you do. You're gonna need a full battery." Clyde could combine a joke with severity and the softness of sympathy, all in one word. He walked over to the window and looked down at the street. Morning rush hour, packed with people and cars. "Today we should talk about your work and progress, about culture and vision, but we won't. That's because I have something that can't wait. Yesterday I had dinner with a college friend. We got to talking about our team and I mentioned your hunger to break big stories. Then, as fate would have it, in walks someone I didn't recognize, but I could tell he was a hot shot, because he greeted everyone in the restaurant in turn. As if he knew everyone. But no, he wasn't the owner." Clyde smiled and moved back behind his desk. "Then up he walks to us and greets my friend. Guess I was the only one in the place who didn't know him. He introduced himself to me as Brad Wellington. He seemed like a worldly guy. My friend joked that this was a man who knows every important person in Silicon Valley. Like me, you might think, but somehow we managed never to meet."

Danny smiled. "There are others like you? Interesting. Then you're not the last specimen on Earth, but just an endangered species."

"Yeah, yeah. But he's an adviser and I'm a journalist. So he sat at a table with someone else. I remembered that I'd read about him once. He was a successful businessman until he was in a bad car accident. He recovered, but made a career pivot, leaving entrepreneurship and shifting to the advising businesses. Well, it doesn't matter. While my buddy and I were talking about you, he mentioned that the man Brad was joining was the director of the American branch of an unusual company. It's out of Europe, he said, and develops fun mobile apps. Insanely successful. They signed on with Brad to help them open up some doors in Silicon Valley."

"Interesting," Danny threw in, but Clyde was on a roll and didn't stop. He was excited about his discovery, but he was doing his best not to show it. His armor had hardened over the decades and few could read him if he didn't want to be read.

"Brad and his guest left but my college friend and I kept talking about them for a long while. Meanwhile, I checked them out online and they really are rising stars. An unusual, special story. The company is registered in Cyprus but the founders are from Slovenia. I mean, Slovenia!"

"Where is that?"

"A small country somewhere in the middle of Europe. I still don't know exactly where it is. Doesn't matter. What matters is that they sound very interesting and all but unknown over here. So I got Brad's phone number from my friend. Called him today." Clyde paused to add a flourish of drama. "I'm meeting him today. I mean, we're meeting him today. To learn a little more about this company. How about those apples?"

Danny beamed. "I love those apples. But why me? You think this'd make a good story?"

"I don't know yet. That's why we need to hear what Brad has to say. He is very open about it and he was delighted when I told him who I am, what I do, and why I'm interested. Maybe our article will make some inroads for them. I'm told they're quite difficult to reach and they don't like to give interviews. None of the important publications have written on them yet. That means we've got no time to lose. We need to know more, ASAP. In two hours we're off to Palo Alto, where I met Brad yesterday. That gives you two hours to see what else you can find on them. Here," he slid a sheet of paper across the desk to Danny. "Here's some basic info. They make apps with some talking animals or something. Can you believe it?"

———∞ ∞———

As they entered the elevator, Danny could feel the blood coursing through his veins. Clyde spied on him out of the corner of his eye and thought he could read the energy returning to his colleague's body. Danny was back! It was just as Clyde had anticipated. He was glad that his plan had worked, but Danny would really need to grow a thicker skin. It wouldn't do, long-term, for a journalist to be beaten to the floor by a negative turn of events. His career would be full of them. But this wasn't just Clyde's recipe for pulling Danny back to his feet. There was something resonant about the story. It was so unusual, could it really be true? And, really, had no one covered it yet? They couldn't wait a moment.

Clyde's ears popped from the pressure change of the elevator's rapid descent from the eleventh floor. He opened his mouth to clear his ears and said to Danny, "Did you Google them?"

"I did. Crazy pants."

"Well? What did you dig up?"

"You were right. They have their origins in Slovenia. That's where the R&D team is still. In the middle of nowhere. The founders are a husband and wife, along with a few other minor shareholders. I didn't find much else, as there isn't much written. The company's leaders live and work in Cyprus. That's about it... I found more articles about their exponential growth and about what they make. How they did it and their background... I can't find anything solid."

They emerged from the elevator and hurried across the marble lobby out onto the street, where an Uber driver in a black Toyota awaited them.

"Going to Palo Alto?"

"Yes. Coupa Cafe on Ramona."

"Perfect. Hop in. You're off to the Coupa? Trendy. Venezuelan, I think. Always full of folks from the valley. I drive people there every day. An interesting mix of local and modern."

"I know," Clyde thought. "I was there yesterday."

"Here you go," said the driver after nearly an hour. He pulled the car up in front of a parking lot for bikes, painted green, on Ramona Street. They got out, rated the driver on the app, and walked toward the entrance to the restaurant. Past red plastic chairs that peppered the terrace, beneath hanging lights, they moved through the scent of freshly roasted coffee.

"That's the smell of Venezuela," Clyde said, as he peeked inside the window. "Looks like we're the first. Let's sit by the window, so we can see him when he comes in."

Danny took a chair at a small table in the corner, while Clyde ordered coffees at the bar. He placed his briefcase on a chair and looked around the room. It was bumping, most people chatting with laptops on their tables, others surfing their phones. The exposed beams of raw wood were offset by yellow walls hung with coffee bags and funky photos. In the windowsill beside their table lay a copy of Forbes magazines, one of its pages marked with a Post-It note. Danny picked it up and flipped open to the page. Clyde arrived with two coffees and set them on the table.

"What are you reading?"

"A copy of Forbes from a few years back," Danny replied. Then he read aloud: "Coupa Cafe, where tech entrepreneurs and investors work and meet."

"No surprise. A lot of important people from the start-up world gather here. Above all they meet venture capitalists and see if they can find some synergy. An interesting place and an interesting business story. That's why it's in Forbes. It's also an IT hotspot. Steve Jobs used to go there."

"Really?" Danny asked, with a hint of doubt.

"Here he is!" Clyde hadn't heard the question as he spotted Brad on the terrace. As he'd done the day before, Brad seemed to know half the restaurant and greeted several people on his way in. "Brad, we're over here!"

"What are you doing inside," Brad asked. "Come out to the terrace, we'll have more space here."

Danny and Clyde grabbed their ceramic coffee mugs and moved outside, where Brad was still chatting with, well, everyone. They sat in the red chairs and watched him deftly work the patio.

"He's got it in spades," Clyde muttered to Danny. "See how easily and personably he talks with everyone? A master at work. We can learn from him."

Brad finally took a seat at their table and introduced himself to Danny first. "So," he said, getting straight to the point, "what can I do for you?"

The next hour passed in the blink of an eye. Brad regaled them with how he'd met the founder of the company, at this very restaurant, in fact, and how they'd agreed to work together. First he laid out a rough description of their business model, explaining what they do and how they're oriented. He explained that they'd not yet gone in for media exposure, but it was time for a story to come out. Clyde and Danny fired in question after question, but Brad deflected most, answering only in general, without precise data and numbers.

"If you're interested in more," he said, "you'll have to find out straight from them. Let's leave it there. I'll call the founders and see if they want to talk to you. They're probably getting ready for bed in Europe now, so I'll call first thing tomorrow. Then I'll let you know. Sound like a plan?"

———————————∞ ∞———————————

"They're ready to talk. I'll send you their R&D team director's email address ASAP. He's also the founders' son. Best of luck!"

Clyde enthusiastically forwarded Brad's text message to Danny. Now it was just a matter of time. The door was open.

CHAPTER EIGHT

Bridging the Divide

Ljubljana, Slovenia, 15 October 2009

The wind chimes above the door at Kali Center danced and sang, as they did every Thursday at the exact same time. Each team member brought a weekly bouquet of fresh ideas gathered during the previous week. The afternoon sun, aiming to set, sprayed orange light upon the shelves and the scribble-covered flipchart in the middle of the room.

Iza closed the glass vitrine with its library of alternative books and switched off the soothing music that had been playing since the previous workshop. Her last clients had left the room just under an hour ago. That gave her time to air out the space. Now she closed the windows and took her green tea down from the shelf next to the Pyramid of Horus. She sat down on one of the folding chairs, which were arranged in a semicircle.

When everyone was seated, Samo got up slowly, straightened out his wrinkled jeans, and approached the flipchart. He skimmed over what was written and crossed it all out, then turned to the group.

"We've been thinking and working passionately for a few weeks now about what kind of app we should develop. But each and every one of our ideas has already been done in one way or another. So we'll have to think deeper. Or differently. If we always think the same way, we can't expect different results. The mobile app market is hyper-saturated. If we want to come up with something new, we'll have to work harder. Either that or open our minds to look outside the box."

The team looked a little uncomfortable. They knew all this, that they needed a new idea, but they'd tested countless promising ones over the previous weeks. None worked because someone else had or was already using them already. They looked from one to another, hoping that someone else would have a breakthrough to offer up. Nothing. Samo pursed his lips in a barely visible way, wiggled his glasses, and looked over at Luka, who was slumped in his chair, legs crossed, staring out the window. In his hands he was mindlessly shuffling a pack of cards, angel cards that he'd taken out of Iza's cupboard at the start of the meeting. He was in charge of product development, so when the team ran dry on new ideas, he felt even more pressure than others.

"Earth to Luka. You still with us? What's on your mind? Anything new to share?"

Luka continued to stare at the setting sun, then straightened up in his chair, which creaked. He fiddled with the keychain, which he wore around his neck, and looked at the scribbled and Xed-out flipchart.

"I'm thinking about what we have that others don't. We know how to develop software applications. Others do, too. We're a really strong, driven team. There are others elsewhere in the world that fit that description. We need to bridge the gap between what we have and what the market needs. That bridge must be solid. Do we have any content that could translate into a mobile app that others don't? Where can we be more innovative?" Luka was silent for a moment, while the others leaned in. "I think we do have something like that."

Everyone was listening with interest aside for Iza and Samo, to whom he'd briefly mentioned his new idea ahead of time. He slowly picked up the pack of angel cards, fanned them out, and flicked them with his finger.

"We have this. Alicia Streep Angel Cards. People buy them for spiritual guidance. If you have a question, you pull any one of them out of the pack and you get a message that guides you. Believe it or not, these are some of the best-selling angel cards in the world. That's a fact. Iza sells them here at the center and they go like hotcakes. Am I right?"

Iza nodded and smiled.

"And if they sell in physical form, why not as an app? The company behind them is called Greyland. I've checked them out and gotten an email address. We can ask them if they'd be interested. Given how our app could increase their profits, they'd be fools not to be up for it."

"It's worth a try," Frenk said. "Did you make sure there's nothing like it out there?"

"I took a quick look, but didn't find anything to speak of. In this case we wouldn't be striking out entirely on our own, but would have this company alongside. Could make for a good partnership. It's a start, anyway."

Frenk gave him the thumbs-up. "I agree. We've got nothing to lose. Send an email, see what they say. If we're all up for it, you can even write to them today. What do you think," he turned to Andrej, who everyone knew was no fan of angel cards and the like.

"What are you all looking at me for?" Andrej said, a bit flustered. "You know I think it's all rubbish, but that doesn't mean that others think it's rubbish. If you tell me people will buy this, I'm all in. We have to start somewhere."

The hour that followed was a tennis match of ideas, bouncing from one person to the other, formulating what such an app might look like and how they should present their pitch to the publisher. The incense-laced space pulsed with energy. Samo stood at the flipchart as they polished their initial ideas and the text for the email.

"I think we've got it now and it seems great. Let this be the start of something big! Luka, send the email tomorrow and let us know as soon as you get a response. Okay? Are your programming fingers itching to get started?"

They were, and the enthusiasm was palpable.

"Great, but we nearly forgot an important item on today's to-do list. Before we reconvene next Thursday, we have our D-Day. Wednesday the twenty-first, right? Iza and her colleagues checked the astrological charts and the date is firm. That is the day the planets align and that is when we should kick this new project off. Those of us still working at Delta Search should leave a bit early that day. The rest of you are already free. First things first, everyone should arrange their capital investment with their bank. We'll all meet at the notary's office at 2 pm. There we'll arrange everything and register the company officially." Samo looked around the room. "No matter what, this has to be done on Wednesday, while the stars and planets are in the ideal position. Is two okay for everyone?"

"Sign here. And here. And... here."

Bereft of emotion, the notary pointed a finger at the pile of papers. Everyone was in a hurry to sign the documents to launch their business and specify the division of shares. The chilly, soulless notary's office was warmed only by the enthusiastic glow of the eight teammates present.

"After all the rigamarole at the bank this morning, this is going quite smoothly," said Andrej, who was last to sign the paper.

"What do you mean?" asked Peter, who'd arrived a few minutes late and missed the story.

"We set the new company's parameters," Andrej explained. "The division of shares was determined down to the cent. I rounded up and paid 3 dollars too much. Who'd have thought that this could create such problems? If it'd been too little, I'd understand, but too much? After that there were...complications... Well, it's fixed now. But after this morning's adventure, we agreed that one of our key focal points would be financial hyper-accuracy. As of today, we pay – and hopefully, soon enough, charge – down to the last cent. No more, no less. No matter what."

Once all the paperwork and formalities were sorted, Samo invited the team for a beer. They sat in an empty bar down the street, ordered a round, and toasted to their new start. "To a success story!"

They clinked glasses and repeated Samo's toast.

"I'm sure it will. And while we're on the subject, we have an idea for our logo. Here are some sketches." Samo laid out some large printouts on the table, which Iza's friend, an architect, had drawn up. "It's interesting to combine a technical font with a light touch. The two Ts in Outfit7 could be made to look like dandelions. What do you think?"

CHAPTER NINE

From 35,000 Feet High

Above the Atlantic, 29 November 2014

A spray of white clouds fluffed their way aimlessly across the blue sky, as a United Airlines Boeing 777-300 barreled past them at 550 miles per hour en route from San Francisco to London. The loud ping and flashing "Fasten Your Seatbelts" sign switched off after a bout of turbulence, and the stewards began their rush to distribute moist, scented towels to refresh the tired passengers, already several hours into the flight.

Danny looked out the window above the wing, which moved ever so slightly up and down, and watched the endless blue, his forehead cool against the yellowing white plastic frame around the window. The dry air on the plane parched his throat and he pressed the call button to ask for a cup of water. This was his first trans-Atlantic flight. Despite his excitement, he tried to keep his cool. But keeping his cool was tough because he wasn't a good flyer. That turbulence hadn't helped his queasiness and anxiety. When he was nervous, he liked to squeeze or fidget with something. His "airplane mode" phone now became the fiddly focus of his attention.

The flight attendants checked in on him with smiles several times. A handsome, polite young male traveler was always welcome. They weren't so sure why he'd spent most of the flight staring at a red and green card, the size of an envelope, which he'd trapped in the netting on the back of the seat before him. It bore an illustration of a smiling gray cat with the words "Have Fun" written beneath it. He had the impression that it kept shifting its smile when he looked away and Danny would smile back.

"May I ask about this cat that you keep smiling at?" a young stewardess asked, conspiratorially, as she served him a drink.

"It's an invitation. I'm going to an important meeting in London. He's reminding me of what's to come."

"Interesting invitation. Not particularly official..."

"Ah, but it is. In its own way, it's quite formal. Everything about my meeting would qualify as unusual. I don't even know what to expect. We'll see, I hope it will..."

"Then good luck, sir," she replied with a kind voice and a light smile on her bright red lips. "I'm sure your meeting will be a success. We'll arrive in about two hours." She placed the cup of water on the small table before him and turned to the guest in the next row.

Danny took another look at the invitation. He'd received it in the mail at the Bay Area Biz editorial office two weeks prior. Then he picked up his phone, which he'd been using in lieu of a stress ball. His thoughts were bouncing around his skull. He looked at the phone. It was hard to believe that there was something virtual inside worth hundreds of millions of dollars. Amazing.

He put the phone in his lap and sipped the water. He looked again at the cat on the invitation. Then he leaned his head back to the familiar spot on the window frame and watched the clouds loaf past.

CHAPTER TEN

A Puzzle Becomes the Picture

Ljubljana, Slovenia, from November to December 2009

"Guys, I just got the reply from the publisher. That took a while!" Luka whispered to Samo and Andrej, his nose buried in his email. They were the only members of the new team who were still working at Delta Search for that final month. They looked around the room at their soon-to-be former coworkers. "Let's go outside to read it."

> *Dear Luka*
>
> *Unfortunately, we are not interested in your offer because we are developing our own application. I would also like to inform you that any potential use of our cards in your application will result in our legal department's intervention. This also applies to the use of any copyrighted work by Greyland Publishing in any other electronic or print media. I ask you to immediately stop working on the development of any content related to our product and not to interfere with our business in the future.*
>
> *Respectfully Yours, Verne Triff*
> *Customer Service*

Andrej turned to Samo in astonishment. "What the heck? What kind of answer is that? I understand that they don't need us, but that's not exactly good bedside manner." He looked at Luka then at Samo again. "Aren't these people involved with angels and positive energy?"

Samo shrugged. "Apparently not…"

—∞ ∞—

A fresh Thursday meant time for the Outfit7 team's next meeting at Kali Center. Still a bit unnerved by Greyland's response, the team had been thinking about what to turn to next. Andrej got up from the semicircle of folding chairs, put his hands in his pockets, and approached the bay window. "Maybe these angel cards weren't the best idea… I think we've got to pivot in a new direction."

"Of course it wasn't the best idea," Luka replied sharply. "That's clear enough. But who knew that the folks behind the angel cards were so testy? It's clear the cards sell well, but the company is weird. That doesn't mean it's not the right direction. I still think we should combine our knowledge with Iza's. Give a whiff of alternative thinking to the app market. It's got a big following already and the New Age and alternative trend can only help us."

Andrej shook his head as he looked out into the street. "I don't know. I'm not convinced."

"What about affirmations?" Peter asked, breaking the silence. "You know, when people repeat an inspirational saying or mantra to motivate themselves? To lower stress or whatever? Isn't that popular now? We could make an app that feeds you positive affirmations. People download the app and chill out or get inspired."

"What should they affirm?" Andrej retorted. "In my opinion, happy thoughts aren't enough to sell well. If you ask me, people are only interested in cash. In how to get rich quickly."

Peter scratched his chin. "Well, maybe that's the twist. Affirmations for accumulating wealth. Positive phrases about the monetary law of attraction. It's supposed to work. Think rich and you get rich. The more you believe in something, the more likely it will happen. Isn't that so?"

"Ah, come on," Andrej rained. "That's totally ridiculous..."

"Andrej, we know you don't believe in that, but look at it from the point of view of all those potential buyers who do. I don't know... Iza, what do you think?"

"I think it's very interesting," Iza rejoined. "And yes, positive affirmations can help, even if they are tied to wealth. Worst-case scenario, nothing happens. There are no negative consequences. They can be only positive, or not, based on whether someone believes strongly enough and works toward the goal. In any case, I think it's worth trying. We have to start somewhere and soon. In one month we need to have full-time, full-on projects. Something. It's okay with me. Samo?"

He was listening with his elbows propped on his knees, three of his fingers on each hand interwoven, rubbing his lips with his outstretched index fingers. "Maybe. At some point we've got to make a decision and just go for something. To get our feet wet and teach ourselves how a useful app is made and prepared for release and download. We need to get a first project through the app store review system and published. None of us have done exactly that yet and we have only a theoretical idea of what is needed. Even if it's not a hit, we'll learn from our mistakes and do better next time. I'm for it, too. Let it be: affirmations for wealth. What should we call it? Affirmations for Wealth?"

"Wealth Affirmations," said Luka. "But let's throw in a subtitle. Maybe: Convince Your Subconscious and Get Rich? Works for me. What about you all?"

The others nodded, with a bit of reserved doubt. They checked the app stores and found nothing similar.

"So we have one idea. Let this one be our tester. A learning experience. Errors are permitted. But just this once. Okay?" Samo was emphatic. "What would it look like? Let's think about the structure, what characteristics the app should have." He approached the flipchart and began to scribble a summary across it. The ideas, though they started slow, began to fly faster from all the Outfitters.

∞ ∞

"Are you sure our tires have enough air?" Iza asked, as she stood freezing in front of the car, which hummed with ignition, up to her ankles in slush. In low boots, with a hood over her head, she cuddled herself in her jacket, rocked back and forth, and watched as her husband worked to scrape snow off the windshield. It had just stopped falling. The car was bursting at the seams with boxes and she was worried about how they would get home. But she didn't want to complain. Samo, she figured, knew what he's doing.

The rear seats of the old, gray Toyota Land Cruiser were fully reclined and the back of the car was loaded to the ceiling, not to mention the additional carrier that they'd borrowed and affixed to the roof of the car. They were fully packed with boxes full of new, as yet unassembled furniture.

"The tires will be fine," Samo said. "We look like refugees toting all this crap, but the tires will be fine. I'll drive slowly. The snowbound road isn't a racetrack."

Iza took her seat in the icy car and shivered. She put the IKEA receipts in her purse. Samo jumped into the driver's seat, rubbed his cold palms together, and blew a puff of warm air into them. "There we go, the last pieces of furniture on their way to the office! Cargo, let's go!"

They drove for two hours, slowly and carefully, pulling up to the curb in front of the one-story building in the middle of Ljubljana. Samo got out of the car, slammed his door, and pulled his phone out of a pocket. Iza didn't want to set foot outside in the cold. With the sound of soft music on the radio and the warm air from the vents, she was nestled inside, looking at the darkened building. Fourteen days ago, they'd chosen it as the team's new office. Or rather, Samo chose it. The headlights illuminated only a few windows, which were boarded up from the inside. The facade was ugly, dilapidated orange brick. At least it was orange, a color she liked. A small comfort.

Everything else was dark. She still got a lump in her throat when she recalled first stepping into this office. It looked to her like an abandoned, decaying coal cellar. Everything about it was old, ugly, and smelled questionable. They'd searched the city for offices the entire autumn but had found nothing that was up to snuff. Every office that was in a more palatable state had a rent higher than they could afford. They'd wasted a lot of time on numerous expeditions. Then Samo brought them to this office, just once, and had said "This is it." And that was it.

Iza immediately told everyone how awful it was and she almost cried while doing so. The others had been silent.

She stared out the driver's window as Samo put the phone to his ear. "Here we are. Last round delivered. You calling the others?"

"Roger that," Frenk replied through the phone. "We'll be there in half an hour."

"Are we actually going up there?" Iza asked, leaning across the gear shift and speaking through the crack in the otherwise closed and frosted driver's window.

"What else? You want to sleep in the car?" He leaned towards the crack in the window and smiled mischievously. "Come on, let's go inside for a spot of tea. The others will be here in a half an hour, then we'll carry everything up the stairs."

They entered a darkened room and flicked the switch behind the door. Neon lights shuddered on, pouring white light across piles of half-opened cardboard boxes and pieces of new furniture bought the week before that were scattered around the room. Iza just couldn't overlook the ancient stains on the gray carpeting. And that musty smell...

Samo stood next to the tea and coffee machine they'd brought from home the day before, selecting the right drink. Iza just stood, scanning the space. It was hard for her to accept that an office like this could be a nest of success. In addition, she felt that Samo was being too much of a tightwad when it came to the furniture budget, and they'd had a proper argument about it more than once. "Well, only for a year, this is it," she considered... The landlord was supposed to demolish this whole building anyway and build a sleek, new business complex in its place.

She had already envisioned how this very humble space could be spiced up with tables arranged in work islands, with stickers on the glass surfaces and brightly-colored carpets. "Red was missing," she thought. It really needed some red for energy, and green for harmony and growth. She pictured flowers in the window sills and a variety of other details that could transform the plain jane space into something homey and inspirational. "Well, maybe it won't be so bad, after all..."

While sipping tea and talking to her husband about where a table might go, where to place the cabinet, and what might hang on the walls, the rest of the team arrived. They wore sweats and other work clothes, and carried whatever tools they had at home: a screwdriver, pliers, a hammer.

The eight greeted each other with good cheer and looked over all the furniture and equipment. They opened the remaining boxes, pulled out the instructions, and made a battle plan.

"You all really are green," Iza joked. "The results of the SDI questionnaire were right on target. Greens do everything according to instructions and prearranged procedures. I would have started screwing together chair legs and only stopped to check the instructions if I noticed I'd added a fifth leg."

Andrej sniggered. "Yes, but the problem is that you, who are red, wouldn't actually manage to assemble anything. That's why you have this team. You organize us well, and we will properly assemble the furniture. Together, we're the perfect combination."

"Exactly." Iza was pleased that it was Andrej who underscored this point, that the results of the questionnaire translated into work in practice. That's what they were designed for, anyway.

"Anyone else for tea?" Hands flew into the air and she walked over to make it. The rest of them, meanwhile, brought in the last load from the car and carried it up the stairs to the first floor office.

Evening tea made way for morning coffee. After assembling furniture long into the night, the team reconvened the next morning, a Saturday, to finish the job. Most of the team had finished working at Delta Search weeks ago, while a few had to see out the month. They were all aching to get started and put their new ideas into practice, but first they needed a functional office. There was time enough for that.

Peter did some calisthenics, stretched his arms, and wiggled his hips. "Geez, parts of me hurt that I didn't know existed. That's what happens when you give IT people manual labor." The others agreed and were happy to make fun of themselves. They huddled around the coffee machine and sent the morning's first hit of caffeine into their veins. Only Samo was already at work, kneeling in the middle of the room, rolling out sections of red carpeting that would mark where the desks would go. Iza had insisted that they cover at least the largest stains left by the previous renters. To give the space at least the illusion of tidiness.

"Check this out, guys," said Frenk, with a smile. "This is a proper IT startup. We're all hanging around the coffee machine, while our director lays down the carpeting for our desks by himself! Best to stay away until he's finished, then we can all go home."

Everyone laughed. They were in an unusually jovial mood this morning, and such jokes and bonding elevated the new team's positive energy. Peter downed his coffee and joined Samo on the floor. "Come on, people, we can't let our director work all alone. Where's the team spirit? Goooo team! Forward march! We've got to finish by tomorrow night. Samo, how can I help?"

"Here, take this double-sided duct tape and stick this piece to the floor." Peter knelt and reached for the duct tape, which was about a meter away from him. This forced him to stick his butt into the air, revealing what is affectionately known as his "plumber's crack".

"Man, put your ass away," someone shouted in jest from the area around the coffee machine.

Peter grabbed the tape, straightened up and awkwardly tucked his shirt back into his trousers. "You can see my ass, but at least you can't see my anus."

Samo laughed as he lay on the floor, his head supported by his bent arms. "They can almost see your anus. And I don't mean the planet."

After a nanosecond delay, the team erupted in laughter.

"You should hide Uranus from our telescopes," Patrik added.

Even Iza found it funny, though she still rolled her eyes. Ah, children... Boys sometimes had humor so dark and strange that it pushed the boundaries of good taste. This wasn't even the first such foray today. As long as the jokes were modestly intelligent and didn't offend anyone, they didn't bother her. They can only contribute to good morale, she reasoned. Where there is joking, there's real energy. This quality gave them a little something special. If they ever managed to translate the good vibes into good apps, then they might really accomplish something. The question was whether the world would accept what they had to offer. Such ventures were always dancing on a razor's edge. Especially when it came to Samo. She was well aware that their success would depend not only on doing things well but doing things differently. That meant approaching the abyss and risking a precipitous drop.

∞ ∞

After two days of hard work, the office was ready. The last monitors were connected and all their software development tools were installed.

"There we are, that's that," said Samo. "On Monday they'll hook up our internet and we'll be ready for action. Then we just have to water the plants. It would be a good idea to make a watering schedule. Otherwise I give the plants two weeks before they look like toothpicks. Iza won't be here every day..."

"That's true. And, to be honest, we're not quite ready yet," Iza added. "We still have the vitrine from Kali Center in the car. We'll need the crystals inside. That will be the cherry on the sundae."

"That's right," said Samo. "Well, let's go down and get it. Where should we put it?"

"There in the corner. That'll let the crystals emit as much energy as possible to cool our overheated heads."

Tomi, Frenk, Patrik, and Andrej went downstairs for the shelf unit, and the others brought up the various crystals, which were in cardboard boxes. The shelves were placed in the corner and then, one by one, the crystals were carefully displayed in it.

Luka stood by the coffee machine and watched. "Now that's definitely something that not every startup has. And people are certainly interested in it. There's something else we should keep in mind. Iza, you said that those crystals are supposed to work remotely, too, right?"

"Yes," she replied. "But the energy has to be well-directed." She took one of the crystals in her hands and showed it to the others. "This purple one is amethyst. It stimulates the mind and emotions. It will bring peace and harmony to the office." She set it down and took up another. "This black crystal is onyx, volcanic glass. It is a crystal of inner strength, will, and motivation. This one will be especially useful..."

Luka recognized the gems and what they were meant to do, but he didn't know if they could work long-distance. "Yes, okay, okay. If they can work remotely, then they can also work virtually. As in, through an app, right?"

"In principle, yes," she replied. "Right now I'm working on a project with two experts on crystals. They'd be able to tell us more and maybe give us an idea. I'll ask."

"Try it. I really think that this could be one of our strengths. It certainly can't hurt. We'll figure something out."

Andrej pretended not to hear all this. "This will be my desk," he said. "She's calling to me. I can feel her vibrations." Pretending to shake, palms extended above the desk, he closed his eyes, and acted as if energy were coursing through him.

"Oh, enough with the sarcasm and choose whichever you like," Frenk snapped. "The one opposite should be mine. That way I can watch you when I get bored. And I can kick you under the desk if you act like an ass."

"That's my dream come true," Andrej replied with a smile.

The office was laid out with six clusters of two white desks on red carpets that covered the plain gray floor. The eight team members would sit opposite each other. The extra two clusters were intended for potential future collaborators. They divided up the work and started arranging their desks the way they liked them. Meanwhile, they also worked on the adjacent meeting room, setting up a shared cupboard and putting vinyl wall stickers on the windows that separated the workroom from the meeting room. It was late into the evening when they were finally satisfied. Their lair was ready a good two weeks before showtime.

Iza pulled the car keys out of her small purse and placed her phone in it. "Guys, I'm off. I have a job to get to tomorrow. You unemployed souls can party late into the night and sleep even later. Some of us have to work. See you Thursday for another barnstorming brainstorm. But no longer at Kali Center. We'll have it here. How cool is that?"

"Ultra cool," Peter replied as he looked around the room, nodding in satisfaction.

CHAPTER ELEVEN

Face to Face

London, UK, 30 November 2014

When Danny's ears popped, he knew that the plane was about to land at Heathrow. About time, too, after eleven hours stuck in his seat. His legs were numb and all he wanted was solid ground. He raised the blind and looked out the window. Just gray clouds blocking any possible view of London. *About as foggy as my head,* he thought to himself. *There's something big but it's obscured at the moment.*

After twenty long minutes of descent, the plane landed softly on the runway. Back in the terminal, he walked towards the baggage claim with a light backpack and laptop bag slung over his shoulders. While walking, he looked at the oversized ads hanging on the wall for banks offering their services. So much money surged and churned behind the scenes. So much power over everything. The whole world is one big business flushed with billions of transactions of all sizes. Someone with just 0.1% of what these brands shining their ads from the wall had would be unimaginably rich.

He retrieved his large red suitcase when it hummed its way around the conveyor belt. He and Nancy had bought it for their honeymoon in Mexico. Finding an ATM, he withdrew some pounds and headed for the Tube, which would take him downtown.

"Mind the gap between the train and the platform," repeated the speaker system at each station. All sixteen of them en route to Victoria, where he had a hotel booked. As he rode, he observed his fellow passengers and tried to categorize them: tourists, locals, white collar professionals, students... He liked to people watch and guess at their life stories. "Is he on this train?" Danny wondered. "Mark Login, the family's eldest son, with whom he'd have an interview tomorrow? No way. People like him probably travel by private plane and chauffeured limo. This mode of transport is for second-class citizens."

He'd heard stories of wealthy Russians living large in London. He'd wager that the Logins were a similar clan. If you managed to pile up so much wealth so quickly, then of course you'd indulge as much as you like in all the luxuries your heart desired. He let fantasy run wild and imagined himself in a similar role. Nicely dressed, in a sports car, cruising contentedly down Santa Monica Boulevard with Nancy riding shotgun. Didn't sound so bad.

"Next station: Victoria," the speakers announced. A gentle female voice. "Okay," he thought to himself. "Danny, wake up and focus."

After a short walk to his hotel, Danny lay down, exhausted, on the bed and tried to sleep. Not happening. Thoughts kept swarming his head like flies. Tomorrow would be the most important step of his career. He'd get a good story that would open doors and move him onward and upward. It would also provide personal insight into how the heck someone can earn so much in so short a time. I have to be well-prepared, he thought. After a few hours of spinning in bed, the sun was already tapping at the window. He got up, dressed quickly, swallowed down a light breakfast, and headed for the Grosvenor Hotel, where he and Mark Login had agreed to meet. At least that's what it had said on the invitation with the laughing gray cat.

He was up too early and had time to kill. When he'd arrived, he'd spotted a comforting sight – a Starbucks in front of the hotel on

Buckingham Palace Road. Perfect. My cafe, right in front of my nose. Now, he could prepare and calm himself down a bit. He placed his Venti Latte on the bar in the window, leaned his umbrella against the wall, and squeezed into the only free chair in the cafe. He smiled politely at an Asian woman sitting in a chair next to him, eagerly typing on her tablet with oversized headphones over her ears. After flipping open his laptop, he let his mind wander out the window onto the busy Buckingham Palace Road, while some apps took their time opening. Meanwhile, he listened to the modern arrangements of French chansons playing on the sound system. He watched one of the iconic, red double-decker buses and many of the likewise iconic black cabs drive by, the drivers sitting on the right – which he saw as the wrong side. "I'm liking Europe already," he thought.

Though he was nervous, with icicles in his veins, he felt prepared. "It would be a beautiful, successful day. I know it will," he affirmed. One more time he ran through the questions he'd painstakingly prepared. Revenues, profits, investments, offices, planned growth, tax optimization. Every question carefully chosen. He'd spent a few days drafting his questions. He was sure he'd left out nothing of import. After all, Danny was an organized kind of guy and that's what an interview like this called for.

He finished his coffee, put away his laptop, stepped outside, opened his umbrella, and headed across the street. The white flags on the Grosvenor Hotel made it stand out from afar. It was awe-inspiring: a luxurious palace from the early 20th century, leaning against a modern commercial building next to Victoria Rail Station. He passed through the revolving oak door and entered the lobby.

Craning his neck, he admired the huge crystal chandelier in the ceiling, among arches and gilded pillars. Magnificent stairs rolled upstairs to the rooms. He walked across a downy-soft Persian rug and past a large bouquet of fresh red flowers atop a carved wooden pedestal. He realized that his mouth was hanging agape. "What a spectacular lobby," he thought. Perfect for a meeting like this. As I imagined it. These people don't skimp on anything. They put the lux in deluxe.

"How can I help you, sir?" a ninja-silent receptionist asked, interrupting his reverie. Danny was momentarily confused, then reached into his coat for the invitation. He read it aloud. "I have a meeting with someone in the Soak Lounge."

"Of course, sir. Please follow me."

From the lobby they turned left through a glass door into a beautifully decorated restaurant with a striking circular wooden bar at its center.

"Would you like a window seat, sir?"

"Sure, why not?" Danny replied, looking round to see if Mark might have already arrived. He snuck a peek at a small photo of Mark he'd been sent by Clyde before leaving home. No sign of him yet. A velvet green armchair by the window caught his eye, so he sat and ordered black tea. He placed his laptop and new black Sony dictaphone on the table – he'd treated himself to it for just this occasion, its maiden voyage. This was the big fish and he had to be ready to catch it. An interview with a member of the Login family – the director of R&D for Outfit7. This story would open his door to the world of great writers, a door he'd yet to see cracked open. He took a deep breath and looked out the window again. Rain had begun to patter on the road outside.

"Hi." A voice beside him. He turned back toward the room. It was Mark Login. "You must be Danny. I'm Mark."

Surprised, Danny held out his hand and said, hoarsely, "Yes, that's me. Nice to meet you."

Before him stood an energetic young man, with piercing blue eyes, dressed in jeans and a gray hoodie. He was even younger looking in person than in the photo. Surely younger than Danny. He slid over to the armchair beside Danny and sat down, crossing his legs and resting his chin on his hand. Danny was a little shaken – a man his own age, or younger, and infinitely more successful. Well, at least this will be easier and a lot less formal than he'd expected.

"You chose a gorgeous meeting place," Danny said.

Mark looked around then quickly replied, "Well, I would've rathered we meet in the Starbucks across the street. That would've been much cooler. But the one across the street is always so crowded. This was the closest second choice that was quiet enough that we could speak in peace."

"Yeah, sure. I was just there. It is really crowded," Danny said. "But anyway, a man of your refinement wouldn't think it's cool to be there, really," he thought.

"So, where should we start?" Mark asked, a bit cynically.

"I think our editor was in touch with Iza Login. I'd love to discuss your story, which would be published in Bay Area Biz. It's a great success story. We're a San Francisco magazine..."

"Yeah, yeah, I know who you are. I've checked up on you," Mark said with sarcasm. Of course, he always did his research ahead of time about the people and organizations he would meet.

"Great, then I'll get started. Is it okay if I record this conversation so it's easier for me to write it up later?"

Mark nodded. Danny pressed the REC button and looked at his questions, which were ready on his laptop.

"I'm interested in everything, from your beginnings to today. From revenue to profit to investment to optimization and so on..." He looked up from the monitor at Mark in search of feedback. Mark just stared back, quietly and calmly.

"Maybe we should start with a short answer question? Why did you move to Cyprus and what benefits did it bring regarding taxation?"

"Really? Is that what you're interested in? Finance and taxes?" Mark's voice was harsh. His smile faded and his blue eyes narrowed. "What about some questions about why we do what we do? Our mission? Our corporate culture? I thought that was what this article would be about."

"Yes, that, too," Danny replied, trying to regroup. Something was definitely off. He hadn't thought up a single question on that subject. He was interested in business. The magazine had the word Biz in the title. "I've got to turn this around, think on my feet," Danny thought. The most important thing in his mind was to extract information about money and growth plans. That was what other journalists didn't have. Along the way they could throw in some fun facts about corporate culture and values.

"If you don't mind, I'd begin with a chat about the numbers, which are so impressive. I mean, you are creating a real-life unicorn. Really, hats off. And if we run out of time, then of course we can talk about the mission another time..."

"What if today we talk about the mission and save talking about numbers for some other time?" Mark replied with acid in his voice. Then he stood up and stared out into the rain beyond the window.

Danny was confused. Mark was losing patience and he hadn't even started. Danny wasn't sure what to do. He couldn't go back to San Francisco without answers to the questions he knew would make the story. The readers wanted numbers. He decided he had to, politely but firmly, insist on following his plan.

"Um, look, I'd rather talk numbers and business plans today. I desperately need this information in order to write my story. You know that's really of special interest to me, personally. Stories like yours are so inspiring. For American readers, particularly..." Danny felt himself stumbling along and tried a smile, to lighten the situation.

It was met with silence. Danny's cheeks began to flush. "This was going all wrong, all wrong..."

Mark spun from the window to Danny. "You know what... I don't have time for this. If you're interested in numbers, contact our PR department. They'll tell you everything you want to know. You wouldn't get any more out of me than what they'd tell you, anyway. Nice to have met you."

Mark grabbed his phone off the table and quickly exited the room before Danny could think, much less speak. Danny's heart pounded and shook him. "What had happened? What the heck? Did I do something wrong?" He looked at the doorway, hoping Mark would pop back in, that it was some weird joke. It was not.

----------------∞ ∞----------------

Iza sat at a small white desk on the second floor of an office on London's Heddon Street. She was running over last month's sales reports. Her omnipresent turquoise ring gleamed under the office lights. The door flew open and Mark stormed in. He sat in an office chair by the window, crossed his arms behind his head, and stared blankly.

"Well," she began, "how did it go?"

Mark pretended not to know what she was talking about. "Did something go?"

"Yeah. An interview with Bay Area Biz."

"There was no interview."

Iza stopped typing and looked up at him. "What do you mean?"

Mark stood and walked over to a picture on the wall, as if to study it. "He was one of those again…"

"One of which?"

"The ones who keep knocking on our door. All he cared about was money and how we earned it. And what we are going to do to make more of it. When will people realize that our story doesn't revolve around finances alone? I've had enough of this. Maybe it would be best if we didn't give any interviews anymore…"

Iza knew just what he meant. Reporters bombarded them with exactly the same line of questions, day after day. Nonsensical questions about material success. She'd hoped today's interview would be different. "Huh. I promised the editor an interview, but we'd agreed that it was going to be about our whole story."

"Yeah, but it wasn't," said Mark decisively, as he still stared at the picture on the wall.

Iza let out a slow exhale and lowered her head. "Alright. I think I'd better email the editor. That wasn't our deal." Iza was known for her quick responses to emails and for never wanting to leave things unsaid. She nudged her mouse to rouse her sleeping computer, scanned her inbox, and began a friendly email to break the news: "Dear Clyde Macmillan…"

———— ∞ ∞ ————

Danny sat in silence for a few more minutes, his gaze fixed upon the chandelier above the bar. His thundering heart had not subsided. His teacup was left untouched as he paid and stepped out onto the wet road. His head was throbbing. He didn't know what to think, couldn't think. Turning right along the sidewalk, he started to walk, destination unknown. The cold rain sailed down the contours of his body, but he didn't feel them. It didn't occur to him to open his umbrella. He just walked, dodging the people who scurried towards him. One question kept rattling around his mind: "What did I do wrong? I was ready with the perfect questions. I don't understand a thing." He shook his head and almost walked into the busy traffic, past a red do not walk sign at a crosswalk. He walked past Buckingham Palace. Though he'd never seen it before, he didn't even take notice, his eyes glued to the pavement, lost in thought.

He passed one of the Royal Guards standing in front of the palace. Then his eyes drifted toward the impressive coat of arms on the enormous wrought iron gate that embowered the palace courtyard. The armorial bore a golden unicorn and a lion.

"A unicorn... Is somebody up there making fun of me? Is this some inside joke about this unicorn of a company that I should be writing a business story about? What are you trying to tell me? And what's with the lion?" He looked away and walked on. All he wanted was to slip away, evaporate like a thin mist under a warm sun, to have no living soul anywhere near him. What a failure.

He crossed the wide road and entered Green Park, gravitating towards a wooden bench beneath a large tree. The bench was wet, but he didn't care. He sat down. Water gurgled and chugged from a triangular monument dedicated to Canadian soldiers. Behind him, Japanese maples were losing the last of their burnt copper leaves to the dregs of autumn.

What now? What happened to my story? What would Nancy say? He could already envision Nancy's father reprimanding him over Christmas dinner. "Didn't I say this wasn't going to work? You'd do well to listen to me. Stop dreaming and find a real job, kid." And what would Clyde say? His coworkers? The company had just paid for a trans-Atlantic flight, meals, and a hotel, and gotten nothing out of it. His career at Bay Area Biz, heck even as a journalist, was probably over. A once-in-a-lifetime chance had floated over to him, like that maple leaf in the surge of the fountain, and had floated away just as quickly. He still couldn't fathom what he'd done wrong.

He looked into the gray sky and felt the raindrops coolly pummeling his warm face. A whirlpool of worst-case scenarios was holding him captive. He had no idea what to do next. Should he call someone? Hide somewhere? Go home as soon as possible and try to forget everything? Doesn't the saying go that everything happens for a reason, for the greater good? If so, how was this good for anyone? If anyone out there has any supernatural abilities, then I'm all in. Just tell me what to do...

Just then, his leg began to vibrate. It took him a second to realize that it was his phone inside his pocket, shaking against his thigh. He pulled it out through wet fabric and swallowed hard when he saw who was calling. Oh no, not now, not yet... Clyde. He steeled himself and accepted the call.

"Clyde..."

"Danny, don't say a thing. I know what happened. But don't worry, we'll take care of everything. You'll be flying to Slovenia in two days."

"What? Slovenia? Why?" Danny was completely floored and couldn't follow what was happening.

"I can't speak right now," said Clyde, "I'm in the middle of a meeting. Barbara in admin will email you all your travel plans. We'll be in touch."

"Clyde, are you sure? Do you really know what happened in the interview?"

"Yes. Like I said, everything's okay, just let Nancy know you won't be home for a few days more than expected. Get yourself on that flight and we'll talk."

"Okay, but are..." But Clyde had already hung up. Danny immediately opened Google maps on his phone and typed "Slovenia".

CHAPTER TWELVE

The Early Days

Ljubljana, Slovenia, 5 January 2010

Slowly she crept through the office, approaching from behind. She grabbed him by one shoulder, lifted the headphone from one of his ears and said, "Hey, bossman, I brought you your pencil sharpener."

He turned around swiftly and, without looking, snatched the yellow and red sharpener from her hand. "Sweet, my pencil sharpener. You're the best, Iza. This was a must for our first day. That's how you kick it off. Thank you."

Samo immediately tilted to the left and fastened the pencil sharpener to the edge of his desk with its integrated vice. He picked up the already well-sharpened yellow pencil that was lying on his purple, palm-sized notebook – the one in which he mapped out his daily to-do list and ideas – which was lined up perfectly on the right side of his keyboard. He inserted the pencil into the sharpener and happily cranked away.

Frenk looked with curiosity, peering around his monitor, then he motioned to Luka, who was at the next desk over. "Check this out, he's already sharpening. On the first day at work! That's a good sign. The more he sharpened when we were at Delta Search, the more successful our projects played out."

"Then let him sharpen away!" Sharp thoughts require sharp pencils. That was clearly a good mantra for him. A talisman and meditational aid rolled up into one. Now if he can sharpen our penetration into the mobile apps market the way he sharpens pencils..." Luka smiled and winked at Frenk. Then he stood up, adjusted his t-shirt, which bore the phrase "Totally out of CTRL", and shuffled over to the other side of the office.

"Samoooo, how's your magic sharpener? All good?" he joked. "Would you sharpen one for me? Some of us haven't written in pencil for donkey's years, because some of us live in the twenty-first century..."

"So far, so good. May it continue this way." Samo lifted his freshly-sharpened pencil into the air, puckered his lips, and nodded in satisfaction. He touched the sharp tip to his index finger and patted it. "Sharp as your future mother-in-law's tongue. If you ever wind up with one. You'd need a girlfriend first, you know. Alas, for IT guys your age, the statistical probability of your finding a girl is, well..."

"Ha, ha. I think your pencil is sharper than the nail that popped your Lotus' tire last week."

Samo sighed and scratched his head. "You may have a point..." He stood and removed the headphones that were ringed around his neck. "Hey team. Since we've already disturbed you and since Iza arrived, why don't we have our daily meeting now? First day in the office, first official meeting. It's already one o'clock and it's a good time to coordinate, so we're not each knitting our own patterns. It's critical to learn to work in a coordinated, and above all goal-oriented, way. Only then can we be truly effective. Should we go to the boardroom to talk? As you know, Iza will only be with us for two days a week, so let's take advantage of her time with us."

The team slowly rose from their respective desks. All but Andrej, who still programmed away, typing at his keyboard, engrossed in his monitor. The idea for the first app to emerge from the Outfit7 team, Wealth Affirmations, whose development the team had just agreed upon, was the one about which he was most passionate. It had grown on him – at first, he'd actually considered it a bad idea. He was blasting rock music through his headphones and hadn't heard a word of what Samo had said. Luka picked up a crumpled piece of paper from his desk, balled it up, and lobbed it at Andrej. "Bravo One, please report to base. Bravo One."

Andrej slowly turned his head, removed his headphones, which thrummed with the volume of the rock music, and looked contemptuously around the office at his colleagues. "Why are you bothering me? I'm putting our app together. It's gonna make users rich and, consequently, us, too, and you're joking around. Hey, do you hear the song that I was listening to? 'Money Talks' by AC/DC. So I'm in the right frame of mind. Such masterpieces must not be interrupted. And, by the way, did you all forget that we're here on our first day of work? A measure of responsibility would be welcome. And need I mention – respect your elders, you little rugrats." He picked up the crumpled piece of paper and hurled it back at Luka. He missed by more than a yard, making his colleagues laugh even harder. Andrej thought it was funny, too, but he scrunched his lips together in an effort to maintain the pretense that he was angry.

"Come on, Iza's here and she won't be every day. Let's put our heads together. Enough playing around for today." Samo picked up his purple notebook and razor-sharp pencil, and headed for the room next door. The others followed slowly. Luka brought up the rear, stroking the glass display case with the crystals inside on his way to the boardroom.

As everyone sat around the large central table, Iza leaned back in her chair and picked up a small paper bag she'd brought with her. "To kick things off, Santa has brought us his first gift. A little late, mind you..." Out of the bag she pulled a gray cardboard box labelled "The Phone Without Compromise". She turned it towards her colleagues.

"Wow, a Motorola Milestone!" Peter enthused. "How'd you get one?"

"Our old babysitter works in Munich now. Since it's not available in Slovenia yet, she bought it in her own name in Germany and sent it to us here. She's a gem."

"Sweet. This is the technological state of the art, right here. The first Motorola to run on Android 2.0. Finally. Now we can fully test our first apps! If we decide to develop Wealth Affirmations for Android, as well, we can upload it soon and see how it works. If it works at all…"

They gathered around the packaging. "Go for it, Samo, open it already!"

He took the box in his hands and slowly opened it. With reverence he removed the black, metallic object within, held it aloft for all to see, then turned it on. The Motorola logo appeared on the screen, then Google's Android system fired up.

"Yup, that is it. The Motorola Milestone is our first milestone. Now we can really get to work. Next week we'll go to Italy for a couple of new iPhones to test out the iOS system. Then it'll be time to submit something to app stores. We have to find our niche, and this is a good way to feel it out."

The team passed the device around. Each of them handled it, tapped the screen, and opened and shut the built-in hard keyboard. Iza happily watched from the sidelines. It was like giving children a new toy. They were all so excited, brimming with expectations. It was just what they needed.

"Come on, enough with the fumbling," Samo jumped in, before he rose and approached the whiteboard, a felt-tipped pen in his grip. The others sat back in their seats and stared at the board in anticipation. Only Peter couldn't tear himself away from the new phone and kept testing it for new features under the table, as if no one could see what he was doing. Samo forced a cough and Peter, as if nothing had happened, lay the phone on the table.

"Today is our first official work day, and things are slowly coming into focus. If, until recently, we didn't know exactly what we were going to build, now our initial ideas are well on their way to realization. We know where we stand with developing Wealth Affirmations. Now we can test it on an Android system. If we get some new iPhones, we can test it on iOS, as Peter said. I think we might already send the first thing to app stores within two weeks. I just want to be sure that the final product is really good. We have an idea of what it will look like, but we'll test it and touch it up until it's perfect. Even if the final product ends up quite different from what we have in mind now. We all know a lot about making software products and now we need to upgrade our knowledge a bit more so that it translates into the world of mobile apps."

"What do you mean?" Frenk jumped in. "We've done a lot of this stuff at Delta Search. What's so different here?"

"Not much. We just have to keep absorbing knowledge and adapting. None of us have yet submitted a product to any app store. We don't know precisely what needs to be done. I'm now going over exactly how we're going to tackle this. In terms of the app, we need to get it through the editorial review process first. Only then will they publish it. In terms of user experience, it's important for us to make the app simple to use, logical, and, above all, beautiful. That's why we'll pick away at it until it is perfect."

"Yes, I agree," said Luka. "My job will be to ensure that the final user experience is optimal. At the same time, we'll be testing what the minimal standards are for our first apps to get into the app stores at all. Last time we considered making an app with a single button, so we'll see what happens. Samo and I have been playing around with that idea since last time."

"Wait, guys, let's finish up with the previous topic before moving on. So, Wealth Affirmations. We know who's doing what. Our submission deadline is in two weeks. Fourteen days from Monday. Provided we get our hands on an iPhone at least a week in advance and everything is tested. Sound good?"

Everyone nodded. They knew there would be a lot of work. Rather, they didn't know how much work there would be, exactly, because this would be their first time doing anything like this. But with all the pent-up enthusiasm shimmering around the office, they had no doubt that they would succeed.

"Let's move on to the new apps," Samo continued. "We have a new idea, this single-button app we discussed last time. Luka and I suggest that we offer the user a simple app entitled Save the World. I found a free photo of the Earth online, taken by NASA. The app would show you a picture of the planet and a single red button with SAVE written on it. When the user presses it, a progress bar appears. When the bar reaches 100%, a caption reads 'Earth has been saved.' That's it."

The team looked at Samo, expecting him to admit that this was a joke. Instead, he stood quietly and looked back at them in all seriousness. "I'm not kidding," he felt compelled to add.

"And you expect them to let crap like that into app stores?" Andrej ventured.

Luka had anticipated such a response from the team, so he quickly moved to Samo's aid. "We don't really know. But we need to see what the bare minimum is. If they let us publish something like this, then we know we can publish anything. But the app won't be crap. We're going to employ nice graphics, it's going to be fun, and it'll allow you to take a snapshot of what you're doing on screen, while 'saving the world', and put it in a gallery. You could put it on your desktop or send it to friends. This'll help it reach an audience more quickly. It's straightforward for the user, but technically not so much."

"This idea strikes me as...what's the word...stupid," said Iza. "But we really need to know the minimum parameters. If they say no, it'll be no and we will upgrade incrementally until they allow it in. But if it's immediately accepted, then we'll know what's up from the get go."

Samo nodded. "Look, we'll try and we'll see. As we've said so often, we're still in the learning phase. Whatever we learn from this will come in handy in the future, I'm sure. Above all we need to learn to make a good product. That's why we'll have to constantly adapt. When an architect designs a house, the builders erect it just as it was drawn. We also have a blueprint for our product, but the final version might not look exactly like it. We'll tinker with it until it's been polished like those crystals we have in the vitrine. Anyway, there's no real rush. When it's ready, we'll submit it."

"Why aren't we in a hurry?" Andrej asked in surprise. "Of course we're in a hurry. The whole world is pumping out similar products. If you ask me, we're already damn late. The mobile app market is among the fastest-growing on the planet. There's so much money in it and all the developers want a piece of the pie ASAP..."

Samo partly agreed with Andrej, but he didn't want them to ram their heads through the wall. "We'll be in a hurry when it's the right moment to hurry. When one of our products goes viral and people can't stop sending it to each other, then we'll be in a hurry. You strike the iron when it's hot. At the moment, we don't even have an iron billet yet. Now's the time to do the right thing the right way, to learn as much as we can for when we're in a real hurry. It's a shame to waste time and energy on products when we don't even know if they're the right ones. Now's the time for tests and power moves."

Andrej nodded, but added, "I still think we're late..."

Luka jumped in excitedly. "I really don't understand your thinking. We're just at the beginning. First day on the job. And we're not at zero, not at all. We're already developing one app well and soon we'll be able to test it on phones. We'll have a second one, Save the World, ready shortly..."

"So what exactly will the user get from using this app? You press SAVE to save the planet? Yeah, right..."

Samo knew that Andrej wanted only the best for the team, but his sarcasm frosted Luka's cookies. "I did say that this is just a test of the bottom line to get accepted into app stores. As for the user, it's a positive message. Everyone wants to save the planet... Even if it can't happen with the touch of a button, it's endearing, right?"

"Yes, but then why don't we make it a little more fun," Frenk suggested, leaning forward in his chair. "What if, when the user presses the SAVE button and a banner says 'Earth has been saved', we could also add 'And now you can go on with your life?' I think that'd be pretty funny."

"Let's do it," Samo giggled. "Let people save the world and then live peacefully ever after. Why the heck not?"

"If only it were that easy in the real world," Iza sighed, looking pensively out the window.

"Okay, we've got ourselves a plan for the first two apps. But we also have ideas for the third and fourth. Check this out. I came up with two ideas based on our past meetings." Samo opened his purple notebook and turned to the whiteboard to begin sketching.

————————∞ ∞————————

Samo crouched in the snow in the garden in front of his house and raised his eye, awkwardly, to the lens of his camera. He rubbed his brown eyes, which ached a little since he was adjusting the focus, and he slowly got to his feet. Then he pushed his glasses up the bridge of his nose and stepped in front of the lens. With his shivering cold hands he flattened a snowbank into a smooth, white tile that would reflect the sun's rays.

"Are you sure the professional photos of these crystals weren't good enough?" Iza asked him.

"They were good. I already told you they were," Samo replied. "They just didn't gleam as well as they should. I can't put my finger on it, but there was something missing. We have to do it ourselves."

"Well, then I'll set it up right here, in the middle of this swath of snow."

From a portable table full of different crystals, Iza took a large, polished carnelian and put it on the snow in front of the lens. The sun's rays reflecting off the snow shot through the crystal, accentuating its orange-red color. He looked through the lens and added, with enthusiasm, "Yeah, that's it. This'll be great. Way better than the one from the studio. The snow adds whatever was missing before."

"About time. Well, let's go one by one, step it up, so we don't freeze out here."

They placed crystal after crystal in the snow and photographed each one several times, until they were satisfied. When they'd finished, shivering, they packed up their gear and headed inside the house. Samo uploaded the photos to his computer, while Iza made them mint tea and sat at the table with two mugs. They reviewed all the photos and chose the best ones straight away.

"Now we're talking. Am I right?"

Iza enthusiastically looked through the photos on the screen. "You were right. They really are better than the studio ones. This is going to be the bomb."

After several hours of work, Samo was visibly relieved. He took a sip of hot tea. "Do you think this is really going to work? A mobile app with remote healing crystals?"

She half-nodded. "I think so. Back when Luka first suggested it, a while ago, I thought it had something. People believe in the power of crystals. And the crystals work remotely. Why not access them via an app? Physically they can be stored with us... Tomorrow I'll speak with some crystal experts who will give us precise instructions on how to connect to them remotely. Then we can start on the app. Users will choose the crystal they need and connect long-distance. We'll add a list of diseases and other problems and lay out which crystals are associated with eliminating them. Healing Crystals the app. There's nothing like it yet, so I don't know why it wouldn't work. I'll draft the content about healing and the descriptions. You'll ensure that the app actually works, looks good, and is user-friendly. Piece of cake, right? You're all experts. Now you'll become true alternative lifestyle geeks," she said with a smile, lightly ruffling Samo's hair with her still chilly fingers.

∞ ∞

Samo looked up from his monitor at the gigantic number scrawled on the glass wall in front of him in green. "$100,000,000." He thought about that goal. 100 million for a better world. Now we're in Phase 1, he considered. His phone vibrated on his desk. He picked it up and slowly brought it to his ear. "Yes?"

"Here I am. I'm downstairs in the parking lot."

"Okay, we'll be right there." He hung up and waved to everyone in the office. They slipped off their headphones, one by one. "Iza is downstairs. Let's go."

Peter rushed to the door in his enthusiasm. "Wow, the goodies have arrived! Again!"

As they did every Monday, just before 1 pm, they had a meeting. Now they hurried down to the parking lot. There was Iza, waiting for them, with the trunk of her red Alfa Romeo popped open. "Here boys," she said, "the free marketplace is open again."

They happily grabbed their weekly supply of fruit, juice, coffee, and tea, and carried them up, single file, to their first-floor office. Frenk was last in line and took a box of mixed chocolates from the trunk. "Chocolate again? You're going to make us fat... You know we sit on our asses all day and barely blink." There was a touch of truth in his words, but what the heck – everyone was happy when she brought sweets.

The delivery was diligently stacked in the fridge and on the shelves in their small office kitchen. Iza followed them. The stagnant air and the odor of stale food made her wince. She looked left and right and flared her nostrils. The floor was a mess of crumbs, the table top was tattooed with dried coffee stains, there were unwashed plates piled in the sink, a cluster of cups in the drainer, and the rubbish bin had garbage protruding from under its lid. In a corner a leaning tower of empty, used pizza boxes offered a fond reminder of last week's takeout lunch.

"You're a bunch of piggies," she commented. "Didn't your mothers teach you anything? I've seen cleaner pigsties!"

The boys did not make eye contact and acted all innocent. Andrej, the only one with visible remorse, pointed to the drainer. "Well, we did wash almost all the cups and dishes. We knew you were coming today, so we tried to clean up as much as possible in anticipation."

"You call this as much as possible? What did it look like before I got here?" She took a cup from the mound of washed dishes, holding it as if it was a biohazard, between her thumb and forefinger. It was still brown from residual tea. "This qualifies as a washed cup? Wow. Come on, people, get out of the way while I sort this out. And wash these dishes...again. Our meeting is postponed a half hour until I can get this mess straightened out. Profuse apologies, but measures must be taken to avoid an outbreak of bubonic plague..."

"She clearly doesn't grasp the concept of creative chaos," Luka whispered in Samo's ear, and giggles issued forth from the kitchen as they sheepishly made their escape.

———————————∞ ∞———————————

At precisely half past one, the team was sitting diligently in the boardroom, waiting for the start of the fifth of their Monday meetings in a row. After more than a month, they'd gotten used to the office and to working with each other. They divided the tasks and developed new apps to test the unexplored terrain of mobile technology.

"To sum up last week," Samo began, "our first two apps, Wealth Affirmations and Exotic Iceland, are both already in the app store. For now, they have not been downloaded much, but it's still the early days, so it's hard to judge whether they are good or bad. But Save the World needs saving. Apparently Apple has a higher minimum level than we thought. They feel that it's too 'simplistic', so they rejected it. That means we have to expand our little Earth somehow."

"Expand it how, exactly? To cover the whole solar system?" Peter joked.

Frenk raised his hand as if to grab at a star. "Hang on, why not? Humans could save all the planets. We add Mars, then Saturn, then Jupiter, then...uh, which are left?"

"Did you even finish elementary school?" Luka teased.

Then everyone started teasing Frenk. "Do you know what 1 + 1 is?"

"Do you know the world's highest mountain?"

Samo interrupted. "Hey, what about Uranus? Uranus...remember when we were taping the carpets to the floor? When Peter gave us a free show of his plumber's crack and we told him to 'save your anus'? That is exactly what we should do. Add an image of Uranus to Earth and press the SAVE button to save the planet. Then the message pops up, 'You saved Ur...anus.' Get it? Isn't that awesome?"

Everyone laughed even though they knew he wasn't kidding, and they were all for it, too. Iza wasn't surprised by his idea, either, as she knew her husband and his sense of humor well. Still, this seemed a bit much. "Are you sure? Even if users liked it, do you think Apple will let it through?"

"If it crosses the line, then at least I'll know where the line is," Samo replied, still smiling. "The worst that happens is they say no. Trying ain't dying. We said all along that this app was just a tester. At the same time, we can upgrade the current app. That's what they want. We'll throw some more programming hours into updating the app and, instead of one planet, we'll have two. Earth and Uranus. Ur... anus. You saved UrAnus! Ha! That's it, let's go develop!"

"Wow. If Americans end up understanding your sense of humor, then I'm Alice and this is Wonderland," Iza muttered, shaking her head.

"Really, Alice?" Samo rejoined. "And where's your white rabbit?"

Through this relaxed banter, they reviewed plans for the future and the week ahead. Samo drew a few more diagrams from his purple notebook on the whiteboard. They carefully reviewed each segment of the new app developments and exchanged views on each step ahead of them. The focus would be developing the Healing Crystals app, and they'd spent more than ten thousand dollars on it over the previous month. They were betting heavily on its success. The plan was for it to be published in app stores and on Facebook within the month. It had to be tested and polished, of course. But the team envisioned it as their first flagship app.

"Okay, we've got our plan, we know what each of us is doing, where we are, and how we're doing so far. As usual, let's conclude with our collaboration and culture. Iza?"

"Yeah, it's high time we start talking about our values. We already know each other well and we need to define what means something to all of us, as a company. That is really valuable for us. Values define corporate culture and are the most important tie binding us and our future colleagues together. If we want to truly succeed, we need to have a strong culture. We will hire and fire based on values. That's why I'd like us to define that foundation today. What is it that really makes us Outfit7?"

She handed out blank sheets of paper and ballpoint pens, white with the Outfit7 logo on them. "Now I'll ask you to take a few minutes and write down what means most to you, what we believe in. Or what inspires us. You can use a single word or a sentence. It can be a saying or a proverb. Whatever comes to mind and you feel would be proper to display on our walls. I'll summarize the list later and choose some of the best options to adorn our office. You up for it?"

It didn't seem too tough for the boys, as they'd spoken about it several times before. They got to work. As if competing over who had the ugliest handwriting, they silently and sloppily wrote on the sheets Iza had given them, while she worked on her own sheet.

"Great, thanks to you all. Next time, I'll show you what we came up with. If I can decipher these hieroglyphics of yours, that is. And one more thing – if you agree, we'll soon make a manifestation of our goals. You know, when we pass on our intentions to the Universe..."

"Iza," Andrej interrupted, zipping his black hoodie up to the neck. "I'll politely decline. I've told you many times that this manifesting mumbo jumbo is not my cup of tea. You just go ahead and enchant without me..."

———————————∞ ∞———————————

The graphic artist entered the office and began applying stickers to the glass partition walls. The stickers consisted of phrases like: "So cool." "Fun!" "Continuous change." "Just do it!" "The sky's the limit." As the team typed away from behind their monitors, they watched their office transform into a space plastered with the motivational phrases and values that they'd written down the week before. Then Samo suddenly pushed his chair back, stood up and lowered his headphones onto his desk.

"We're shutting down the Exotic Iceland app. Everyone working on it should stop now. What's done is done."

"What do you mean?" Frenk asked in surprise.

"Just what I said. We're done with it."

"But we're just starting to work on it. We can't just stop in the middle of everything. It hasn't even been in the app stores for two months..."

"I know, but all the same... The download stats are abysmal. And I know why. How many people really need an app that guides you through Iceland? First they have to be tourists traveling there, then they have to need a guide, then they have to have a smartphone, then they have to find our app. How many potential users does that leave us with? A thousand? Ten thousand? Either way, it's far too few. We made a mistake at the start in estimating its potential. We need to focus on the billions, not the thousands. We'll stop working on it. Keep it in the app store until Apple kicks it out. We're not upgrading it anymore. If it has no potential, then it doesn't make sense. Let's focus our energy on other projects. The soccer World Cup is this June. Maybe we should do something with that..."

"Is he serious?" Peter whispered to Frenk. "We can't just cut off an app that we haven't even properly worked on yet..."

Frenk, too, was visibly surprised. "Apparently he's serious."

Samo saw his colleagues looking at him in disbelief, so he continued. "A lot of companies eke out a living from apps like our guide. We do not want to be one of those companies. We've got bigger goals. If we trouble ourselves with maintaining something that lacks potential for exponential growth, then we're just tying ourselves up in knots. We have to work only on products with great potential. This is a really critical aspect for startups and I'm going to hold us to it. Now and down the line. Whenever we find that something no longer has a shot at reaching the goal we set for it, we cut it off. Even if it's already in production."

Iza looked around the office at the surprised and concerned faces. No one said a word. They were all staring at their feet without following his rationale.

"Samo," Iza began, "will you join me for a minute in the boardroom?"

"Of course," he replied curtly.

They entered the boardroom and shut the door.

"What the heck was that just now? You're serious?"

"Of course I am. Why?" Samo looked at her as if all were as it should be.

"Just like that? They should just stop working on something that they've put hours and hours of their time into? And they should stop in the middle of a project?"

"Precisely. And we're not in the middle of that project. From this moment, it's at its end. Racking up losses every hour is not a justifiable expense. If users think the app is boring, then there will be no downloads. That means no money. And when you wrap your head around that, you'll realize that every minute invested in that project is actually money down the drain. Not only that, but it means we could be doing something else with more potential during that lost time. That means more money in the end."

Iza fought to restrain herself and reduced the tone of her voice. "Yes, but just last week you were excited about the new upgrades to the app."

"I'm aware," Samo replied firmly. "Now, however, I've found that we haven't really done anything better for the user. So we need to stop working on it ASAP. One day, when we're already a colossus with unstoppable momentum, we won't turn around. Then we will move forward. Now, while we're a startup, we have to constantly search out the right path and adapt to the situation, moment to moment. Every minute."

Iza nodded slightly and thought aloud, "Okay, all of this is clear to me and if you decide it doesn't make sense, then I support your decision. But next time, be sure to pay better attention to how you communicate your decisions. According to SDI, almost everyone in this team is green. They work precisely according to plans and diagrams. You can't just interrupt their flow like that. It's like cutting their legs out from under them. I understand you're being driven by your red, action color, in this case. And because of the lack of blue in your chart, the importance of relationships doesn't motivate you much. But I'll tell you this: your team in the other room is in shock. Seriously. You're going to have to iron this out."

Samo seemed to understand that he'd gone a bit too far. "Yeah, maybe really... Well, you see it a lot better than I do. Would you talk to them to alleviate this, as you call it, 'shock'?"

Iza sighed and nodded. He took the sponge in his hands and resolutely erased the development diagram for the Icelandic app from the whiteboard. "Okay, that's it. I erase it and we move ahead. Now we've cleared some space for a new project..."

––∞ ∞––

The days flew by and Outfit7 spent their time dedicated to concocting new ideas. A corner of the office was converted into a social space. They'd affixed a whiteboard to a long bright green wall, which was artfully decorated in stylized, printed dandelion seed heads – an aspect of the company logo. Nearby a white loveseat leaned against a glass partition wall, and on the other side stood the vitrine displaying the crystals. The center of this part of the room contained a low, round white table, above which hung a large IKEA light, also resembling a dandelion. Every time someone wanted to sit in the loveseat, they would whack their head against the light. This became a habit, to see the large flowery paper cluster rocking back and forth in the wake of an inadvertent headbutt.

The clock on the shelf indicated that it was almost 6 pm. The boys grabbed their black office chairs and rolled them over to the green corner, where Iza already sat on the loveseat in a long blue dress. Everyone but Andrej sat in a semicircle around the central table. Iza sat up, elongated her posture, straightened a renegade lock of red hair, and looked at each person in turn.

"We all know why we're here today. We've talked about this frequently. Well, now it's showtime. We'll make our first manifestation of our company goals."

Tomi raised his hand, as if he were a student. "Is this going to work without Andrej? Doesn't it only work if the entire team believes in it?"

Iza shook her head slightly. "Not necessarily. What's most important is that he doesn't block our manifestation. If he were to proactively do so, then it would indeed be very difficult to meet our goals. Look, even if he doesn't say it out loud, I believe that Andrej stands with us in our desire to meet these goals. It's just the technique of manifestation that he doesn't believe in. So he's neither assisting us nor inhibiting us. All but one of our team is manifesting the goal and, if we are pure and honest in our objectives, then the Universe will provide." Iza looked around the room at her colleagues and read their faces. They were satisfied.

She continued: "You all already know something about this, but let me repeat it for the sake of clarity. This is primarily about conscious creation. If we trust unconditionally and our trust is not dismantled by a limiting conscious or subconscious belief, then we are all capable of creating whatever our hearts desire and our minds can conceive. We can manifest anything we can imagine."

"Can we manifest a load of cash?" Frenk inquired.

"We can, but today is not the day to do so. We will manifest what will consequently bring us money. The number of downloads that we would like. Remember this: the manifestation must be ethical. In our case, money is the goal, but it must have a broader rationale. To help the planet and humanity wake from its self-destructive stupor."

Peter scratched his forehead. "Okay, so let's imagine something, manifest it, and wait for it to come about?"

"Not exactly. We can manifest something we are passionate about, that excites us. If we do it correctly, then the whole Universe will be on our side and support us on our path. But that doesn't mean we can be passive. It's necessary to work proactively in the set direction. Above all, we must be careful not to block our own manifestation. First, it must be something we can imagine. Then we have to take decisive steps towards bringing it about. Consciously and subconsciously. The bolder and bigger the desired end, the bolder and bigger our steps must be."

"Well, our goals aren't small. We can only manifest them if we can conceive of them and are committed to them, right?" Samo directed this question to the group more than to Iza.

"Of course," Luka replied confidently on the group's behalf. "Should we write them on the board again, so they'll be totally clear?"

"Sure." Samo got up from the loveseat and smacked the paper light with his head. "I see the light!" He grabbed the swinging light with both hands to stop it from moving and approached the whiteboard.

"So," he continued, "we said we'd like to have at least ten new apps released this year. We'd like these to generate a million downloads. And that's by the end of June, over the next three months. Is that right?" He wrote these goals on the board. "Then we said we'd like to get it up to ten million downloads by the end of the year."

The numbers on the board looked impossibly large. Inconceivably so. So many zeros...

"We currently have a few thousand downloads," said Frenk, with a hint of doubt. "All in all, nothing at all to show for three months of work. But now we'd like to have a million by the end of June." He looked at Iza. "Those numbers look impossible to reach."

"If they seem impossible to us, then they certainly won't be reached. We are blocking ourselves with our own disbelief. Only if we believe whole-heartedly in them does the path open for us. Then, of course, there's a lot of work that goes into actually making it happen. This is the first step. Do we dare believe that we can reach such figures?"

Everyone looked at each other and half-nodded.

"Okay, so these are our goals," Iza continued. "It is crucial that we fully believe in them. Each one of us must truly believe. If even one of us has doubts, then we need to talk about it now."

Silence.

"Good. If there's any negative feeling during the manifestation, then we need to extinguish it quickly. We must stay positive. And one more thing – the manifestation works best when it is triggered in a theta state of consciousness. That's when brain activity has a frequency of 4 to 7 Hertz. This means that we must first be completely calm and only then manifest our goals. This makes it more effective. I'll lead you in meditation now, then together we will manifest the goals written out on the board. Ready? First, get really comfortable..."

Iza turned off the lights in the office and lit a candle on the table. The others settled themselves, closed their eyes and listened.

"We inhale into our heart and exhale down through our feet, down through the earth, beyond the rocks, beyond the crystals, into the very center of the Earth..."

Gradually, everyone melted into a state of peace. After a few minutes, they visualized their goals together, passed them off into the hands of the Universe, and slowly woke back into their original state. When they turned on the lights, they felt a little embarrassed but they also felt good. It couldn't hurt, right?

Frenk broke the silence. "Now we can only hope that, in the next three months, this really moves forward and we can check off those enormous numbers on the board. From a few thousand to a million."

Iza looked at him out of the corner of her eyes. "Of course we will. Because we just manifested them."

CHAPTER THIRTEEN

Open Up
or Go Home

London, UK, 1 December 2014

Danny walked into his small London hotel room and hung his oversized overcoat on a hook on the back of the door. It was dripping onto the cheap carpet. The room felt even smaller now than it had this morning, before he'd left for the meeting with Mark Login. It was already getting dark outside. All day, Danny had wandered the streets of the English capital, pushing through the rain and cold. He felt his stomach rumble, but he did not associate this with hunger. He threw his soaked clothes into a corner and stepped into the bathroom, to warm himself with a shower. Looking in the mirror, he saw his lips were blue, dark circles hung under his eyes, hair all over the place. Well, he thought, I sure managed to pour cold water all over that interview…

He stood in a steaming hot shower for a long while, running through the day's events, but he couldn't piece them all together. It couldn't be less clear to him what had happened and why. He threw on some sweatpants and rolled into the bed, up against the wall, phone in hand. For the first time since his brief, enigmatic morning call with Clyde, he looked at the screen. He saw a text from Nancy that had been waiting for him for hours: "How was your million-dollar interview, honey?" After exhaling long and hard, he looked up into the void of the ceiling and shook his head. He did not answer immediately, instead opening his inbox, where a single email was waiting for him. It was from Barbara, the secretary at Bay Area Biz. He opened it.

> *Hi Danny.*
>
> *Attached I'm sending you a plane ticket from Stansted Airport to Ljubljana, the capital of Slovenia. You fly the day after tomorrow, in the morning. You also have a bus ticket from London to Stansted and a hotel reservation in Ljubljana for a few days. Clyde will tell you more. He needs your confirmation that you'll take the trip. Call him. Please send me your shirt size, too. I have no idea why they need it, but they do. Hope you have a nice flight (it's about two hours). BTW: did you know that you're only going to be a two-hour drive from Venice? If you have a free afternoon, you can hop over and check it out.*
>
> *All the best, Barbara*

What the heck was he going to do in Slovenia? Not that he wasn't truly interested, but he just didn't have the energy to call Clyde, now. He opened his wife's text and replied briefly: "It could've been better... Talk to you tomorrow." Then he pulled the blanket over his head and, restlessly, fell asleep.

∞ ∞

The room shook as if an earthquake had hit when a heavy freight train rumbled past the hotel window towards Victoria Station. Danny slowly opened his eyes to the roar of the windows, still jangling from the vibrations. He yawned. It was as if he'd had turbulent dreams but couldn't put his finger on what he'd dreamt about. He got out of bed slowly, crouched and limping. Sluggishly he made his way to the small window, rubbed his eyes groggily, and looked at the tracks that led into the station. Then, piercing the morning murk, the next train passed by and the world shook again. Man, I feel like a train ran me over, he thought.

He threw himself back down on the bed and turned on his phone. 5:15 AM. Another text from Nancy indicated that she was a little worried, and Clyde had messaged that he should give him a ring. I should call them both right away, he thought. If it's a little after five in the morning here, then it's late evening on the West Coast. Last chance to call them.

He brushed his teeth quickly in the miniature bathroom and marveled at his disheveled image in the mirror. After boiling some water in the room's kettle, he made himself an instant coffee and grabbed his phone. Who first? Ah, I'll do the harder one first. He pressed his contact for Clyde.

"Hey Danny," Clyde answered. "How are you?"

"Uh... Yesterday was really not okay at all. And I don't know exactly why it went so badly. I had everything worked out to the last detail, but when I started asking him questions, he got angry..."

"Yes, I know. And I also know why."

"I'd love to hear it. Because I really don't understand."

"I was in touch with Iza Login. She's the Deputy CEO. She explained that the issue is that journalists call them every day and all they want to know about is their financial success. Just about business and money and how they got so much of it. And how they plan to get more. They're totally fed up with this line of questioning, from others and from us."

"Okay, I get that. But isn't that exactly what interests us, too? At least, that's what interests me..."

"Sure, but they feel that the point of their business lies elsewhere. They operate with a very special corporate culture and a sophisticated managerial process. Money is not the ultimate goal and validation of what they do. For them it's just a means to get what they really want. At least the two principal owners. And if you ask questions more in that vein, you'll definitely get some good answers. I'm guessing that all of your questions were about finance?"

"Yeah, but..."

"Look, I ironed it out. Iza and I agreed that, despite yesterday, you'll get an interview. And not only with Mark, but with whomever you want. Including her and her husband Samo, the company's CEO."

"Really? How did you pull that off? That's amazing!" Danny was enthusiastic, but with a twinge of doubt. "Wait, how did you pull that off?"

"Look, we talked. First she sent me an email that briefly explained the situation. Then we got on the phone. She saw that I understood where they were coming from. And I gave them my word that you would understand, too." Clyde recognized that this was going to be a good life lesson for Danny for the future. He left a few seconds of silence for this to sink in. "They have one condition."

Danny anticipated something else. "What condition?"

"That you try to understand them as a whole, not just as a money-making machine. And that you then present this correctly to the American public. That you try to understand the purpose of the project, their corporate culture and mission. Only then will it be clear to you what role money plays in their work, and how they get it. Vast mountains of money..." Clyde heard Danny's deep exhalation over the phone.

"Okay, but I'm not sure I totally understand. That was my goal yesterday, too. A chat about finance and then a bit about the rest.

I'm not clear exactly what they want from me. I certainly don't want to screw it all up again."

"They want you to get to know their corporate culture first and foremost. Only after you understand that thoroughly will you get the rest. That's why you're flying to Slovenia. They're inviting you to their winter team-building event, which is the day after tomorrow. That means you'll pretty much come directly to their event."

"What, I'm joining them for team building? Now I'm a little confused," Danny added with a touch of sarcasm and without thinking. "Did I come to Europe for business or pleasure?"

Clyde took a deep breath and began to speak louder and with fed-up emphasis. "Son, you listen to me and try your best to follow what I'm saying! This company is unlike any other. They're something special. Their message is about doing something to make the world a better place for all of us, for society at large and for humanity in general. If you want to understand them, you will have to take a big, grownup step forward and open up your mind. And your heart. Maybe your heart above all. Your current limitations are not going to cut it. I have confidence that you can slake these blinders of yours and see the bigger picture. And do it with your heart. And you've gotta 'translate' this story for our readers. Now, I can't force you to do that. You're going to have to decide on your own. I've been telling you this for as long as I've known you. Now it's time for you to either step it up, or lose your chance. Decide. Right now."

Danny was taken aback by Clyde's tone, as well as by everything he'd said. Am I that narrow-minded, he wondered? I really don't see the bigger picture? Given what had happened to him lately, he reasoned, maybe he didn't see or understand things properly. It took him a while to respond. Clyde waited patiently on the line. He hoped that Danny could open up and accept the challenge.

"Okay," Danny began softly. "Maybe you're right... I'll do my best to understand. I've got nothing else left, anyway. It's either this or I just come home. That's not an option. At least, not yet. I'm going to Slovenia and whatever happens happens."

Clyde felt a sense of relief when he heard Danny's words. There was still hope...

"Through the team building you'll get to know their culture and values. Their background, the way they work, what they do, what their employees mean to them, their vision, their leadership, how they work as a team. After that, the interviews. Everyone will be there. The managers, who live in Cyprus, and their employees from offices the world over. They gather twice a year for meetings and training, followed by a two-day team-building program. I'm told these are really megalithic events, so don't think of them as your 'well-deserved entertainment'. See what the team building is designed to communicate, what sort of culture it establishes. Got it? Barbara will shoot you over all the details for participation. I'll keep my fingers crossed for you."

"Okay. I'll do my best. Thank you, again, for this. You really know how to support your people and extend a hand when we need it most."

"That's what I'm here for, son. You just keep your eyes, ears, and feelings wide open. And believe. The rest will fall into place. Good luck."

"Thanks, Clyde."

As Danny hung up, he felt a strange sense of peace. The cyclone of feelings and thoughts that had whipped around his heads were replaced by a serenity that felt foreign and rare. Sitting on the bed, he leaned his head back against the wall, closed his eyes, and slowly breathed. With each exhalation, his body relaxed more. It was an unusual feeling, the opposite of anxiety, that filled him now. He sensed a shift within. It was a direction he'd not known before.

Just open yourself and swim with the current. Whatever happens happens.

Dawn bled in through the window in gentle rays that dappled the blue carpet of the hotel room floor. There was no trace left of yesterday's rain and cloying clouds. Just a morning adorned in orange and yellow against the blue sky.

He suddenly felt a warmth in his heart and a strong need to speak to Nancy. He picked up his phone.

"Hey darling, what's cooking?" she greeted him anxiously.

"Oh, Nancy, I don't even know where to begin. So the interview... it didn't go well. But then Clyde stepped in and sorted everything out, and paved the way for even more interviews. And get this: I'm going to do them at the R&D site of Outfit7. Tomorrow I fly to Slovenia. To the capital."

"Bratislava?"

"No, that's Slovakia. I'm flying to Ljubljana. It's the capital of the only country in the world with a word in its name that matches how strongly I feel about you."

"Yeah? What's that?"

"Love. You can't spell Slovenia without love."

"Aw... That's a bit cheesy, but I like it. Tell me more..."

CHAPTER FOURTEEN

Reshaping the Box

Ljubljana, Slovenia, 12 April 2010

"Damn it!" Andrej smacked his hand down on the table as the printer rolled out the latest download number for Outfit7 apps. "Pathetic." He grabbed the paper and reluctantly headed into the boardroom to join the team.

"Any good news?" Peter asked.

"Nope. A few hundred downloads. That qualifies as very bad..." Andrej held up the papers for all to see. "We've published six apps on various platforms, but not one has taken off yet. And forget about earnings. The crystals app brings us a few dollars, the rest zilch. The grand total we've earned from all this is around ten thousand dollars. That's not even a third of the money invested in its development. The rest is right around zero."

The room was tomb silent. Only the gurgling of water through the old radiator pipes could be heard. No one knew what to say. It'd been the same story for the past few of their weekly meetings, the same bleak numbers. They knew that their salaries, rent, equipment... everything that they needed to work...it was all being paid for out of

Samo and Iza's personal savings, which surely weren't infinite. Each team member paced the empty thoughts in their minds, trying to outrun the bleakness of the situation. Despite the low morale, they all expected Samo to somehow swoop in and save the day. If anyone could, it was him. Surely he already had some ingenious plan that he simply hadn't shared with the group yet? He has a plan, right?

Samo broke the silence. "Yup, we're gonna have to get some revenue from somewhere sooner or later. Not just revenue but proper profits. We've gotta keep looking for a good, unique idea. An idea that will function as a reasonable compromise between potential profitability and the investment required to develop it. The fact is that the best current category for the mobile apps market is games. It's the most used and the most profitable. That means it has the greatest potential."

Samo picked up his phone. With his glasses at the end of his nose, he looked at the screen and typed. "Look at this. You probably know it."

He turned the phone around to show his colleagues. On the screen flew funny red, black, and yellow birds, while green pigs stared at them grumpily. "Angry Birds from the Finnish developer Rovio. We all know them. This is the most profitable creation on the market, if you ask me, and the one with the greatest potential for growth. They've certainly already reached five, maybe even ten million downloads. I'm sure they'll hit the billion mark in the years to come. Unfortunately, we just barely missed the start of mobile app game development. If we wanted to make a game like this, it would probably require an investment of around a million dollars. Maybe more. We don't have that kind of money. To be perfectly honest, we also don't even have the knowledge. The risk would be too great. Anyway, it's a moot point because we haven't got the money. We need to find some other solution."

Samo put down the phone and sank back into his chair, crossed his legs, and took a deep breath. Meanwhile Iza kept her eyes on the reactions of the young team members, in their raggedy old sweatshirts, as they sat around the table.

"This is pretty pathetic," she said in the peppiest voice she could manage. "What's with us? No one died... Come on, let's shake it off. We've only been working together for four months. This is nothing yet. Did you expect us to morph into Google overnight? Well, we just haven't found the right formula yet. We need to keep looking. Seek and ye shall find. Maybe we've hit the bottom, which means we can only go up from here! Wallowing in despair will help no one. Maybe this is the moment to bounce back?"

Samo bit his lower lip and looked at her sideways. "Well, yeah... There's one thing I haven't shared with you yet. Then we can decide if we've hit rock bottom."

He stood and leaned his weight on the table, pressing with both hands. "As you know, we've been investing heavily in Facebook app development in recent months. The connection between mobile apps and Facebook looked promising. Back in 2009, everyone played games on Facebook, and even now they... Well, it appeared to be the right direction. It is not." He looked from eye to eye around the table, took a breath and continued. "They just released a series of restrictions for app developers. A lot of them. One is crucial for us: they've banned free promotion of external apps. From now on, you have to pay for everything. I'm afraid that this means a dead end for us on this platform. We just cannot afford such expensive ads. We'd end up in the red. In the future, Facebook will no longer be a focus of our time, money, or energy. It just doesn't add up."

"What are you saying?" asked Frenk. "That all our input and work invested into Facebook was in vain?"

"I'm afraid so," Samo confirmed, adjusting his glasses. "Let's call it a good learning experience..."

"I can't believe..." Frenk continued, before Samo cut him off.

"Believe me, Frenk, no one said this path of ours would be easy. That should be clear to all. Remember, we're a startup. Our advantage is that we can constantly and quickly adapt to market needs and look for niches. With Facebook or without... And Iza is right. Maybe we're at the bottom of the curve right now? It's got to get better, right? And even if it doesn't, at the moment we have little which means we've got little to lose."

"Well, except for our jobs..." Frenk muttered to himself. Tomi, who sat beside him, listened to this exchange and swallowed hard. Just a week before he'd signed on at the bank for a big mortgage to buy an apartment. Losing this job would hugely impact his life. As it would all of the other team members, too.

Samo saw that the team needed their general to lift morale. "Chins up, boys! I'm still convinced that we're on the right track. We're just missing that elusive X factor. We'll find it, I'm certain. We just have to keep on chipping away. Now, let's go through the current state of our apps and project plans, then hit the computers! And everyone can take a slice of vegan pie that Iza baked for us yesterday. To infuse us with a dose of positivity and motivation. She can do that, even if she uses sweets to get to us."

Samo finally got his team to smile, at least a little, washing away their sour faces. He wanted them to be in a good mood, to raise their motivation, but he knew that if he didn't believe in his words himself, then no energy would transfer to the team. Not even humor and vegan pies would help without belief. Samo was well aware that the situation was less than rosy and was looking for some other way to get things started. This wasn't the way forward, not in the long run. He had to find something that no one else had thought of. He was still convinced that he would find it when the time was right for him to do so. Apparently, it simply hadn't been the right time yet. This just meant that he'd have to work even harder and that he had to think further outside the box, and be even more attentive to every opportunity.

As soon as he'd heard the news from Facebook, he decided, before the meeting, that he would dive deeply into the market and potential positive directions for his team's investment of time and energy. He believed in them. But he no longer fully believed in the path they had been treading thus far. "I need to find something new," he thought...

After reviewing the plans for the week, the meeting ended. Samo closed his purple notebook, rose from his chair and headed back to work, the others close behind him. They drifted back to work with mixed feelings. Luka, who had kept silent throughout the meeting, approached Iza and pulled at her sleeve. "You got a minute?"

"Sure."

The two of them went back into the boardroom together and closed the door behind them.

"What's up?"

Luka paced nervously in front of the window. "I'm a little worried. It was months ago that we manifested a million downloads by the end of June and ten million by the year's end." He looked up at her with questioning eyes.

"Yes, and?"

"Yes and it's mid-April and we aren't anywhere near there. I mean, I strongly believe in the power of the manifestation, but the numbers suggest otherwise. I don't know what sort of miracle could bring us to a million in just two months. Does this manifestation thing work at all? Did we do something wrong? Should we repeat the process with different goals?" He scratched his head, feeling awkward. "Look, do you two have enough savings to fund us all while the company is more or less bleeding money? I know that Samo made a lot selling his share in Delta Search, but all the same... Everything that we've done so far, and we're still just a big black hole of expenses. Isn't that right?"

"Luka, listen to me. It's mid-April. It's not the end of June, is it? Let's wait until then and we'll see. Acting from a position of fear during a manifestation certainly won't help. Doubt blocks goals. That's the first thing we need to know. We have sincerely passed on our intentions to the Universe and now we must trust that the Universe will help us on our path and remove those obstacles from it. At the same time, we need to work hard in the right direction and create consciously. By no means should we get stuck behind a set of numbers and just dance around them in fear. Then truly nothing will happen. We have to work towards the goals and they will manifest. Believe. June is a long way off." She smiled at him and gently touched his shoulder.

Luka just nodded, silent.

∞ ∞

The days to come spun on monotonously, each indistinguishable from the next. The team felt trapped, devoid of both space and time. They worked diligently on their assigned tasks and maintained their existing applications, adding new functions to them. But the numbers remained more or less the same. The fun was draining out of work, their trademark humor ever less frequent. It was a pale shadow of the joy and optimism of their first days.

Samo's absence didn't help. He was mostly quiet during the day, immersed in his work, and on ever more occasions he opted to work from home, not even showing up at the office. The whole situation was eroding morale.

Iza made a concerted effort to remain positive and encouraging. At the same time, she watched Samo's quest for something that could push them forward. Day after day, he stared at the computer's small monitor, scanning for niches. More like looking for needles in haystacks. It was the same at work and at home. He'd sit on the living room couch until late, working until he began to snore. She wondered what was going on inside his head, but he was the only one with a legend to that map. When Samo was deep into his work, it looked as if there were some extra dimensions behind his computer monitor that only he could see and comprehend. If the average person looks at a monitor and reads information from it, Iza felt that Samo saw some alternate series of algorithms, like he was looking through The Matrix, trying to decipher its contents and reassemble them into a different form. When he was at maximum concentration, it was as if he, the computer, and the internet itself were one endless, undefined, inconceivable whole. Colleagues, but Iza above all, had seen him enter this zone on several occasions, but now it was all the more obvious. It was clear that he needed his time, so he was largely left to his own devices and disturbed only if the matter was urgent.

He was trying to remain focused. Samo appreciated that the team was giving him space and he was sure that they were doing their best on their own, in parallel to his efforts. He didn't waste a moment. Most of his time was spent trying to find answers to questions he thought he'd answered long ago. How to properly invest in the development and promotion of certain types of apps. How does promotion work and what's necessary for it to take off? What are the key differences between paid and free apps? Many questions, few real answers. The firm edging into the black was not within his sightlines yet. He plumbed the very depths of development, marketing, and the potential of mobile apps. Above all, he hunted for the key to virality. He reviewed all the apps he could that were successful and sought ways to mirror their success, as well as to invent new ways of getting users familiar with a given app. Whatever the app was, there was only one important thing: it had to go viral. Something about it had to encourage people to send it to one another, doing the promotional work for them. The term "viral" was right on – it was a positive virus, passed from person to person, not through paid ads. If they wanted to embrace the world, this was the only way.

Precious few moments were left for Samo to devote to the non-virtual world around him. On a number of occasions, while enjoying a vegan dinner at home with the children, Iza tried to coax out of him some of his interiority and what progress he might have made.

"A Mister Kern called a few days ago," Samo said, breaking the dinnertime silence.

"Yeah? Who's he?" Iza replied with curiosity.

"I don't know, I don't know him. But he said that he'd heard of us and he'd like to work with us on an app that would include 3D animation. He wanted to work with us because he doesn't have animators."

Iza looked at him. "Okay... But we don't have animators, either."

"Yeah, I know. That's the most interesting part. If this Mister Kern, who has no idea about animation, can make some products that contain animation..." he sipped some white wine, then continued, "then I don't know why we couldn't do the same."

"That's true," she replied with interest. "So, what now?"

"I told him we couldn't work with him because their proposed collaboration didn't seem right to me. But it did make me think. I also checked what already exists in the animated world and what doesn't. I've pored through the app store's Entertainment category, as well as Gaming, which is the most saturated. There are some apps that literally flew off the virtual shelves with no serious investment in marketing. And we could actually afford a campaign that didn't have serious investment in marketing," he smiled, then set down his fork and leaned back in his chair contentedly. "I think I've found a niche that would suit us perfectly. 3D animation within the Entertainment category."

Iza felt like Samo had been numb for quite some time. This was new now, finally a sense of optimism. She'd been waiting for him to open up again and impress everyone with a big, new idea. She knew it would come, sooner or later. But this particular idea? It struck her as very unusual. "Okay, but how could we pull it off without animators?"

"We couldn't," he replied warmly. "We need to take on an intern and try. Are you interested in what they would do?" Iza felt a wave of energy emanating from this question, like an invisible explosion. Samo's pupils dilated, like a treasure hunter staring at a chest of gold. She knew he could hardly wait to show her something.

"Yes, of course. I'm all ears."

Samo reached across the wooden table, where his phone lay. He swiped it open, tapped on an icon, and passed it on to his wife. She lifted it and looked at the screen curiously. An unusual app was open before her. At the top of the screen she saw a blue sky, followed by artificially drawn clouds, green grass on the ground, an unusual green awning, and a red box, which had stylized hands, a large mouth, and a pair of round, squinting eyes, one on each corner. She looked up at Samo, to be sure he wasn't joking.

"What's this?" she asked, skeptically. Meanwhile the red box on the screen opened its cartoon mouth wide and repeated, in a high-pitched voice, "What's this?" Iza was so surprised that she did a double-take and stared at the screen, watching the strange animation. "Does it repeat everything I say?" she asked.

"Does it repeat everything I say?" the voice parroted.

"Yeah, he repeats after you. This is Talking Carl," Samo said enthusiastically.

"Yeah, he repeats after you. This is Talking Carl," said the phone.

"Now turn it off before it gets annoying," scolded Samo.

"Now turn...," but Iza had already closed the app.

"Uh interesting, I suppose," she said. "What do you think we can do with it?"

"This feature, that it repeats your words, seems good to me. This is a technological masterpiece at the moment, but I think we could make it even better. So I'm on the lookout for some different character, something prettier, more likeable, and more popular than, well, a box. Just today, I was browsing TurboSquid. It's an online store for 3D drawings. But I haven't found anything right yet. It seems to me that this box is something we could upgrade and take to the next level. If the app were more fun, if it had a more elaborate sense of humor, it could certainly go viral. I think the Entertainment segment is our future."

With each sentence spoken, Samo was more enthusiastic about the idea. It was infectious.

"I think I've found what I was looking for," he continued. "At least the right direction. We'll sort out the details, of that I'm certain."

∞ ∞

Something in the air told the team that this Monday's meeting would not be like all the others. Luka had already spread rumors that Samo was onto something new. On Sunday they'd spoken over the phone and Luka scattered a few crumbs of information around the office to raise hope and expectations. But he didn't want to ruin the surprise for Samo and give away the news. It was finally an encouraging step that would help to clarify the company's vision.

Iza brought in the weekly supply of coffee and fruit, but for this occasion she made them a small raw cake. As soon as they'd brought the libations from the car into the kitchen, the team stopped working and gathered in the boardroom, brimming with anticipation. Morale hadn't been that high in weeks. The smiling faces quietly waited for whatever Samo had cooked up for them. He'd been mentally absent for more than two weeks, and everyone was happy to see him back, full of enthusiasm and positivity. Wearing a brown zip-up sweater, he stood before them.

"Guys, I found something. It could be interesting..."

The projector whirred and from his computer he cast a picture on the pull-down screen. A funny-looking red box.

"This is a paid app called Talking Carl. In addition to a few minor features, it repeats everything you say into the phone. It was only recently released into the app store. It was a hit straight away."

"Is it a mailbox?" Andrej joked. Everyone, Iza included, laughed, as that was indeed what it resembled.

"No," Peter rejoined, "it's a plastic backpack for school children."

Samo let the levity fill the room – they'd been missing it for so long. "Think what you like. The animation is basic, simplistic. In other words, there's still a lot of room for improvement. But the point is what it does." Samo pulled his phone from a pocket, opened Talking Carl, and showed everyone the app's features. "Don't look at the graphics and user experience now. Focus on what it does, and how we can do better."

Phone in hand, Frenk spoke with enthusiasm to his new red friend and then added, with interest, "I actually have no idea about animation, but I think we could upgrade this considerably. Why do you think this is such an opportunity for us?"

Samo nodded and began. "The Entertainment category is by far the least saturated at the moment and we can do a lot without paying high promotion costs. I think this is the way to go. The key is that

Awyse, the firm that developed Talking Carl, have managed to get very high on the charts in Western countries. And remember, this is a paid app. Getting to the top of the charts with a paid app is at least a hundred times harder than with a free one. We all know that. The point is that if they can do that well with a paid app, then with a free one we could reach higher, faster. We should develop something with similar features, honed to the minutest detail. We'll publish it for free and we'll win. Trouble is, you can't make a living from a free app. We need to figure out some monetization model. Ads are the most obvious and we need to consider that carefully. In-app ads are still in their infancy, but I think integrating ads is the best recipe for us. Luka is firmly against that approach, but I've yet to hear a better idea and I'll stand firm with my instinct for now."

Luka nodded slightly as he listened, his chin balanced on his palm, watching Samo present.

Samo continued. "The app must be free in order for it to spread quickly. If we get a hundred times more downloads with a free app with ads, we'll get more for the same effort than the paid app developers get. And that's right from the get go. I spent a lot of time researching this and all the data leads me to the conclusion that this is true and that this will work. Don't forget, too, that people have much lower expectations from a free app than a paid one. If a free one is really top drawer, then it could easily multiply the number of downloads by a thousand. For me, this is a no-brainer. It has the true potential we've been looking for. We just need to test the theory and then make changes as needed." Samo's enthusiasm snowballed as he spoke, causing his glasses to slip down towards the end of his nose.

"It sounds very interesting," Andrej remarked. "What do you think we should do differently?"

"First of all, I think we should add a character that's a little more human. Carl is very technical and doesn't have a proper personality.

Second, we should refine the repetition as much as we can, to optimize the user experience. I already have an idea about how to do that. I spent days browsing online for the right character, someone users could feel close to. This is what I found. I bought it for $65 on TurboSquid." He pressed a button on the computer and an image was projected onto the screen. "Here he is. Meet our new friend, Tom."

A cute, gray kitten with oversized friendly green eyes appeared. He stood on a street corner, on the gray asphalt sidewalk, against a backdrop of orange brick tagged with graffiti. An old metal trash can was to his left. He smiled charmingly and looked out at the team, which studied every detail of the projected image with interest.

"Any thoughts?" Samo asked.

Andrej replied first. "I think it's very nice, but I don't have a good sense of what will work on the global market. I'm no graphic artist, nor am I your average earthling."

"If I understand correctly, we're supposed to animate this cat, this Tom, as you called him. And he would do the same thing that the red box did? Repeating the user's words?" Peter asked. "You think that has a chance of succeeding?"

"Something along those lines, yes," Samo replied. "We still need to agree on what exactly he would do and how, but that's the gist of it, yes. I'm certain this could go viral. Especially if the app is free. The only thing we need now is an animator or two to help us. Iza is already on the line with some potential interns and we can choose one or two to help us. Have you found anyone yet?"

"Not yet," Iza replied, "but we have quite a few candidates. They'll come in this week for interviews and we'll decide then. We need capable collaborators who will fit into our office culture. Unfortunately finding and integrating the right people takes time. As for Tom, I can honestly say that I don't like him. Well, the cat alone is maybe okay. It's the background that I find really off-putting. It's morbid, like he's standing in some godforsaken place. I would add more color and make the environment more natural."

"But that's just what I like about it," said Samo. "The contrast between an adorably cute protagonist and the ugly, dark surroundings. A lot of people in the world would identify with this. Especially youngsters. Well, at least I think so."

"Possibly. But why a cat?" asked Andrej. "And why is his name Tom? Don't you think this is a little too close to the cat from Tom & Jerry?"

"I don't know exactly why I chose this cat," Samo replied. "Intuition, I suppose. He seemed so human and likeable to me. I don't have any real rationale for it. It just struck me as cool. I like the name Tom for a cat because Tom Cat means a male cat in English. A talking cat. The fact that people already associate the name Tom with a cartoon cat can only be an advantage. "

The April sun was already shining shifting to its sunset orange, and the meeting still rolled on. They debated all manner of ideas, exchanged opinions, and sought arguments and counterarguments. They weren't convinced that this cat was really the way forward, but Samo believed so strongly in the idea that it was hard to resist his passion. It was definitely something new and totally different from what they'd been attempting to date. Since their past efforts had not borne fruit, then it was worth trying something new. They also knew that Samo would not have proposed such an out-there shift if he hadn't studied its potential in great detail. Whether or not it would go viral was something no one could really say in advance.

The debate ran on and Samo let it play out as long as it needed to. After another hour it slowly ground down, and he concluded. "So that's it. We'll start working on this new project tomorrow. For now we'll call it the Talking Tom Cat 1 project. We'll put a little less emphasis on our existing apps, aside from those already in development. Roughly speaking, we'll divide into two teams. One will work on Tom. The other, led by Andrej, will continue to work on the balls already in play. We'll keep several irons in the fire. We'll divide up the tasks tomorrow morning. Sound good? Then we'll see soon enough if we've backed the right horse or if the horse has taken us off on a dead end." Samo shrugged, closed his purple notebook and switched off the projector. He looked around the room and added, in all seriousness, "I personally think we will start building a highway tomorrow that will take us to our promised destination soon. I can't be certain, of course. Whatever happens happens."

Luka and Iza glanced at each other across the room and shrugged. Whatever happens happens. Samo knows best.

Iza stood at the table in the boardroom, reviewing the resumes of the potential intern who had applied for the 3D animator position. There was a knock at the door and Peter poked his head in. "The first candidate is here," he said.

"Okay, send him in." She straightened her long skirt and sat. The door opened again and a young man entered, looking a bit sheepish. He walked around the table, looking at the slogan stickers on the walls and the text on the whiteboard. Iza looked him over. Some lonely wisps that wanted to be a beard poked out of his chin and his brow was crowned by a shining pimple.

"So you're Jani?"

"That's me."

"Take a seat. You can call me Iza, we're on a first-name basis in this office."

"Thanks," Jani replied, visibly relieved, and he sat opposite her.

"I read your resume and it looks great. You have all the skills we're looking for. Is your resume, you know, accurate?"

"Yes, yes, of course," he stammered. He had expected a barrage of questions since he knew he was very experienced for someone still officially a student.

"Well, that's an important first step. Trust. If we don't trust each other now, then it will be hard to find trust later. And trust is the foundation of all great teamwork. You've probably already taken a look at what we do. We make mobile apps. Now we have a new project and we could use some help from someone with your skill set. Let's get started. Let's say I invited your best friend over for coffee and I asked him who Jani is. What would he say?"

Jani swallowed, surprised at the strange question. He began to talk about what he liked to do, how he saw the world, how he treated others. It was hard to believe how relaxed and open this interview was, how he was able to, encouraged to, talk about personal things in front of a stranger and potential employer. She gave him an unusual sense that he was safe, so he was happy to tell her candidly about anything and everything. Their chat ranged from hobbies to how he tackled projects and what gave him greatest satisfaction. In return, he asked about what his duties would be, and what hourly rate of pay he should expect. The half-hour conversation was more like a chat with a classmate than a job interview. At least that's what it felt like.

"Okay," Iza finally said, "I think we talked about all the material I wanted to cover. Do you have any other questions?"

"Um, yes. Are there opportunities for advancement here?"

Iza smiled. "Opportunities for advancement? Our hierarchy is very flat. As you know, there aren't many of us. We want it to stay that way. We anticipate that this company will never have more than twenty employees. So I really can't promise hierarchical advancement. But we do have huge goals. And people whose main value is responsibility will progress within them."

"Responsibility? Sorry, so what exactly do you mean by that?"

"We see responsibility in the fact that you are the owner of each task you receive. If you take on a task, then you have to make sure that the task is done and done well. Of course, this doesn't mean that you can't ask the person who assigned you the task for help. You can and should. But the responsibility is yours. If, for any reason, you are unable to complete your task on time, you must immediately inform the rest of the team and explain why it won't be possible. We know that not all tasks are feasible in the time allotted. That's why it's your responsibility to communicate this as soon as you see that it won't work as planned. The person assigned must do all they can do to carry out the task the best way possible, using as few resources as possible. And everyone affected by the task must be kept abreast of how things progress. Does that make sense?"

"Yes, yes, I understand. And I agree with all of it."

"Well, as I said, a responsible colleague will have unlimited opportunities to advance within the context of our collective goals. The responsibility for everyone on the current team is very high. Each colleague gives 100% to fulfill what they promise. The team here really owns their shit."

"And so do I," Jani said, pleased.

Iza reached out her hand. "So that's it. I've got a few more interviews to do and then we'll talk."

As he left, she watched him and felt his energy. She was almost certain that their first new colleague was just leaving the office.

———————————— ∞ ∞ ————————————

The coming weeks were marked by the preparation and development of the new app. Jani was hired and quickly onboarded with the team. Another intern followed, someone who was also an animator, so the two could share the workload and progress more quickly. The office buzzed with positivity once more and noses were to the grindstone. Most of those noses were focused on this new animated gray cat. They reviewed the technical and marketing options for rapid product development and made a clear plan, whose key tasks were penciled out in Samo's purple notebook. The pace was fast and exhausting, but it never felt like work, as everyone was having fun. The acerbic humor and bursts of laughter were back and a key part of daily conversation. Team spirit wound around and interlaced their collaboration. They worked ever longer hours, but felt less and less pressure. They were doing what they wanted to do, what they excelled at, and they were humming along like a well-tuned instrument. The direction was clear and collectively agreed upon. The only thing that they'd been missing was animation skills. But the two interns, young as they were, worked admirably and learned quickly. They were adopted into the team straight away. A few weeks into their time together, the team had the tools and knowledge to develop an animated 3D app and have a minimum viable product by the end of May.

Since the existing apps didn't bring in any income to speak of, and since the new project required so much work, only Andrej maintained their extant apps while everyone else worked on Tom. Financial investments also increased with the addition of two staff members, and those came straight out of Iza and Samo's pockets.

Luka kicked off one of their Monday meetings soon after that. "I have a super important question for everyone," he began. "We know that the unique user experience is one of the most important things a new app needs. We have to work it out to the last detail. In addition to Tom just repeating the user's words, we've now added the ability to pet him on the screen, to pull his tail and to, uh, whack him, well, let's call it to gently poke him." Luka demonstrated all this on his forehead as he spoke. "Samo had a good idea and now we need to decide if we're going to implement and develop it in our app. So... drum roll, please...should Tom fart or not?"

"Whaa....?" Iza half-asked, not even sure if she heard the question correctly. Everyone else laughed.

"May he fart often and loudly," Frenk said immediately. "People fart. That's a fact. Men, women, children. Most people think this is funny. So if we want to have a human-like character as our star, then he should be a farter."

Luka smiled, nodded and turned to the others. "What do the rest of you think? Let's do it democratically. Raise your hand if we should add a button that you can press to make Tom fart."

All hands shot into the air immediately. Only Iza abstained. The meeting plowed on with a hot debate over what symbol and color best suited a feline fart button.

Luka and Iza sat on the steps in front of the office building, surrendering themselves to the warm June sun as they ate their lunch.

"Iza, it's already the middle of June."

"I know. That's why it's so warm and that's why the birds in the tree over there are so happy."

"You know what I mean. We manifested our great success to come about by the end of the month. But there's no indication that we're there. Our current apps bring in next to nothing. Talking Tom looks promising but it doesn't launch for two more weeks. We've gone through more than 200,000 dollars since the start, 30,000 just on developing Tom. I just don't see any chance of making a breakthrough within two weeks to hit a million downloads. It can't happen. It just seems that our manifestation isn't working as promised. Also...do you two have the finances to keep on investing in us? Your bank account presumably has a bottom somewhere, right?"

"We've spoken about it many times, Luka. It's okay that we took some time to refine the app in all its details. The fine tuning is really boring for developers, but you of all people should know that, in the end, everything has to work well. The user experience has to be maximized. Adding ads was also its own odyssey, but that's the only way we can make money. Look at it this way: we have shown that we only need a good month to develop a really strong product that contains everything we need. That's amazingly fast. We're ready to publish in two more weeks. I looked at the astrological charts and June 24 is absolutely the optimal day for it. All the planets will be ideally positioned. Any day before that would have been much worse. That gives us six days till the end of the month, right? I still firmly believe that the manifestation will work."

"A million downloads in six days? Yeah, right..."

"Luka, please don't block the manifestation by doubting. If we said by the end of June, then it's by the end of June. You said it yourself, we're only in the middle of the month, so there's still time. Believe in it and work towards the goal. But to answer your question honestly, Samo just told me that this is the last product we can afford to invest in. If Talking Tom doesn't succeed, we'll have to shut down and end our startup story."

Luka was devastated to hear this, at the prospect of it, but he'd been contemplating it for weeks now. "Oof, really? Are you also thinking along those lines?"

"Are you kidding? I told Samo, no way! We threw enough money at app development to buy a house. Not to mention our time and energy. I told him that I don't care how he does it, he'd better just make it work. There's no option but for this to launch us. Pedal to the metal."

———————————∞ ∞———————————

Peter shifted nervously at the table. "Too bad that Andrej isn't here. Poor guy is on vacation in Greece while we're launching something, all hands on deck. Talking Tom Cat 1 is done, now we'll see the fruits of our labors. He's missing a big moment..."

"He's more than earned his vacation," said Samo. "While we were working on Tom, he carried everything else on his shoulders. Let him enjoy himself. He really knows how to unplug, I will say that. Not answering emails or his phone. A proper vacation. When he comes back, we'll need him well-rested. Iza will be heading off in a few days, too. Then the others."

"Yes, I go on Thursday. Beach, here I come!" Iza enthused. "We dropped the kids off at camp yesterday, and then I'm off for a few days. That's been my tradition since I worked at Microsoft. A little rest after this ordeal will do us a world of good. My only problem is that I can't disconnect as readily as Andrej."

"Well, here goes nothing. Let's send this over to Apple for approval. Whatever happens happens. Right now? Click and send?" Frenk asked with his finger trembling, poised above the mouse button. He looked around the room. His team nodded to him. Send!

He clicked. "Godspeed, Tom Cat!"

CHAPTER FIFTEEN

I Feel sLOVEnia

Ljubljana, Slovenia, 4 December 2014

The small passenger plane looked like an orange dot shot through the blue sky over the snow-capped mountains. The sun's rays dazzled as they reflected off the white peaks of the Alps as the plane descended towards Ljubljana. The mountains slowly receded before dense coniferous forests. Danny could see the first villages bound by a twine of gray, winding roads that threaded the wide patches of green. What a view!

After a soft landing at the teacup-sized international airport, he deplaned and walked to the main terminal building, standing in the line for non-EU citizens. A stern, brunette immigration officer picked up his passport, looked at the photo, and then looked at him. "What is your purpose in Slovenia? Business or tourism?"

"Um," Danny began, not quite knowing what to say. "Probably a little of both. I have an interview with a few businessmen. In between, I have a few days off. I'm writing an article about one of your companies."

While scanning the passport she glared at him. "Really? Which one?"

"Outfit7. You know, the ones who made Talking Tom? That cat who repeats..."

"Yeah, yeah, believe me, I know who Talking Tom is. My kids can't stop playing it. Ever since they downloaded it, they've been glued to the phone. I'm not sure how I feel about that..." She returned the passport to him, maintaining a straight face. Then she nodded. "Good luck."

"Thank you very much," Danny said, as he headed for the baggage carousel. While waiting for his suitcase, he studied the various ads promoting tourist attractions in this country that was unknown to him. Sea, mountains, karst caves, spas, castles... "What don't they have here? And the country is so small..."

Most of the posters bore the slogan, in white against a green background: 'I feel sLOVEnia.' "Interesting," he thought. "Maybe I should be feeling love here, too..."

The red suitcase finally bumped along on the carousel. He grabbed it awkwardly and rolled it the very short distance out of the airport building. Stepping outside, he took in a lungful of fresh, cold wintry air and looked up at those snow-enrobed mountains, looming above, so close. A short man in a blue down jacket approached him.

"Mister Keaton?"

"Yes, that's me."

"Great. I'm your driver for the next few days. My name is Milan. Like the city in Italy with the fashion shows. You know what I mean?"

Danny nodded, not sure what to make of it. "Of course. Milan."

"Super, super. Now you'll never forget my name." He winked at Danny, smiling broadly and toothily. "Our car is right over here. Shall we? Was it a good flight?"

"Yeah, it was nice. Especially the view from the plane on this beautiful, sunny day."

"That's right, now you're on the sunny side of the Alps," Milan replied proudly. "We're in the northern part of Slovenia. We'll be in Ljubljana in twenty minutes. If I step on the gas too long, we'll be in Croatia. We are a very small country, you see," he added, teasing.

"I don't know much about Slovenia, but I really like it so far."

"It'll only grow on you. This is truly the pearl of Europe. Well, if you have a day off, I can take you around a bit."

"I'd like that. I'm told we could even go to Venice?"

"Sure. It's about two hours from Ljubljana."

"Well, maybe we can. What's the plan for today?"

"You'll be staying at a hotel right by a big shopping center in Ljubljana. It's very close to the Outfit7 offices. You'll be able to go on foot. But you're not going to the office today or tomorrow. You have today free and on Friday I'll take you to Maribor, a city in the east where the company's having its winter team-building program. It's just an hour and half."

"Okay. And what are we going to do there?"

"That's a question no one has the answer to. It's a complete surprise for employees every time. Only two or three people at the company know what's planned. The others don't even know they're going to Maribor. I only know because I have to know where to drive you. Secret service. Employees were only told when to show up at the office and when they'd be back there at the end of the program. This has supposedly been the tradition since the company began. Their team-building events are the stuff of legend. They really invest a lot in their employees."

"Wild. I've never heard of anything like it. 160 people go to a two-day business event, but they don't even know where or what they'll be doing there?"

"Yup. This is the winter event. In the summer they go for three days. Same deal. No one knows anything. A complete surprise."

"How do you know so much about them?"

"I've been working with them for years, almost from the start. I'm part driver, part delivery guy, part everything else they need. That's why I know them so well. I'm ready whenever they call. And they always invite me to their team-building events. They're very open and take great pains to ensure that everyone feels connected. Maybe I'll even work for them full-time someday. Not a bad idea..."

"Doesn't sound bad at all," Danny intoned, his mind wandering, absorbing. He looked out the window at the infinity of green spruce forest that rushed past. "If a driver who doesn't even work full-time for the company knows so much about them," Danny thought, "and is so devoted to them, with such a high opinion of them, then I wonder what the insiders think? What a fascinating few days I'm in for..."

∞ ∞

He opened the dark wooden door to his tenth-floor hotel room. "Wow," he thought, "this is a big step up from London!" He threw his red suitcase onto the bed, tucked in the retractable handle, and placed his briefcase, which contained his laptop, alongside it. The bed was big enough that there was still room for the blue paper bag that sat upon it, bearing the words "Talking Tom & Friends" and accompanying images. A small, handwritten card was attached to the bag by a string.

Danny, welcome to Slovenia. Something to read, something to eat, and something to wear at our team-building event on Friday.

Very thoughtful. He sat on the soft mattress, pulled the gift bag onto his lap, and peeked inside. Three books, a small vegan chocolate bar, and a clear plastic bag that contained some black fabric. First he pulled out the three books, each heavy and colorful. Each was an extensive manual on the animated characters in the Outfit7 family. He flipped through them. Each character was described in detail, including personality traits and notes on appearance. True attention to detail. "Geez, I'll need a whole day's work to review these." The last book was yellow and its title was Getting Started with O7. He placed it on the bed, then read the subtitle. "A brief but thorough guide to the magical world of Talking Tom and Friends for those of you who are here to work your asses off and have fun while doing it." This brought a smile to Danny's fatigued face. "Is this some kind of handbook for new employees? And right from the start they tell you you'll be working like crazy? And having fun doing it. Isn't that an oxymoron?"

Next, he opened the plastic bag. Inside was a black polo shirt and a white tie decorated with a cat's paw print in red and green, an element of Outfit7's logo. "Ah," he thought, "so that's why they needed my shirt size. The plot thickens..."

Taking the tie, he tied it awkwardly around his neck while looking into the mirror. It wasn't easy for him, and he kept ending up with the wider end shorter than the thinner one. "Hello handsome," he joked as he looked at himself. He took a selfie in the mirror with his phone and sent it to Nancy with the note "I feel sLOVEnia". He wondered what she would think. She hadn't seen him in a tie in ages. Danny felt so relaxed, more than he had for a long time. What felt odd for him was that he couldn't quite define why he felt this way. For the first time, somewhere deep inside him, he believed that he was working in the right direction. He also felt a warm tingle of anticipation about the events to come.

Danny looked out the large hotel window. Ten floors below, an enormous outdoor shopping mall stretched out, punctured by a tall gray glass skyscraper in its midst. He guessed that this was Crystal Palace. The office building was home to the R&D department of Outfit7. Beyond it, the white chain of the Alps looked like frozen waves in the distance. The mountains were truly magnificent. He hoped that the team building would bring him closer to them.

CHAPTER SIXTEEN

The Tipping Point

Krk Island, Croatia / Ljubljana, Slovenia, 29 June 2010

Talking Tom made it through the Apple review process. It's live in the app store!

Iza had been expecting this text message from her husband all morning. Satisfied, she set down her phone and turned her eyes to the horizon and the sea, which twinkled above her bright red-polished toenails. So it began.

A large cargo ship sailed slowly along the faint line linking the sea and the sky, and she allowed herself to just watch its slow flow westward across the calm horizon. She adjusted the towel beneath her back on the lounger, put on her oversized sunglasses, and tilted her straw hat down low to shade her face from the powerful summer's morning sun. It felt very good that she had not forsaken her traditional mini-break in late June. The kids were at camp, her husband was at work, and she was on the beach. Ideal. The vacation suited her, especially after such a tough slog, balancing her own projects, her children, and doing what she could to help with this new animated cat app. She felt certain that this was a turning point for Outfit7, no matter which direction it would turn. She did not doubt that it would be a positive one. The manifestation had been made, the niche market looked promising, the product was good, and the team had done a great job with developing the app. The only possibility was for it all to move positively forward. She picked up a thick novel, opened its soft covers, and found the page where she'd left off. A few sentences went by before the phone beeped again. She put the book down and checked the text. Samo again.

TT already has its first downloads. Still trickling in.

"I'm delighted. Keeping my fingers crossed that it'll continue," she typed back. She raised her head again and looked into the distance. The cargo ship's dark silhouette was slowly melting into the surface of the sea. She'd always wondered what it would be like to be a sailor on such a ship. For months you'd be onboard with the same people, all working to reach a distant destination. Such a ship seemed like a good metaphor for any organization. All the sailors work together to achieve a common goal. If each sailor turned the rudder on their own, they'd never get anywhere. She wondered if Outfit7 was one such ship. Of course it is. The goal is clear, we have a great captain and a dedicated team of sailors.

She opened her novel again. It was just starting to engross her in the mystery when her phone beeped again.

We earned our first $50 from ads.

"I'm happy to say I told you so. We knew that this was the right path," she whispered to herself as she replied to her husband's text. She finished off her lemonade, leaned back, and continued reading.

Beep. The phone, again.

Downloads are flying. Another $100.

"Our fruit, tea, and coffee for next week is covered. We'll soon have enough to fill our winter pantry." She texted back and smiled to herself. The thought of fresh fruit made her thirsty under the heat of the sun. She raised her hand and called over the waiter to ask for another lemonade. Once more she lifted the book and was about a paragraph in when...

Beep.

Fruit, coffee, tea for 2 weeks: covered. Winter = realistic possibility.

The waiter brought a lemonade and set it down on the table next to her lounger. He had noticed how often she'd started reading only to be interrupted by her phone, and he thought it was a little comical. She either has a boss who won't leave her alone, the waiter considered, or a secret admirer. Or both, and they're one and the same.

Over the following few minutes, the texts kept popping up.

$200.

Another $150.

$300.

Iza stopped replying, as they were coming in too quickly. She tried to read but she was pleasantly distracted with all the excitement and the beeping messages. All she could think about was that they'd finally hit the jackpot. The manifestation had apparently begun to work its wonders. She looked into the sky and gratefully inhaled the briny sea air. "As we requested, by the end of June."

She couldn't take it anymore. So she picked up her phone and called. "What exactly is going on over there?"

"It's a madhouse," said Samo. "The numbers are going wild. We're already into thousands of downloads and we're not even through the first day! I think we're at the start of something big!"

She'd not felt such optimism and positivity in her husband's voice since he'd sold his stake in his previous company. This made her very happy and she sought to emphasize the importance of this moment. "Of course it is. That's exactly what we manifested and worked so hard for. Did you expect anything else?" She giggled sweetly, adding. "This is great to hear. How are the boys taking it?"

"They're jumping around with excitement." Samo held the phone up away from his ear. "Are you in the saddle, boys?"

"Yeah!" was all she heard from a cacophony of voices. He put the phone back to his ear. "Everyone's a little crazy. We're trying to get hold of Andrej but he won't answer his phone at all. He really checks out of the planet when he goes on vacation."

Iza tried to imagine the scene in the office and how her colleagues, along with Samo, were tensely following the numbers and looking forward to each new leap. At the same time, she had Andrej in mind, casually lying with his family on a rocky beach with no idea what was happening. "Let him enjoy his peace in the company of his loved ones. He deserves it."

"Yeah, I know, but he's really missing something special. I would love to share it with him. It's growing like mushrooms after the rain. Cra-zy..." He boiled over with excitement.

"Hey, I'm so happy for us. A cat with a morbid background. Who would've thought...?"

They exchanged a few more words and then hung up. Iza lifted the brim of her straw hat, removed her sunglasses, and stared up at the clouds in the sky. She was permeated with warmth, and not just from the sun. Every cell in her body felt that they had accomplished something significant and right on track for their overarching life mission. She closed her eyes and from deep within her soul she thought, "Thank you."

———————— ∞ ∞ ————————

A hot cup of tea singed Andrej's fingers as he stepped into the office. It was his first day back after a peaceful family vacation by the sea. An empty fuel tank that morning had prompted him to stop at a gas station on his way to work. Since he knew that would make him late for work, he indulged in his morning black tea in the car. When he entered the office, it was empty, as everyone was gathered in the boardroom. Through the glass wall he saw everyone standing around the conference table. Peter was doing some weird dance around the room. Frenk and Iza were laughing out loud. The others were staring at Samo's laptop in the middle of the table with ear-to-ear grins and bulging eyes. "What the heck was wrong with everyone? Were they all drunk on a Monday morning? That must be it." He walked straight to his desk, sat down and turned on his computer. "Let's see what's new."

He was looking at the numbers on the screen and each line put him in a darker mood. All the apps he'd been working on, combined, had generated just a few hundred downloads while he'd been on vacation. Leaning back, he crossed his arms behind his neck, and slowly exhaled. He knew that things couldn't keep going on like this. He was really concerned about this company's future and its financial stability. Aside from Iza and Samo, he was the only member of the group with a family. He had responsibilities and, if this didn't work out, he'd have to look for another job. How else could he put food on the table? He should talk to Samo as soon as possible...

"Andreeeeeej? What's up, my man!" Peter leaned out the door of the boardroom. "Come on, come here. Frenk just opened a bottle of whiskey. Let's toast!"

Andrej was already annoyed, and this was a step too far. "Have you all gone mad? Our ship is sinking and you're toasting over breakfast!? Instead of solving this miserable situation, you're goofing around. You all are out of your minds!"

Peter was totally blindsided by this outburst and looked at him oddly. "What are you talking about? Of course we're goofing around. We have to celebrate."

"Celebrate what? A few hundred miserly downloads? Almost nothing has happened since I left. These numbers are appalling and numbers don't lie. I really don't want to celebrate..."

Peter couldn't believe what he was hearing. "What on earth are you talking about? Don't you know what's going on?"

"Nothing's going on. Just a bunch of weirdos goofing off, drowning their misery in alcohol."

"Andrej, you really didn't check your emails or your phone? Man, you do know how to take a vacation. Talking Tom is a hit. Since its launch we've already recouped its entire development budget."

"Look kiddo, don't fuck with me! I'm not in the mood. Some of us have families and there's nothing funny about this."

"Look at me, Andrej. I am not kidding. Come and see the numbers. They're growing by the second. We're now at over 400,000 downloads. It's a proper hit. That's why we're celebrating."

Andrej was still wrestling with his mind, which was unprepared for this turn of events. He found it hard to pivot from melancholy to excitement. "Are you sure?"

"Come and see for yourself. It's nuts! Samo just told us to cancel all our old projects. We'll just hang onto the crystals app, but the rest are toast. All our energy from now on goes into the cat."

Completely confused, Andrej got up and quickly walked towards the boardroom. Without greeting anyone, he stormed up to Samo and looked at his laptop screen. The others studied him in silence, curious as to what he would say. His pupils dilated and his locked jaw softened. All the tightness he'd felt in his shoulders, the physical repercussions of his burden, instantly evaporated. "You've gotta be kidding. It's true?"

Samo crossed his arms and looked deeply into Andrej's eyes with great satisfaction. "Yup, it's true. We found a niche and we filled it quickly. It's already going viral. Exploded like a supernova over the weekend. It seems that our gray cat is going to be an international blockbuster!"

∞

7 UNICORN DRIVE

Part Two

CHAPTER SEVENTEEN

Orchestrate

Maribor, Slovenia, 5 December 2014

The brakes squealed softly as the gunmetal gray BMW stopped in an empty square in front of a large building. The orange glow of street lamps illuminated the old trees that lined the square, and the lonely park benches beneath them. Not a soul could be seen and the only interruption to the absolute silence was the muffled sound of classical music.

Danny leaned forward in the back seat of the car. "Is that it, Milan?" The driver turned to face him. "Yup, that's it. Maribor Opera House. This is where it'll go down."

"Okay, but where is everybody? Looks like a ghost town."

"This ghost town is about to turn into an anthill. Trust me. They're not here yet. The buses from the hotel are on their way. The organizers are inside the opera building and they know you're coming. Find someone inside from Teambuilding Academy, the agency that organized all this, and they'll tell you what you need to know. I'll see you later at the party. First, I'll bring your luggage to the hotel. You have everything you need?" Danny checked his shoulder bag. Documents, wallet, phone. All accounted for. He also slipped on his white tie, the one with the cat's paw print on it, which he'd received in the gift bag at the hotel. His black shirt had wiggled its way out during the two-hour drive, so he tucked it back into his pants. He glanced at Milan:

"I have everything. How do I look?"

"Like someone going to an Outfit7 team-building event," Milan replied with a grin.

"I'm not used to wearing a tie, but I feel pretty good in it. You can't go to the opera without a tie, right?"

"Certainly not. And fear not. Soon many others will be here to join you, all with the same clothes. I delivered almost two hundred of these ties last time. Can I do anything else for you?"

"I don't think so, no. I just need to rev myself up. I've gotta say that I'm a bit nervous."

"A little nerves might be good for you today. These programs of theirs are designed to shake people out of their comfort zones. To overcome fear together as a team. Everyone will be under stress, you'll see. You just unite your energies and you'll win the day. Above all, have fun with it."

Danny emerged from the car into the sharp, cold air. "Okay, I'll work on that. You seem to know them very well. You're not your average driver, Milan, I'll tell you that! Thanks for everything, you've been great. See you later."

"Ciao." Milan waved through the open car window then sped off down the empty street, disappearing around the corner.

Danny pursed his lips and blew a puff of warm air into the gloom. That's it, eh? Okay, pull yourself together and let's do this. He put on his hat and slowly walked the empty path that led to the staircase and the entrance to the old opera house. The large chandeliers were visibly aglow through the tall windows. He tried to focus while also thinking as little as possible. The memory of his meeting with Mark

Login, and how awkwardly it had ended, gnawed at him. He tried
to dismiss it altogether and surrender to the moment. There must
have been a reason that it had gone down as it had.

The leafless branches above his head whistled in the winter wind.
With each step he took towards the entrance, the sound of the wind
became wove ever more through the strains of classical music
floating out of the opera house. He pushed open the glass door and
entered the foyer.

Not a soul in sight. Just quiet music emanating from one of the rooms.
He followed the sound and came to a soft, red carpet that led to a
large door. A quick pull on the handle and the door creaked open.
As he stepped inside, his foot almost slipping on the well-worn floor,
traces of the thousands of visitors whose tread had smoothed the
path over the years. He looked around the concert hall, which was
lit by huge crystal chandeliers high above him. The pleasant scent
of old wood reminded him of the long hours he'd spent as a student
inside the old Presidio Library in San Francisco. "Ah, college life…"

On the other side of the hall, he spotted some people immersed in
their work. They all wore green ties and leaned over a large mixing
table, checking the sound system. He approached. To his left and
right, chairs were arranged in semi-circles throughout the room.
There must have been some two hundred of them. He noticed music
stands among the chairs, as well as microphones of the sort used
by radio presenters in fancy studios.

"Vam lahko kako pomagam?" A voice inquired in an unknown
language.

Danny turned and saw a tall young man with glasses. Like Danny,
he was wearing a black polo shirt but his tie was green, as were
those of the others in the hall.

"Sorry, I don't speak Slovene. I'm looking for an organizer from the
team-building, uh, team."

"Ah, you must be Danny. Our director wanted to greet you, but he is busy at the moment in the building next door. We've got a half an hour before the participants arrive and it's a bit hectic. He told me to take care of you. I'm Blaž, a team-building trainer and part of the organizational team." He offered a hand and shook Danny's firmly.

"Nice to meet you."

"And you, Blaž. What exactly is going on here? Does the team building involve watching a concert?"

Blaž just smiled. "I'm going out for a last cigarette before showtime. If you don't mind joining me, I'll explain everything to you."

"Of course."

They stepped into the cold of the staircase in front of the building. Blaž lit a cigarette, the flame flickering in the night wind. He exhaled happily. "So, what do you know about what's happening today?"

"Practically nothing," Danny replied. "Just that I have to come here and I should wear this shirt and this white tie with the paw print."

"Classic," Blaž smiled. "No one knows anything... That's how it's been ever since their first team-building events. Anyway, today's program lasts all day. This morning we picked up the staff in Ljubljana with a rented, private train. On their way to Maribor we went through a series of team activities on the train, focused on corporate values. They were all connected with music in one way or another. The program is called Note to Note. Well, they arrived in Maribor and we took them to a hotel. After check-in they drew numbers out of a hat to split into six groups and each group went to its own conference room. There, a surprise awaited them. Classical instruments were laid out in each room, along with a professional musician. In short, the goal was for each group to learn to play a classical instrument in an hour and a half."

Danny tried to learn to play the piano when he was a little boy, but unsuccessfully. He soon gave up, as he had learned almost nothing after more than a year of lessons. With this in mind, the task seemed impossible. "An hour and a half? What instrument, the triangle?"

"An hour and a half. Six groups, six instruments. Violin, viola, cello, trombone, clarinet, percussion. We have a system that teaches them to play the basics in a very short time."

"Sounds like mission impossible. What if they've never played an instrument before? What if they're tone deaf? And what do you have them play? Something simple, like 'Jingle Bells?'"

"Yeah, yeah," Blaž smiled and blew a puff of smoke into the night air. "They'll play part of the 'Carmina Burana' by Carl Orff. Not exactly easy. But our teaching system is airtight. Each of them will learn a few basic tones. Even with no prior musical experience. And when one hundred and sixty people play together, then the whole thing sounds the way it should. But yes, starting to learn is always terrifying. In the end, though, it all comes together nicely. Proper synergy. Teamwork. All in an hour."

"Well, I'll believe it when I see it. The team was probably in shock when they learned what awaited them. The very idea of learning to play trombone...in an hour..."

"Yeah, their eyes got pretty big when they saw the instruments. But I'm sure it'll work. Now they are supposedly rehearsing. Slowly the groups will come here to play together for the first time, as an orchestra."

"Crazy. I can't wait to see this. It's hard for me to imagine it all coming together."

Blaž stroked his beer belly. "Yeah, it's quite something. But if anyone can pull it off, it's these guys. They're a good team. This sort of program simulates their organization's whole business process quite well. Everyone has to take responsibility for their task, their instrument, their team, and all the teams must play together as one, well-coordinated orchestra. With good mentoring and teamwork, it is indeed possible. We'll see soon enough..."

Blaž's cell phone rang. He answered quickly and exchanged a few words in Slovene. "Shit, the director tells me they're almost here already. Let's get inside quickly. It's showtime."

Just as they stepped inside, the first bus appeared on the far end of the square. The others were close behind, four in all. Soon the empty, tree-lined square bustled with a crowd of people with black shirts and white ties peeking out from inside their overcoats. Smiling faces glowed in anticipation. Each participant had a case containing their instrument. The river of novice musicians flowed towards the entrance of the opera house.

One hundred and sixty participants took the chairs in the concert hall and started readying their instruments. Danny sat beside three technicians in a corner behind the mixing table, watching the group, which bubbled with positive nerves, talking to each other, teasing, and glancing at the empty black stage before them, in anticipation of the start. Danny was amazed at how young the Outfit7 team appeared to be. He could have mistaken them for a gathering of college students. Something didn't add up when he tried connecting the team that milled around before him with the company's astronomical financial numbers. He quickly picked out the faces of the Login family who, just like the others, sat in the hall, waiting with their newly-learned instruments in hand. Iza was in the front row, holding a viola. Her sons, Mark and Nikolas, were at the back, with their instruments, along with Samo on drums. They appeared to be equal team members, participating just as all the others did. If Danny hadn't studied their photos, he'd have no way of differentiating the owners from the staff. He couldn't distinguish who was a manager and who was entry level.

The crystal chandeliers were switched off, the soft background music on the speakers went silent, and a strong spotlight shot down upon the empty stage. An MC, wearing a green tie, appeared.

"Welcome to Orchestrate, the highlight of today's event." He spoke in English. "I also warmly welcome our colleagues and partners who have joined us from across the globe. Let's give them a round of applause!"

Loud applause and whistles shook the room.

"We all know why we are gathered here. In the next few minutes, we will play together as a classical orchestra, proving that the impossible is indeed possible. And who would know this better than you, the Outfit7 team?"

The hall again burst into shouts, claps, and general conviviality.

"Let this event symbolize your teamwork at the office. Let it symbolize your connectedness, transcendence of boundaries, your drive to meet your goals, your international business sense. Show what you are capable of as a team, even if you're tackling something you've never done before. Programmers, animators, salespeople...today, at least, you're musicians. Let the Outfit7 orchestra indulge in the playful tones of the introduction to the cantata Carmina Burana, the overture known to the world as 'O Fortuna.' And don't forget one of your core values: have fun! I invite Maestro Luigi to the stage!"

To a soundtrack of applause, a small conductor in a black tuxedo stepped up to the stage. With his baton, he tapped the music stand before him. The hall silenced.

"Hello and welcome. Before you came, I practiced with you in sections, each section with its own instrument. Now we will play together. As one big team, as a classical orchestra. You will soon hear a musical matrix that will provide you with the rhythm. You will play 'O Fortuna' at my signal, with the help of your mentors in each section. So, first we'll go through two practice runs. Then we'll record our performance professionally, both audio and video. That's why you see these professional microphones set up in between your rows of chairs. That's why there are cameras around the hall. The very best of luck to each and every one of you. Are we ready?"

The participants shifted restlessly in their chairs, adjusted their ties, and awkwardly fiddled with their instruments. Maestro Luigi looked toward the mixing table. "Lights, sound, we ready?"

From a corner of the hall, someone gave a thumbs up sign and a basic metronomic beat emerged from the large speakers. The conductor wove the air with his baton and the first instruments sounded. Over the seconds that followed, the vibrant tones of classical music filled all corners of the hall. Danny watched as a wave of strange, but wonderful emotions filled his body as he swayed along. The sound made his skin tingle and goosebumps popped up. He'd never seen or heard anything like it. He couldn't believe his eyes or his ears. A group of non-musicians were actually playing like a symphony orchestra...

The first two practice runs already sounded good enough that it would've been hard to say it was played by absolute amateurs. There were some off notes here and there, of course, but all entirely forgivable. They were ready for the big run. The conductor praised them and signaled to start recording. "Well, now it's really showtime!"

He waved his baton and, over the next few minutes, the orchestra played an almost flawless rendition. The final, brassy tones led to the piece's climax. This was followed by an explosion of applause, shouts, and whistles throughout the room. The enthusiasm was palpable and indescribable. Danny, the technicians, and the organizers in green ties stood on their feet in ovation for the amazing feat the young team had pulled off. The conductor also applauded, then bowed deeply and left the stage. On came the MC.

"Congratulations to you all for this success. You were great." He looked around the room at the satisfied faces. "We have a beautiful recording that you'll be able to enjoy for years to come. You have proven that you know how to take the bull by the horns and get done what needs to be done. You really know how to own your shit! Are you happy with your results?"

The adrenaline-flushed participants whooped and clapped.

"I agree. You were that good. Now, let me give you a little surprise. Your ultimate goal has not yet been achieved..."

The smiles on the faces of those assembled faded somewhat and expressions shifted toward curiosity and wonder.

"As you know, 'O Fortuna' is not just an instrumental work. So far we've just professionally recorded the instrumental part. That's just halfway there."

The audience guessed what was coming next, whispering among themselves and shaking their heads, while smiling.

"We have a hall set up for you in the building next door. A group of professional singers are eager to teach you something beautiful. Within an hour, we'll reassemble here and you will sing the vocal part of 'O Fortuna' on this very stage. You'll sing along to the recording we just made. Then we'll edit everything together to form a complete cantata performed by Outfit7."

Someone from the audience playfully shouted, "What!? We have to sing, too? Not a chance!"

"Yeah, yeah," the MC teased. "The second part of the test awaits. Are you in or are you out? And that's not all. When you return, an audience of strangers will be waiting to listen to your performance. We promised everyone an unforgettable experience. And for your return, you'll be joined by another, very special, conductor."

The Outfit7 staff left the hall with a mixture of sounds and emotions and headed to the other building. An instrument was one thing, but singing in Latin in front of an audience of strangers was something else entirely. The staff was mostly introverts and already felt that they'd swallowed a stone of trepidation.

Blaž crossed the empty hall and approached Danny. "How do you think it went?"

"Wild. You really don't see that every day. It was beautiful. Now what? Will they really have to sing?"

"Absolutely. We wanted an activity that would really move them out of their comfort zone and still be fun. This is it. Every really good team needs something like this. It also helps them connect with each other more, helps them bond. That also gets them both expressing and internalizing their values. Overcoming fear and discomfort together, really helping each other, encouraging each other... It's a test of their mettle. It's an outward expression of their internal culture. Proof that, as a team, they can do anything."

While the staff was in the other building learning to sing, the organizers shifted the chairs in the hall, while others frantically edited the audio recording over which they would soon be singing. Danny watched with interest, wandering around and asking questions as he thought of them. The organizers were friendly but busy, so the answers were short. During his walk around the hall, he spied a giant projection screen up near the ceiling, behind where the audience would sit.

"Hey Blaž, what's with the projection screen being behind the audience? They won't see anything."

Blaž looked up from a laptop on which he was checking his connection with the projector. "That's not for the audience, but for the performers on stage. Remember when the MC promised a different conductor? Well, we hosted Maestro Luigi a few weeks ago in the recording studio. Together with a bunch of Outfit7 animators, we dressed him up in a motion capture suit that charted his movements while conducting. We then converted the data on his baton and body movements into animations and transferred them to Talking Tom. So their conductor for this second part will be their star character. Pretty cool, huh?"

"I'm speechless. How did you even come up with something like that?"

"Yeah, we're special, what can I say? And Outfit7 is a very special client, one that is happy to work with us to test the limits of the possible. They really invest a lot in the quality and efficacy of events for their employees. Their people are their greatest asset. As you've probably noticed, they are well aware of that."

On either side of the central red carpet, fifty white wooden chairs were prepared, the audience members waiting in anticipation. Behind the chairs, a large wooden door was closed. The head organizer, in the adjacent building, was sent a message that all was prepared. The Outfit7 team could return to the opera house. In a matter of minutes, on the other side of that wooden door stood a nervous mass of black polo shirts and white ties. The atmosphere was heavily charged but positive, everybody wondering whose bright idea it had been to make a bunch of programmers sing in front of a group of strangers. Their veins were flush with more adrenaline than blood. What could be less pleasant for the organizers to have concocted for them? But they knew that they could make it happen if they worked together as a team. They knew perfectly well that this was precisely why this particular event had been organized for them. To prove that teamwork moves mountains. At work and in life. They cheered each other on, giggled nervously, and waited impatiently for the door to open. The black folders containing the Latin text for "O Fortuna" shifted and creased in nervous hands.

The door swung open theatrically and the MC up on stage announced to the audience that they would enjoy a performance from the Outfit7 choir. A performance like never before. The team swallowed hard and entered the hall one by one. On their way to the stage, they were cheered on by wild applause from the audience. Nervousness and trepidation were shed with each step. As they lined up on the platform on stage, now facing the audience, Talking Tom suddenly appeared on the projector screen at the back of the hall. Loud classical music blared from the speakers and Tom began to conduct. One hundred and sixty mouths opened in unison.

"Semper crescis/Aut decrescis..."

Each verse they sang encouraged the team to project their Latin words louder and prouder. The consonance of coworkers soon raised their voices into some cosmic connection with the sky. After less than two minutes of song, the weight had slaked off their shoulders, replaced by a balloon of pride. The final applause from the audience was an exclamation point to this highlight event of their year. Most of them had just gone far beyond all borders they previously thought achievable. They had a sense that, without their colleagues, they never could have done it, but with them, they could do anything. In just four hours altogether, they'd learned to play a classical instrument, recorded a concert, learned to sing, and performed as a choir on stage in front of an audience of strangers at the opera house. Meanwhile, the event was recorded for them to enjoy later. It wasn't until the adrenaline subsided that they fully grasped what they'd achieved – and realized how tired they were.

But the day wasn't quite over. Everyone knew that an unforgettable party awaited them after dinner, a party with a theme. That had been the case at every team-building event to date. Only a few of them knew what the theme would be, just Iza and a few folks from HR and marketing. The staff slowly wound their way to the four buses waiting outside and headed back to their hotel, where a lavish, plant-based, buffet dinner awaited. They had a half hour to shower and change before the party began.

Danny sat silently by the mixing table, trying to grind down all he'd just seen and heard, to distill it in his mind. It had been something utterly unique. He watched the team-building trainers scurry around the hall like ants, tidying the instruments and returning the hall to its original state.

Blaž approached. "Well, that's it. The main show is behind us. Are you coming with us to the hotel? Most of us will join our colleagues who are finishing their preparations for tonight's party, while the rest of us will clean up here and head back to Ljubljana."

"I'm happy to go with you," said Danny, still shaking his head in awe. "Okay, there's a van waiting outside the opera. We'll head out ASAP as the timeline is pretty tight."

They walked through the dressing room, where Danny picked up his jacket, then headed down the stone steps toward a white van idling in the square. Seven smiling trainers with green ties waited, too, happily collecting impressions of the concert.

Blaž introduced him. "This is Danny, an American journalist. He's the one writing a story about Outfit7."

"Hey guys."

"You're welcome to join us," one said. "Are you ready for a party to remember?"

"I was born ready. Given what I've seen so far, an interesting evening awaits."

They climbed into the van, each with some equipment balanced on their laps for transport to the party.

"May I ask what to expect next?"

"Now we can tell you," another trainer replied. "A few days ago, Outfit7 launched a new app. It's called My Talking Angela. It's a white cat, sort of like Tom's sweetheart. The whole party is dedicated to her. In fact, we've done up the entire app in physical form."

Danny nodded. "I know Talking Angela. But what do you mean, in physical form?"

"These people are involved in designing and programming apps. Everything is digital. We, on the other hand, made versions of all the digital elements in the app, but real ones, designed to integrate into team activities. For example, in the app, users collect pictures and paste them into digital albums. We printed the pictures and made similar albums so the pictures can be pasted onto large panels. They'll basically be playing their own game, but in a tangible format. The entire hall is decorated like the rooms in the app. So they'll be able to actually walk into the digital world of Angela. The party's called Angela's Dream Show."

"In-tense. That's like someone climbing right into your imagination."

"Exactly. On top of that, the program will serve as internal promotion for their new logo. At the end, everyone will get polo shirts with the new logo. And, of course, the Outfit7 cake. This has become a proper tradition at such events. This cake will be extra special. Angela has these gold, high-heeled shoes in the app. We commissioned a pair of identical shoes from a real shoemaker. They'll be placed atop the cake, and Iza will get them as a gift at the end of the evening. I can't tell you how many iterations we went through before we matched the shoes in the app perfectly. They're tailor-made to Iza's size. Well, you're about to see how it all came together. It's gonna be the bomb."

"You're all crazy...in a good way. I can say that with confidence, even though I've only known you all for a few hours," Danny smiled. "I've never seen, or even heard, of anything like this, anywhere else. And the fact that there's a company in Slovenia... or anywhere, for that matter... that offers something so special to their employees is... I've heard of companies staging insane events to keep employees involved and to hammer home values, branding, products... But none of that's even close to this. Normally the CEO would hire an orchestra to play for the staff, not the other way around... And I can imagine all this ain't cheap..."

"No," chimed in the director of the organizing team, "it is not cheap." He'd been sitting quietly behind the wheel up to that point, driving the van to the hotel. "They really invest a lot in their employees. Not only financially, but also substantively. And we really like to go the extra mile for them. Their culture is so unique and it so elevates the importance of their employees and their values that we really work with our hearts to make these events the best they can be for them. And we feel how grateful they are. None of our other clients are even close to this level. And Outfit7 works with all external partners, like us, just as they do with their own employees. They are incredibly demanding and want the very best, but working with them fulfills us. We're ready to collapse from exhaustion and stress, but we're delighted to do it. Interesting, isn't it? Something special. They know how to get the best out of their collaborators. We give our best, they get more than they could've hoped for, and we're all happy. Win-win."

"Sounds like perfect symbiosis," said Danny. "How long have you been working with them?"

"Almost from the start. We did our first team-building event for them back when there were just thirty people at the company."

Given that they'd been working together so long, they must know them really well, Danny considered. "I'm really interested," he said, "given that you've been able to watch their story unfold all along, what do you think the recipe is for their enormous success?"

"Huh," said the director, "a good question. Apart from working within a profitable market, I think it's a combination of factors. You've got the true and genuinely good intentions of the founders. People-first leadership and the right values. You've got the scrupulously-planned construction of the corporate culture that holds their ship together, even through storms. They function as one and live the vision of the company together. You saw this for yourself today. They are truly out of this world. That's Outfit7 for you."

———————————∞ ∞———————————

Danny slowly opened his heavy eyes and lifted his even heavier head from the soft pillow. His ears still hummed from the loud music of the previous night. His unsupple body, for decades now unaccustomed to dancing till the wee hours, gradually rose to a sitting position and peered out the hotel room window. He rubbed his face with his palms, wishing to make certain it hadn't all been, and still was, a dream. What a night! Mental. These people know how to have fun. Work hard, play hard. A cliche, perhaps, but Outfit7 was proof of concept.

The last time he'd partied that much was at the end of his studies. He smiled at the flashed memory of his college days but quickly gathered his thoughts. It was time to pull himself together and concentrate on why he was here. Yesterday was a blast, but important interviews awaited. First with Iza and Samo, whom he'd met briefly at the party. He couldn't focus, not yet. Not before a hot shower and a strong coffee.

CHAPTER EIGHTEEN

Values at Crystal Palace

Ljubljana, Slovenia, 8 December 2014

The dark grey, freshly-cleaned BMW turned off the highway loop towards the large outdoor shopping center on the outskirts of Ljubljana. The car undulated its way over speed bumps towards the parking lot. Monday morning fog peeled away from Ljubljana and its surroundings, and the first rays of winter sun refracted off the glass facade of the office building in front of which the car stopped.

"Here it is," said Milan. "Crystal Palace. Not much compared to American skyscrapers, mind you, but it's the tallest in Ljubljana." He spoke with pride. "The Outfit7 reception desk is on the eighteenth floor. They're expecting you. Just call the receptionist."

"Thanks, Milan," Danny said. "You're a good guide. Our little excursion to Venice yesterday was a particular treat. I'm glad we made the most of my free day. It also helped my post-party headache..." Danny still felt nauseous when he thought about the amount of vodka he'd consumed at the spontaneously-formed "slammer" bar in front of Angela's Hall at the team party in Maribor.

"I'm happy you're happy," Milan replied. "I was happy to take you around, myself. Well, I'm off. See you in a few hours. Good luck with your interviews!"

Danny entered the building and stepped into the elevator. As it slowly ascended, floor after floor, he had a view of the skyscraper through the elevator window. As he rose past the height of the mall's buildings, the white mountain peaks suddenly appeared in the distance just beyond the city. "Wow, look at those mountains," he thought. "What an unforgettable view." He walked to the office's entrance and pressed a bell on the wall next to a picture of Talking Tom's smiling face. The door opened.

"Welcome to our office," a receptionist said. "Take a seat and Iza and Samo will be ready shortly. Coffee or tea?"

"I'd love a coffee, thanks," Danny replied, settling down comfortably on the soft red couch by the reception desk, which was lined with colorful crystals and a large bouquet of fragrant flowers. Above the counter on the wall, he spotted several white wall clocks showing the time in various places: Ljubljana, Cyprus, London, Los Angeles... Beyond reception lay a huge, open office space with floor to ceiling windows. Several tidy, white tables were lined up, separated by green partitions. The walls were bedecked in colorful graphics of various Talking Friends characters. Danny estimated that more than twenty people were in the office, all eagerly typing away and studying large, silver monitors. It was surprisingly silent. He'd been in a lot of offices, but never one that felt so...peaceful. Just the opposite of that raucous event of a few days ago. Work hard, play hard.

At Friday's party, an Outfit7 employee had told him that, when they'd moved into Crystal Palace, the office equipment had been set up according to strict Feng Shui principles, that ancient Chinese art of landscaping and layout. She'd explained that the purpose of Feng Shui was to increase the flow of energy. That's why it was important where things were in the office. She'd gone on to say that all the Outfit7 premises were "energy cleansed" at least once a month. He didn't know what energy cleansing was, exactly, but whatever it was worked. There was a really good vibe in the office. Peaceful, creative, positive.

The open office in which he sat was surrounded by small, glassed-in offices and a few aquarium-like conference rooms where employees could retreat for individual meetings. All the glass walls in the office were decorated with decals containing motivational phrases, underscoring the company's values in bright colors. Danny peered into one of the corner offices and saw a decal in red: "Make it happen."

"Man, they really live their slogans," he thought. "They certainly do make it happen."

Just then, the glass door he'd been eyeing opened and a familiar face stepped out. Danny's stomach clenched. It was Mark Login. Danny had a sour memory after their recent almost-interview in London. At Friday's party, Danny had avoided Mark spryly, so they'd not spoken since that fateful meeting.

"Oh, hey Danny!"

"Hi," Danny replied, tensely.

"How's it going? Did you have fun on Friday?"

"I did. I'm still recovering," Danny said, embarrassed.

"It's good to see you again," said Mark, with what sounded to Danny like kind sincerity. "I know our last meeting wasn't quite as smooth as it might've been. Please understand that we are swamped with calls from journalists asking us only about money and the market. By now I'm guessing you've seen that money, for us, isn't everything." Danny had to agree. "Yeah, you are very different from any company I've visited before. And what I saw raised more questions than answers."

"Oh, I believe it," Mark replied. "Not to worry, Iza and Samo will be the right port of call for all your inquiries. I'm sure you'll do well."

"I hope so. Thanks for the encouraging words."

This short chat changed Danny's mind about the young director completely. Friendly, warm, open. As if he'd met an entirely different person back in London. He didn't know if Mark had changed or if he now understood the whole situation in a new way. Either way, something was different, and for the better.

Mark put on his jacket, nodded farewell, and walked past him onto the orange-red carpet. When he'd gone, Danny opened his bag and pulled out his green plastic folder, which contained his papers for today's interview. He eagerly flipped through the questions, which were scarred with cross-outs and corrections. The sum of all the various possible scenarios flooded his mind. Foremost in his thoughts was simply: do not mess up again.

As he sipped his organic coffee with rice milk, Iza and Samo Login entered the open office space. They greeted their colleagues at the nearby tables and approached Danny. He watched them with mixed feelings. They were dressed smartly but comfortably. The two exchanged some friendly words with the receptionist and handed her some instructions.

"Hello, and finally for real, right?" Iza said with a wide smile on her red lips.

"Hi," Samo followed.

Iza seemed very open and positive from the start, but Samo's expression was hard to read. He had deep brown eyes behind narrow glasses that seemed to pierce Danny with skepticism. Samo offered his hand.

"Hello," said Danny finally, rising from the couch and shaking hands with them both. They entered one of the seminar rooms, this one behind glass with a blue decal stating "No limits". Settling into comfortable conference chairs, Danny noticed a surprising scent in the air. "Lavender oil," he thought, then he traced it to a diffuser in a corner of the room. Glasses and a jug of water sat on the table, as well as a large, handheld flashlight. "What might they need a flashlight for? Was anyone camping out here overnight?"

Iza played with her turquoise stone ring. "Well, what are we going to talk about today? Oh, yeah, by the way, what did you think of the team building?"

"Oof, Friday was unforgettable, I'm happy to admit. I'm slowly starting to understand what you all are up to here."

Iza half-smiled, but Samo was still serious, looking at this reporter with his arms crossed. "So what did you find out?" Samo asked. "What *are* we up to?"

Danny looked up from his papers, a bit surprised by the question. "Huh, it suddenly feels like I'm the one being interviewed," he thought. Danny was surprised by this line of inquiry but he didn't let it throw him off. "For one, I can say that you are considerably different from other companies I've gotten to know so far. I'm most impressed by how connected you all are. That and the fact that you really know how to have a good time. Especially considering last Friday night..."

Samo's pinched lips finally spread a bit. Iza added, "Of course we know how to have fun. In fact, 'have fun' is one of our corporate values. Without fun, everything is boring, and if you're bored, you can't be creative."

"That's true. Every aspect of Friday was unusual. I was most impressed by the holistic nature of it, that every aspect was dedicated to teamwork and underscoring key lessons and values."

This pleased Iza, who was happy whenever someone from outside the team understood their story. She added, happily, "Friday was like a distilled version of what happens in our offices all the time. The values of 'work as a team' and 'have fun' come to the fore, of course, presented in a different way than we can manifest at the office. After a team-building exercise like that, it feels like the company has been totally revitalized and people can work in a completely different way. This bond forged between coworkers remains and we feel it in our everyday work."

"Wow," Danny jumped in awkwardly. "Sorry, I forgot to ask if it's okay if I record our conversation so I can make a transcript?"

"You can, of course. When will it be published?"

Danny placed a small Sony dictaphone on the table and pressed the red REC button. Samo looked at him, amazed. "Ha! Who still records with a dictaphone these days?" He immediately realized that the question may not have sounded very polite.

"I'm a bit of a traditionalist," Danny said. It wasn't the first time someone had commented. A few months ago, he'd been recording an important interview on his phone, and the entire recording got somehow erased. It had shaken him and Clyde had been furious. From that moment on, he'd used a dictaphone, sometimes also in tandem with recording onto his phone, so he'd have a backup. He didn't feel like explaining this to the Logins, so he quickly continued, "This records more clearly and reduces background noise better. The article should be published in about two months' time as the cover story for Bay Area Biz. Of course, in the end, it's all up to our editor-in-chief."

"Clyde?"

Danny nodded.

"I'll talk to him if need be," Iza said teasingly. "We've gotten along pretty well over the last few days and I think our deal will bear fruit pretty quickly."

"Uh, what deal?"

"Oh, it doesn't matter. He'll explain it to you when the time comes."

Danny was confused but just shrugged. He didn't want to press too hard, as he was still afraid of saying the wrong thing and scuppering the interview. It seemed she wasn't about to say anything yet.

"Well, if I may... Let's talk about your other values. I saw 'make it happen' on the wall. Are there more key phrases and what do they mean exactly?"

"The first two values, 'work as a team' and 'have fun,' are rather self-evident. 'Make it happen' refers to goal orientation and the execution of assigned tasks. Then we have a value, 'no limits,' which is the one on this glass wall. It refers to thinking outside the box. We must transcend both ourselves personally and the boundaries of the organization. Be audacious. Our staff undoubtedly fit this description. And the final value we added a little later: 'own your shit.'"

"Own your shit?" Danny repeated what he thought he'd heard with a hint of doubt.

"Yes. Own your shit. This is the most important thing for both current projects and company development. It refers to the responsibility we all share and bear. As individuals, as departments, and as an organization. If we are responsible for pursuing a vision, a goal, if we are responsible for performing our tasks, for supporting our colleagues, and above all else for ourselves, then success is guaranteed. Responsibility is a crucial, living value for us. It drives our success. That's why we only work with responsible people. That goes for us personally, for our employees, and for our external collaborators."

"Okay, responsibility within the organization makes sense," Danny continued with interest, "but what does it mean for people to be responsible for and to themselves?"

Iza thought how to explain her perspective in a simple way.

"I see personal responsibility more broadly," said Iza. "I believe that we are responsible for the trajectory of our own lives and for everything that happens to us during their course. No one else makes things happen to us in life. We are the directors and lead actors of our own film. We reap what we sow. It is our responsibility. To ourselves and consequently to others around us."

"Wow," Danny said. "If everyone looked at their lives that way, the world would be a very different place..."

"Without a doubt," Iza began. "Just look around. Think of your friends, your coworkers, your relatives. Think of how most people explain their problems. Who's to blame, in most peoples' eyes, for life's challenges and difficulties, its trials and tribulations? People are used to complaining and looking around, outside of themselves, for explanations. Most blame others for the bad things that happen to them. It's easier, of course, to blame someone else, to find a reason outside of yourself. People are afraid to look within themselves and are afraid of change. If we complain and throw the blame elsewhere, we might make things easier for ourselves. We play make-believe that it's not our fault, that someone else is responsible for our failings. People then surrender to their own failure, thinking 'what can I do, it's out of my hands?' and feel trapped in this situation," Iza made air quotes with her fingers, "this trap of 'I can't change.' Because we believe that we're not the ones responsible. This is the point of origin of all stress, tension, anger... If everyone cleaned their own house first, most conflicts would be avoided. Not to mention how beneficial it would be for personal growth, success, satisfaction and happiness. If we are truly responsible, we'll look inside ourselves first of all, and only later around us. We want to have such people in our organization."

Danny listened and realized that his jaw had dropped in the midst of Iza's speech. He thought about how often he'd blamed others for his failures. How often he'd mourned that he couldn't change anything on his own, even if he'd wanted to. A few moments of loaded silence hung in the air.

"Everything okay?" Samo asked.

"Yeah," said Danny, shaking out of his reverie, "yeah, everything's okay. You've just gotten me thinking. These ideas are really deep."

Iza leaned forward in her chair. The large, silver heart pendant on her necklace jingled against the table. "It's not such a complicated idea. But it's difficult to internalize and to act on. We humans are often complete strangers to ourselves."

"That rings true. And it hits home on a personal level. But I imagine it's even harder to encourage on a corporate level, for all employees."

"We try to help people grow here, both in business terms and personally. We are all part of a big corporate family."

"Most companies I know have clearly defined corporate values," Danny continued. "The question is how realistic they are and whether employees really live them. It's really funny sometimes, just something to read on the walls when, in reality, not only do they fail to appear in practice, but sometimes the staff winds up doing the polar opposite. How would you comment on this? I guess the question is about...some sort of corporate insincerity?"

Samo smiled. "Maybe... Corporate insincerity. I think you've hit the nail on the head. I believe that all corporate values are defined in good faith and with positive goals in mind. Once they're defined, it's up to company management whether they are followed and introduced in practice. If management doesn't push them to the fore, then they slowly recede into the background and become just a catchy slogan on the wall that nobody thinks deeply about."

Danny was pleased to hear Samo finally speak, and so passionately. Up till that moment he hadn't been sure if Samo's reticence was because he disagreed with Danny's approach, or if there was a larger issue. Now he probed deeper. "What does it mean for management to implement these values?"

"It means that they permeate every aspect of the organization. They're not just stuck on the walls for decoration or thrown onto a website. They must be palpable at every level, in every corner of the company's corporate culture, from the way people greet each other in the hallway to our relationships with clients and partners, from corporate events to work processes to how we reward and compensate people for going the extra mile. Everywhere. It's essential that employees are committed to and accepting of our values, even if they don't share them personally."

Danny found himself in complete agreement. He'd heard and read a great deal on the subject, but in practice he seldom saw it realized at anywhere near this company's commitment level. "How do you think companies should keep their values alive?"

"I can't say how it works elsewhere," Samo replied. "We strive to hire the right people and we part ways if they don't live our values. Hire and fire based on values instead of only on performance. We had to say goodbye to several promising employees at all levels because of this. This isn't easy, as I'm sure you'll appreciate. But it's essential if we want the organization to function as a single organism. If employees do not click, mesh, gel, then the engine we're running will not move forward smoothly. Gears that go against the grain must be removed or they will inhibit the operation of the whole, and of each component around them. Employees have to fit smoothly into our corporate culture. We pay a great deal of attention to that. Our HR manager might tell you more if you two end up chatting."

"When did you define your values?" Danny inquired. "Have they been present from the start?"

"They've been pretty much the same since the beginning, but they weren't always phrased this way," Iza replied. "These are the personal values that Samo and I live by, anyway. We would never promote values that we didn't have inherent already. If we ever set up another company in the future, the values will be very similar, if not identical. We live the values that we want our employees to embrace. That's key and a mistake I see with other CEOs – they don't live the values they define for their own firms. I don't know how they can expect their staff to behave a certain way if they don't believe in it or adhere to it themselves..."

"I know what you mean, I've seen that before," Danny agreed. He recalled plenty of visits to companies that he could quickly tell he wouldn't want to work for, as the CEOs would say one thing in interviews and their employees in the hallways would say something else entirely. "If only more companies in the world had the Outfit7 attitude," he thought...

"The basis of good corporate culture is that the values management stands for are defined right off the bat, and that they remain firm no matter what happens to the company."

Danny nodded and glanced down at his papers, scanning his questions.

"Well, if we're talking about the origins... I've read something about this before, but I'd rather hear it straight from you. How did it all start? Where did Outfit7 come from, how and why?"

"Get comfortable," said Samo, with a smile, "this is going to be a long story. It all began when I sold my stake in Delta Search..."

Iza and Samo explained the whole story, from selling Samo's stake in the previous company to meeting the co-founders at the restaurant in Ljubljana, assembling the first team, finding the right business niche, the string of failures before manifesting and finding success. Danny augmented their story by asking sub-questions and an effervescent conversation ensued. It seemed to him that both his subjects were unusually emotional when explaining the origins. For them, this wasn't just a business endeavor. It was a part of them. It was their baby.

"...and we finally launched the first Talking Tom," Samo concluded. "That's the first app that really went viral. What followed was a turbulent period. By the end of the year, the company had made several million in profits."

CHAPTER NINETEEN

First Months on a Rocket

Ljubljana, Slovenia, 8 December 2014

As he recorded the interview, Danny took notes on the papers in his green folder, jotting down all the most important facts and quotes. He was impressed at how relaxed and open the Logins were about every detail, from the financial to the personal. They seemed to have nothing to hide from the public. Given how they'd more or less avoided journalists and public exposure thus far, their openness felt unusual. Their story simply overwhelmed him. He couldn't believe how many completely different and unusual incidents lay behind those blindingly enormous numbers that were the sole focus of that part of the public who read their business reports.

"So, you launched Talking Tom and it was instantly a global sensation. What would you say was the difference between the month before Tom launched and the month after?"

"Huh," Samo nodded, "a big difference. First of all, our confidence skyrocketed because we saw that we'd finally boarded the right train. It all happened abnormally quickly. Also, the amount of work rose precipitously. All of a sudden, we were in the office day and night. If we wanted to ride the Tom train we'd built, we had to constantly develop new apps. We immediately stopped working on all other projects and let them slowly fade from app stores. We focused only on Tom and developing the apps around him. It was our winning card, so we went all in."

"What does that mean, developing the apps around it? Did you copy Tom and make more, similar apps to keep the market share?"

Samo shook his head. "Not quite. We were the first to develop a special cross-promotion system between our apps. This system relieved us from relying solely on earnings from advertising, which in turn required editors to put us on the front pages of the app stores. Instead we built apps that had a large user base and then cross-promoted other apps we developed within the existing apps, thus achieving a synergy. This helped us push our apps to the top of the world rankings."

"So, if I understand correctly, you were the first to promote your new apps in your old apps?"

"Yes. When you launch a new app, it gets a quick jump at first but then its popularity slowly declines. So you can't miss this opening opportunity. If your success is based on cross-promotion, you have to publish impressive new apps with a certain frequency and there should be no time lapse between them. Well, at least the interval between new apps should be about the same each time. With Tom, we launched a new app about every three weeks. This, of course, required a death-defying pace. But it led to quick, parallel successes. By the end of the year, we had released several apps that were not just variations on Tom. Each had something new in it, both technologically and in terms of content. Soon after Tom, for example, we launched Talking Hippo, an app for younger children, then Talking Harry, an environmentally conscious hedgehog who picks up garbage. Then Talking Roby, the robot you see on the wall over there. And quite a few others. We ended the year with Talking Santa. That was especially interesting. We wanted Santa to show his naked butt whenever the user wanted, but that probably wouldn't have gone over well at Apple. So we made it so you could get him to show his butt covered in red polka dot boxers. It was good fun..."

Danny laughed, wondering how many times Santa had to drop his pants for all the world's users. "I see that your sense of humor comes in handy."

"It's a mainstay at the office," said Iza, enjoying the flashback to the early success four years earlier. "Whenever we could, we plugged some of it into our apps. If you want to go viral and stay viral, you have to dance along the edge the whole time. Our brand of humor was just right for that. Some of Samo's ideas were pretty far out there," she concluded her nostalgic trip down memory lane. "After Tom, we realized how fleeting success could be. One day you top the charts, the next day you can be forgotten. We didn't want that. So we worked all we could and created new, innovative apps, churning them out."

"It's one thing to launch a lot of products, it's another to earn something from them. I know you've had and still have free apps, so you need to run ads. How did you capitalize on your app releases?"

Samo replied. "Advertising itself is not an easy process if you want to make the most of it. Just as we honed our apps down to the smallest detail, we did our homework when it came to ads, as well. In recent years, I think as early as 2012, we developed our own advertising platform that was no longer dependent on others."

Danny hadn't known that. "What platform?"

"Something we made in-house, which automatically decides for us which ad provider it will accept in which apps. Whoever offered the most at that moment got the slot. We currently have about thirty ad providers in our apps and our system independently decides how to arrange them with relation to the slots available. This mediation algorithm maximizes our revenue. At the same time, there were already several similar systems on the market, but we found that ours worked best." Samo smiled a little with pride.

"Amazing," Danny said. "So you did something that maximized revenue through something that worked in the background of your products. Something the user doesn't really see at all?"

"Yes. The user only sees a small ad somewhere on the screen."

"Is that your only income? Not that this is small, but still…"

"That certainly was our biggest income source," Samo continued. "Almost all apps also have the option of in-app purchases. With different characters, users can buy different things. For example, cookies, diamonds, gold coins, hearts, that sort of thing. We also have a licensing program in place to sell physical products with our characters' likenesses, but that's more than just an add-on. But we do generate most of our revenue through in-app ads."

Danny was a little surprised at all that was going on behind the scenes of the apps. But he also considered this perfectly logical, given the kind of revenue the company accrued. "Were all the apps successful? Did they all go viral?"

Samo had been thinking about virality for years, about trying to discover a magic recipe for it, but he couldn't put it into words. This meant that Danny's question brought a bitter taste to his thoughts. "Some more, others less. We soon learned that there's no absolute recipe for virality. If anyone says they know it, they're lying. But we found that there is a prerequisite for our segment, namely that apps must be beautiful and design-consistent. If they are beautiful, you immediately have a far better chance at success. We really went the extra mile here. As you've probably noticed, our apps are graphically refined, in each detail. They have to be fun and endearing. In my opinion, these are the keys to their success."

Iza added, "But we found something else, too. To create the Talking Roby robot, for example, we took into account user opinions. Before that, we asked the audience what kind of app was still missing from our portfolio, what we should make next. Plenty of them replied that they'd like a dancing robot. So we made one. This app was not as successful as the others, by our criteria. We learned from this that, when you listen exclusively to users' wishes and adapt your product to the desires of a vocal subset of users, you don't get a good new product, but at best an average one. Since then, we've relied on our own ideas, even if that's not what the market's looking for at the moment. We actually determine what the market wants by launching new apps."

To that point, Danny had only heard positive stories about Outfit7, so this piqued his interest particularly.

"So, after all that, it didn't all go like clockwork... If we look at this superficially, it looks like your main successes were riffs off Tom?"

Iza pursed her lips and nodded. "So many people view our start with interest, but it was not just luck, not just something that happened by itself. If we look in retrospect, it all went according to a carefully laid out plan. Better than anticipated, of course. Talking Tom and our other apps grossed nearly five million in profit in their very first year. If we zoom in, though, things weren't straightforward. On the one hand, thanks to cross-promotion, we had to release new apps at the speed of light. Running parallel to this, we had to overcome some significant technological challenges, as we were launching something totally new. Each app was special and innovative in its own way. It was a lot of work. The boys worked through the night on many occasions, or just slept in the office so we could meet our final deadlines. We're talking about months on end without a proper break. On the other hand, we dealt with non-technical challenges and we learned to expect the unexpected."

This piqued Danny's interest even more than the tech side of the equation. "Unexpected challenges? I'd love to hear more."

She took a moment to think of a good example. "Well, let's look at Talking Roby. We bought the 3D model of the robot, like all the others, online. But then we learned that the character was actually copied from the logo of some Turkish appliances manufacturer. That came as a nasty surprise. We'd never even heard of them. Within days of releasing the app, they wrote to us threatening litigation. Luckily they were reasonable and we agreed to switch Roby's color from orange to match the white of their logo, and we added their company's name to the app and ran free ads there for them, so everyone was satisfied. This is just one example of how we had to adapt on the fly. There were many other cases along these lines but we never let ourselves get intimidated. We found creative solutions to each new hurdle. We were as agile as amoebae, adapting to new circumstances as they arose, like water shifting to the shape of its vessel. It was almost a daily exercise. What's new, what needs adapting to? We morphed and flowed as necessity arose. And if even there was no actual change needed, then Samo would come up with something new!"

She turned to her husband and laughed. "No matter what, our biggest challenge was always the sheer quantity of work, like a tidal wave. There were moments when we thought we'd go nuts, that it was all too much. But to be honest we had fun and were happy about our success at the end of the day. Even during our supposedly free time, we were constantly thinking of new products or how to solve the latest challenge. It was a job that was on our minds twenty-four seven. I'm sure we were all dreaming of apps... It wasn't easy, but we pushed and pushed, always forward."

Danny couldn't wrap his head around how they kept up this pace. He couldn't imagine why they didn't bring in more staff. "Did the team grow along with the increase in work and income? I noticed somewhere that, early on, you said you didn't want to grow larger than twenty employees."

"It's true, our original intention was to keep our team small. Despite the amount of work. But since none of us had any 3D animation experience, we hired two interns, as well as another one for admin. One of the new hires immediately became our lead animator, because he was so good from the start. The one we hired for admin began by just helping us around the office. The team had so much pressure piled on them that it didn't make sense for me to insist that they wash their own coffee mugs. Samo once told me that, if our staff's mommies hadn't taught them to clean up after themselves, then it shouldn't be our job, either. Samo, remember that?"

She laughed again and lovingly put her hand on Samo's shoulder. "That's why we hired someone to help keep the office ship shape, so the team could just plough ahead with its work. Meanwhile, I closed my business and started working for us full-time. Otherwise it simply wouldn't have worked. That small, core team remained in place until the end of 2010."

"What was your specific role in the team? If there were so few of you," Danny inquired, "I imagine you juggled a number of roles?"

"Yes, Samo and I were really multitaskers. He was the CEO but he was also in charge of sales, market research, product management, and handling contracts. If that weren't enough, he also tested all the apps. It was funny, he'd write up the errors he spotted in the app on plain white paper or in his little purple notebook. We were so high-tech, but not for that task. Everything was done in an informal, homemade style. We didn't waste anything on the unnecessary. Or did we, Samo?"

"Not at all," he replied. "It wasn't necessary and I was all for this approach. Why buy expensive tools if you can write everything in an analog notebook with a pencil and talk about it face to face with your small team?"

"Ah yes, your legendary purple notebook," Iza teased. "He wrote everything with a plain, old pencil, which he'd sharpen fanatically with his desk sharpener. I can still hear the scratching." She poked Samo and winked. "Well, I took over all HR duties and finances, and I was officially the deputy CEO. Suffice to say we were not bored."

"What about abroad? If I'm not mistaken, you set up an office in America soon after?"

"We opened an office in Palo Alto, California on 14 January 2011," Iza, without missing a beat, replied. "A few months before, we'd met a Slovenian who lived in Palo Alto and had some contacts at Google and Apple. He convinced us that it was imperative that we be present in the US. So in early 2011, he took over as director of our US subsidiary. His perspective on the company's growth was very American. You get an investor, set up management, hire a huge team of developers, and hit the ground running with rapid growth. Either you max out and succeed or you utterly fail. Go big or go home. Needless to say, that wasn't the path Samo and I envisioned. We were pretty stubborn about it. We had several offers from American investors on the table at the time, but we didn't opt for any of them. Investors can interfere with values. That wasn't something we were comfortable with. And, as it happened, we were doing perfectly well without them. We wanted to keep doing things on our own and in our own way."

Iza couldn't hide the spark behind her eyes when she related this. "That's when we stepped on the brakes. We didn't want to expand the team. We would not grow. We were a team, a crack battalion. The best there was. At the time we were utterly convinced of that."

"So you had only a small office in the US. What about Cyprus?" Danny asked. "How did that chapter begin?"

Samo's phone rang. He looked down at the screen. "Oops, I have to take this. Forgive me, I'll just pop out for a sec."

"Should we take a short break," Iza suggested? "Let's take ten. We can resume with Cyprus after. Anyone need a drink?"

CHAPTER TWENTY

Project Cyprus

Ljubljana, Slovenia, 8 December 2014

After a few minutes, they returned to the meeting room and took their seats. From a wooden box they each selected a tea bag and dipped it in the hot water in the mugs before them. Iza placed a large white paper bag decorated with Talking Friends characters on the table and pushed it towards Danny.

"What's this?"

"A little something from us to you and your wife Nancy."

"Uh, how did you know I have a wife. And that her name is Nancy?"

Iza smiled. "Clyde told us a lot about you."

"Oh really," Danny replied. "He didn't say. Well, thank you for this." He opened the bag. Inside were a pair of large beach towels bearing the image of Talking Tom, one gray, the other green.

"Well, now you'll be able to advertise for us on California beaches," Iza joked.

"Great!" said Danny, delighted. "Pescadero Beach is now richer by two cats. Thank you."

"Our pleasure. So, where did we leave off?"

"In Cyprus. How did that enter the picture?"

"Cyprus, yes," Iza said, looking over at Samo. "We moved Outfit7 there in January 2011."

"This was purely for Cyprus's tax benefits over Slovenia's, right?" Danny asked.

Iza looked at Samo questioningly again. He looked back at her and gently nodded.

"Moving to Cyprus of course helped us a bit in terms of taxes. Cyprus is in the EU, though, and so falls under the same general European tax policy. They do, however, offer especially favorable tax relief to young companies that create their own intellectual property. At that time, it was actually difficult to operate a truly international business from Slovenia. The market was not particularly open and there were no companies like ours that worked in a similar manner. International business practices were limited and underdeveloped from both a legal and financial standpoint. It was tricky to conclude international agreements, and accounting for transactions abroad was complex. We'd been looking around with consultants for some time to see where we might advantageously relocate the company. We seriously considered just moving to the US. Cyprus was also on the list of serious options. No matter what we did, every one of our transactions and practices had to be totally legal. Not a touch of gray anywhere. From the start we emphasized that everything we did must be in strict accordance with local legislation. Everything. Considering what many companies were doing at the time, our approach was laughed off as 'backward thinking' more than once... We still insisted on it. We didn't want to jump into anything hastily, so we continued to work from Ljubljana. Then, a situation arose, which was really the main reason we moved to Cyprus..."

Danny looked at her in astonishment. Her tone indicated that he was about to hear something more personal, something that had not yet been made public. "A situation? What kind, if you don't mind my asking?"

Iza swallowed. "We've been discussing for a while now whether or not to share this information. We decided to tell it, in spite of everything. It's not a big secret, but it's very personal."

Danny's ears pricked up.

"You know we have two sons. Mark is the elder one and there's Nik."

"Yes," said Danny, "I had the chance to meet both..."

"Well, at the time, Mark was a high school senior and Nik was still a freshman. Nikolas, Nik, has always been a rebel. Even as a child. That rebellion intensified as he entered his teens. When he entered high school, he started hanging out with the wrong crowd and we grew somewhat estranged. It felt like he'd been swallowed by some black cloud. Everything changed so rapidly and the situation seemed worse by the day. It was...a difficult period. One evening I tried to move his jacket, which was hanging in the closet, and I felt a small bag of marijuana in his pocket. Samo and I were always keen to clear the air and work through everything within our family on a regular basis, so we just wanted to talk to him about it. We sat down that night to chat, but we ended up having a really nasty fight. It pushed me and Samo over the edge. We had this feeling that we would well and truly lose our son if something didn't change soon, and that change had to be significant."

Iza lowered her eyes, which had grown teary. "That night we hardly slept. In the morning, Samo said that things weren't going to be as we feared. Family comes first and no business should interfere with it. He immediately suggested that we all move abroad. Changing Nik's environment, and with it his social group, was the only thing we could envision to protect him and shift him onto a better path. Did I explain it as you said it?"

Samo nodded. "Yeah, that night I realized that my family was more important to me than anything else and that we would have to sacrifice something to keep us all together. Going abroad seemed like the only way. I didn't see another solution. The problem was that Outfit7's articles of association specified that if any of us stopped actively working, we had to sell our share to the other founders. With a very heavy heart, we decided to sell our share in the company, regardless of the potential we'd developed, and move our family abroad."

Danny listened, rapt, hardly believing what he was hearing. Both the story and their openness in sharing it with him. He could never have imagined that this was the reason for their move abroad. "But that didn't happen? I mean, you're still co-owners?"

"Yes, we are," said Iza with evident relief. "The next day, Samo announced our decision to the other founders. Needless to say, they were speechless. Just imagine it. In the midst of the company's biggest growth spurt, to hear such news... After that it was the weekend and that's when we all got together for a meeting and talked it through. That Monday, Luka, one of the founders, came to us and said that the others understood and respected our decision, but they also could not and did not want to move forward without us. He said that they'd all talked it over and suggested that we remain in the company after all. That we should work as much as we could from wherever we might move to. We quickly accepted this warm and generous offer. That's when we started actively searching for where. And we chose Cyprus. It's in the EU. It's still close to Slovenia. It has a legal system and a tradition that is friendly to international business. As mentioned, it has certain tax benefits. And it has gorgeous beaches. I'd always wanted to live by the sea. We packed one suitcase each and went to Cyprus without even knowing what our new homeland looked like. We just felt it was so right and that we needed to move quickly. Luckily, we chose the right spot. And we've lived there ever since."

"You all moved at once? The whole family?"

"No. Just us and Nik. Mark decided to remain in Slovenia. He had a serious girlfriend here. And to be honest, it came in handy for us, as he took over managing our property here. It meant we didn't feel the need to sell the house. But...a significant responsibility for an eighteen-year-old."

"I can imagine," said Danny. "How did the company react? The move must've been quite a shift for all of you. Such a tightly connected team and suddenly you had to do things remotely. How did that pan out?"

"It was quite a big sidestep that we hadn't planned. Especially in the midst of such a wild period. But we got on our feet quickly. In Slovenia, we needed someone to keep the team together and run things. We didn't know exactly to what extent we'd be able to run the company from afar. Since we were in a hurry, we didn't complicate our search for a manager, as we had a good solution right in front of us. See, when the team went on our first team-building excursion, sailing off the coast of Croatia, Samo and I invited our family friend, Robert, to serve as skipper on the boat. He was working for another IT company at the time. I must say that he got along well with the team from the get-go. Soon after that, someone suggested that he might serve as our Slovenian office director. He was always in good spirits, a really positive, people-first leader. And he even plays guitar well... So we called him. At first, he wasn't sure. He said that he had his doubts, and that he didn't want to run a team with more than twenty people. Technically and strategically, he said, he certainly couldn't do our job. We told him that we did not intend to grow beyond twenty anyway, and that technical and strategical knowledge wasn't a problem. In any case, Samo and I planned to continue to handle most strategic functions. What we really needed in Ljubljana was someone to deal with the team. It was most important to us that he fit into our culture and get along with the team. This was prioritized over a laundry list of competencies. We used the same approach for all future hirings. When Robert took the wheel, we moved to Cyprus with peaceful minds."

"But you soon grew larger than just twenty people," Danny added. "By quite a margin. When did you change your mind about the size of the group?"

"In principle we never actually changed our minds," Iza replied. "We always wanted to stay small and agile. Even now we're slowing down our rapid growth in employees as much as possible. But the market demanded more and more from us. If we wanted to stay in the saddle, so to speak, we had no choice but to increase the size of our team. Truth be told, we were still quite small compared to the competition. At the moment there are just over 150 of us, but we produce the work of a thousand. The important thing is the end result, not the number of people who get you there."

Danny felt skeptical about this answer. They couldn't all be superheroes, surely? "How is that possible, logistically? I know you're hardworking, committed..."

Samo scratched his chin. "Most of our competitors develop apps through to the final product. Then they go and test them. If they find that the product isn't paying off with the numbers they'd envisioned, they shut it down before it officially goes to market. They repeat this until they feel they've found a product that tests show should bring big revenues when it hits the market. From Talking Tom on, we haven't thrown away, well, I don't think we've thrown away a single product we developed. Everything we've put on the market has pulled its weight and then some. From this point of view, we've been incredibly efficient. This is the main reason we've been able to keep a relatively small development team and be as successful as firms with far larger teams. As Iza said earlier, our performance is currently comparable to companies that have more than ten times the number of employees."

"Not to mention how demoralizing it is for a product to be shut down after a team has worked so hard on it," Iza added. "Imagine working on a project all year. You finish it and then your company shuts it down because a test run suggests it won't have the return they'd hoped for. We really don't want to do that to our people. Everyone is so committed to our projects because they know they will definitely see the light of day."

"I see. After all, you've grown into such a solid unit. What happened to that other director, then? Robert? He'd said he didn't want to lead a larger team. Is he still with you?"

Samo had great respect for Robert and they were still on excellent terms. He took a moment to think about how best to reply. "Let me say this. Up to twenty people were great. Up to thirty was somehow still manageable. At forty, well, it was pretty chaotic. A lot of people to coordinate, and a lot of strong characters to manage..."

Iza continued, teasingly. "We still have some of those, well, stronger characters. The team isn't all saints. Without a really open and accepting culture, some of our people would have bitten each other's heads off ages ago." Samo smiled, thinking of exactly who his wife was referring to. "At that point, a soft touch leader was not sufficient. We needed a manager who, in addition to being competent as a leader, also had experience navigating complex business processes. So we mutually agreed that Robert should move aside, and we brought in someone new. Or rather, we started looking for someone. And of course, we couldn't find anyone. Classic, right?" Iza laughed. "We had a long list of potentials, but we just couldn't decide. We wanted someone who would be more than a manager, who would truly grasp what we were going for, who would believe in our corporate culture. And he had to speak Slovene. Since we couldn't find someone who fit the bill, we had to think outside the box. Then, one day, our son Nik said, 'What about Mark?' I'd actually thought of him a few times. He was organized, committed, knew the company, had the right values. Most of all, he was someone we could trust one hundred percent. To top it off we'd be investing in the development of our own child, which was a big plus. But I hadn't dared say aloud that I was thinking he should be made director. Just leaving him to manage our property in Slovenia when we left for Cyprus felt like it was too much of a burden, let alone running the whole Slovenia branch of the company. Imposing such responsibility on a young boy was pushing it. We knew he had the right competencies, but he was entirely inexperienced. It would be a significant risk. Since we didn't know what to do, Samo and I spoke openly about it with the founders. They agreed we should give it a shot. Oh, our little twenty-year-old..."

Iza was again overwhelmed by the recollection of the weighty decision they'd been obliged to make. "Shortly thereafter we asked him. What else, right? He took a month to think it through. We spoke about it a lot. In the end, he agreed and became our new director. And he still is. And he's been a very successful one, at that. He honed his abilities, accrued valuable experience, and is doing great. Of course there are issues here and there. There would be with anyone. But he always has us on his side. We spend a lot of time on phone and video calls."

This information leveled up Danny's respect for Mark and his perception of him. "Fascinating. We didn't have the ideal start in London, but now that I hear this... All I can say is 'respect'. And who were the others who joined you in the early stages of growth?"

"The previous new director, Robert, was first. We got him an assistant to help with photocopying and filing and the like. She began to work with us before she'd finished college, at entry level, so to speak. Now she's the head of our HR," Iza said with pride on her colleague's behalf. "You can speak to her tomorrow morning. Then came a few more programmers, then the first full-time lawyer, and so on. Samo and I juggled several functions at once for a long time. Eventually it just became too much. For us both. To give you an example, I was still in charge of all the finances when we had six companies set up around the world. Can you imagine how much paperwork that is? I worked day and night. The paperwork never stopped. We really needed a financial director, a position we called VP of Finance. One of our advisers asked me, straight up, if I was really sure I could hand over all our finances to someone else. I took nearly a month wrestling with the question. It wasn't easy to entrust everything to someone I didn't really know. But in the end, I realized I needed to. If we wanted to move on, it was the only option. So we slowly, slowly delegated most of my operational tasks. I'll never forget when Samo said I could hand over all of my various positions, but the one I had to remain in charge of was personnel. This was so strategically important to us that I wasn't 'allowed' to pass it off. Even today, I personally handle all our personnel policies."

"You rarely see a company that makes HR its top priority," Danny added. "For the most part, HR managers are more bureaucrats than strategists..." He turned over his papers searching for the remaining questions. "So if we were to summarize this period, what would you say that your move to Cyprus really meant for the company?"

Samo thought for a while. "You have to understand that our move was not the only important event that befell the company at the time. It came in parallel to exponential revenue growth and a comparable increase in workload. So our physical absence and the demands of the market dictated some changes, but we didn't turn things upside down. I'd say that we upgraded rather than changed. Previously we'd done a lot of things shooting from the hip. We did far less from that point on. But still, most of the strategic issues were collected in one of my purple notebooks, and most of the administrative and financial matters were in Iza's spreadsheets. Well, the biggest change immediately after our move was the precipitous increase in video calls that became our daily routine. As the company grew, the entire system had to be ever more regulated, procedures that we'd done on the fly had to be standardized. We were lucky then, or whatever you want to call it, that we had two excellent advisers to guide us. In addition to Brad, who I think you got to know personally in Palo Alto, we found one in the US early on, just after we said goodbye to our first director of the American office in 2011. The other one we found in Slovenia. These two helped us tremendously in setting up the structure of the company, which is still in place today. At the time, we didn't know much about running a growing corporation, or about strategic marketing. We learned on the fly. As with app development, we tested what worked and what didn't. We kept what seemed to hold water and threw out what leaked. Both advisers helped us find the best solutions. The main thing was that we no longer learned only from our own mistakes."

"What were they doing, specifically? Or maybe the question is rather what did they suggest you do differently? Did you rely heavily on their opinions?"

"Of course, Samo always decided on his own in the end," Iza joked, poking Samo again playfully. "Am I right or am I right?"

"In principle, you are right," he replied. "And that's as it should be. In the end, the big decisions should fall on the founder's shoulders. The adviser makes suggestions and the founder makes the decisions. That's being responsible. If a company is really good, then there should be a few to no advisers who know better than the founder. If the founder wasn't any good, then the company wouldn't be successful. Good advisers help by not being emotionally involved in decisions. They advise to the best of their ability and, in the end, must not be offended if their advice is not accepted. This is key. No emotional involvement and full respect that the final word goes to the founder. For us it was interesting to have one adviser with an American mindset – go big or go home – and the other with a more traditional, European approach that often resulted in two opposing pieces of advice regarding the same question. I'll give you an example. They helped us set up our first organizational structure. A diagram of Outfit7 and its departments. The diagram each one suggested looked totally different from the other's. In the end, we applied common sense, put our heads together, and decided on our own. That seemed fine to us. And it seemed fine to them, too. That makes them good advisers."

Danny knew a lot of advisers. Silicon Valley bristled with them. He had to agree with Samo's idea of what makes for the best. He couldn't think of many who fit Samo's definition. "Did they advise you on other matters as well?"

"Of course. They helped with all sorts of things, I can't even remember the extent of it. Especially the American, who was really more than an adviser for us. He wound up joining the team full-time for a while. Together we set values, structures, managerial processes... He was also brilliant at marketing, especially brand building. We were really underdeveloped in that area at the time."

"I'm curious. You mean you didn't promote your brand well?"

Samo shook his head. "Well, we knew something about that, otherwise we wouldn't have made it as far as we did. When things developed, we had to focus and push it harder. After Talking Tom, we released quite a few 'talking' apps that had good cross promotion in the background. In terms of brand, however, they didn't match up well with each other. That's why we released more apps and new characters in the second half of 2011 and in 2012, which we merged into a brand: Talking Tom & Friends. That's when we created Angela the cat, Tom's sweetheart, the inventor dog Ben, the fun and funny green parrot Pierre, the loveable giraffe Gina and Ginger, the naughty kitten. Each was a unique character and, at the same time, they were a group of friends, together. It was only then that the apps began to fully support each other, a constellation instead of random stars. They worked together, as one, in all aspects. We have to thank our advisers for helping with that."

"I have to add something," Iza jumped in. "We not only had a business relationship with them, but also a friendship. Perfect trust. That's part of our culture. We have open and warm relationships with everyone, employees and subcontractors alike. This trust across the board is the foundation of all the successful projects we've run. And speaking of Cyprus, our American adviser also, I would say, forced the first official, in-person management meeting, and he suggested we hold it, in Cyprus."

"What do you mean by forced? You didn't want to have the meeting?"

"No, no, I mean we were going to have some kind of meeting. But it would probably have been more casual, without as much structure. Not a meeting proper. We also wondered why we should have the first strategic meeting in Cyprus? It was as if they wanted to sunbathe a little. That's how Samo saw it, anyway." Iza looked at her husband and giggled. "That adviser put a lot of pressure on me, because he knew I already had experience in big corporations. First on me, then I pressed on Samo. So we finally got together. The first leadership meeting in Cyprus. November 2011. From then on, meetings in Cyprus have been the norm, and we hired an entire management team based there in the months that followed. But that first meeting was quite exotic for us and a big milestone for the emerging corporation."

Danny imagined a group of young managers packing their bags and hopping on a plane for their first meeting on a sunny Mediterranean island. "What exactly did you talk about there?"

Iza rummaged through her memory. "Everything we mentioned earlier. From values to structure to processes, we established then the way they still more or less remain today. It's only been three years since then, but that's like dog years in our fast-paced industry. After that meeting we began to operate like a proper company. And none too soon. When you're growing so quickly, you're filing a mad amount of work, you're extinguishing fires here and there, and you forget about important big picture things. A lot of startups never address them. Without the right structure, you can be killed by your own growth. I've seen this happen to many companies and it could have happened to us, as well. We're grateful for the pressure from our advisers, who both had objective views of the whole thing, both had experience at past companies and both said that we had to do this and right away. We'd been so over-focused on staying strong and successful in the market by developing new products. Striking the iron while it was hot. But we didn't have a well-defined hammer or anvil. Apart from culture, development, and sales, we couldn't see anything else as important. So at that meeting, we built a really solid foundation upon which everything since has rested. We're still building on it today. Otherwise everything could have crumbled like a house of cards. We could have vanished before even realizing it. And, coincidence or not, it was right about then that we got the swift, sobering kick in the butt that we needed. It was an invaluable lesson. Apple said, 'No more talking apps.'"

"Wait, what?" Danny wasn't sure he heard correctly. "No more talking apps? What does that mean?"

"Yeah, that was a weird story," Iza continued. "I'll explain it to you over lunch, if you're up for it. It's noon and I'm hungry already. My treat at our restaurant on the first floor. You game? Samo, will you join us?"

CHAPTER TWENTY-ONE

Yin & Yang

Ljubljana, Slovenia, 8 December 2014

They left the meeting room and entered the main office. It was as peaceful as before, though Danny could see that everyone was hard at work. Amazing. He looked around and spotted Mark Login through the glass wall of his small corner office. He'd just looked up from his computer and made eye contact. A quick wave and Danny waved back. How quickly the London meeting had formed a warped and wrong impression. What he'd just learned about the young director totally shifted his opinion. "If we don't have the right information," he thought, "we can devise the weirdest stories in our minds that lead to fear and conflict. How unnecessary." He thought about how he should really air out a number of his more strained relationships. "The awkwardness could all be in my head. Mark Login is proof of how we can get it wrong."

Danny and Iza walked to the elevator, while Samo excused himself and ran off to another meeting with product managers. The elevator carried them smoothly to the first floor. Iza leaned against the wall mirror and fixed a buckle on the waistband of her purple dress.

"Did you know that our restaurant is vegan?"

"I heard that, yeah. And the spread at the team-building event had some vegan options."

"Not just some," she said, "it was all vegan."

"Huh," Danny said, "I didn't notice."

"That's the point. We try to make people aware of nutrition, but we know we'll never succeed if the food doesn't taste good. Most people still think that vegans only eat grass, like we're a bunch of bunnies. If you think like that, it's hard to imagine a life without meat on your plate. That's why we work hard to make the food tasty, so even the carnivores won't notice the difference. That's the only way we can show people that a change in diet is possible without excessive sacrifice. Even if you are a serious foodie."

Danny occasionally ate meat, but he was a vegetarian at home, following Nancy's preference, so he knew what she meant. "Why do you want to see people change their diets? For health reasons?"

"It does result in a healthier life, but that's not the main reason Samo and I are such advocates for plant-based food. It's really about our future. The future of the planet. Humans slaughter some fifty billion animals a year, and we use almost a third of our total land area for breeding and grazing. Mass industrial breeding heavily pollutes the environment. According to the latest data, the meat industry produces twenty to fifty percent of all greenhouse emissions on Earth. Far more than any other pollutant. To produce one pound of beef, for example, you need about twenty-five pounds of grain and fifteen thousand liters of water. If this were devoted instead to human consumption, nobody on the planet would be hungry. If we look into the future and continue as humans eat today, then the end of the world is in sight. In our opinion, a change in diet is key to individuals' health and well-being, but also to the health, well-being, and probably even the continued existence of the human species as a well. Since it's obvious that we have no other option, we're hoping to be advocates for the only change that could save us. Before it's too late for us all."

"It's pretty unusual for someone to think about that before ordering a burger."

"I'm afraid so. That's why Samo and I feel it's our mission to change that. You know that this company was also established to support environmental projects with the money earned, especially in healthy and sustainable nutrition. That's why we support such a diet for our employees. We serve strictly vegan meals at all corporate events and in our canteen. If anyone wants, of course, they can eat meat. We're not forbidding anyone from doing that. But they won't get it in our cafeteria, which is free to employees, and they'll have to pay for their own lunch."

They walked down a corridor to a glass door. Iza touched her ID card to a sensor and the door opened. Instantly Danny was hit with the delicate scent of curry. In the yellowish light of the cafeteria, he saw several people chatting casually at wooden tables while they enjoyed their meal. "More youngsters," he thought. "It could be mistaken for a student dining hall." He looked around with curiosity, taking in the details. It was a nicely decorated business restaurant, similar to the ones he'd seen visiting the Googleplex in Mountain View, California. But their menu was different. Here everything was strictly vegan and organically grown. He and Iza plated the food that caught their eye and sat at a free table by the window.

"Dober tek," she said. "That's how we say 'bon appetit.'"

"Thanks," Danny muttered through a mouthful of lentil risotto. "Have you two been vegans for long?"

"For a long, long time. We basically stopped eating meat shortly after we moved to Ljubljana together in college. Before that, we ate it daily. First we experimented a little, and then quickly saw that it was easy to switch. There was something else that encouraged us, too. When Mark was in kindergarten, he became very ill. As a young mom, of course I did my best for him. Then I received a gift. It was a book whose title I'd translate as A Cookbook for the Soul and Body. It was full of research about how harmful sugar, meat, and the like can be. That's when I started to think about giving up sugar. Samo and I discussed it and decided to give up meat, too. Since then it's been a way of life for us. We started by only eating meat when we were invited to our parents' homes for lunch. We didn't go anywhere else, because we didn't have the money to eat out. We slowly gave up cheese, then eggs, and so on."

Danny had heard similar stories before. "You say you stopped initially because of Mark's health? Did that change in diet help him?"

"Of course. Shortly after changing his diet, he was completely healthy. It also helped Samo. He'd had severe asthma since childhood. He could never play any sports. If you asked me, he couldn't have run a mile. Half a year after changing our diet, his asthma had completely vanished. Now he goes running and plays whatever sports he wants. The change was really amazing. And we remain healthy to this day."

"You mentioned that you and Samo have been together since you were college students. When did you start working together?"

Iza thought back. "We first got together just before we began studying computer science. Because we were classmates, we learned a lot as study buddies and got along well. But then we figured out something else together. In senior year of college, we developed a project called Even Toddlers Can Read. It was a multimedia program designed for young children to learn how to read. It sold well at the time, and we sold the rights to it for a good amount back then. That project made us realize how well we worked together and that we were capable of creating something new and successful from scratch. We were a little sad when we went our separate ways professionally. I worked for the Swiss healthcare company Novartis, and later Microsoft, Samo went to Delta Search. It was a happy reunion when we were back in business together at Outfit7. But Samo had made quite a bit of money with his programming projects before all that. If you're interested in learning more, he can tell you himself when he finishes that other meeting."

"Of course, I'd love to hear it!" Danny's enthusiasm erupted a bit more forcefully than he felt was cool. Who wouldn't want to hear how millionaires earned their first buck. "I'll ask him, but if we can return to you two... As I see it, you are such a wonderfully connected couple. The others I spoke with see you as a single, solid entity."

"Yeah," she replied, "we're a pretty good couple. We have strong complementary skills and the same vision, which is why we support each other so well. Of course we quarrel, sometimes intensely, because we're not perfect. That's okay if the conflict isn't destructive. We accept conflict as a key driver of change and development. In the end, we always come together because we know that together we can achieve so much more than we ever could flying solo. We're like yin and yang, black and white. Love and our shared mission bond us together. We are each our own person and at the same time we are one."

Danny's mind drifted to his relationship with Nancy. Were they like that, too? Did they support each other like the Logins do? Did they have the foundation for happiness and success in life together? Answering that would require more thought than this moment allowed. "Do you think that your relationship has influenced your business's success?"

"Of course it has. Our personalities are like bulldozers. We're both allergic to inefficiency. When we're together, this only intensifies. We've found people around us who know how to connect with that energy and help us push forward, swiftly, writing a new story that many would have written off as impossible. Then we have a real weave of female and male energy. Yup, yin and yang. No matter how I look at our relationship, I always end up citing Chinese philosophy." She shrugged and took a bite of rye bread.

"I'm curious what you mean by a weave of energies."

"According to Chinese philosophy, yin and yang are seemingly incompatible forces that complement and stimulate each other. The same goes for female and male energies. One cannot function properly without the other. Not in business and not in other spheres of life. I'm not just talking about gender. Each gender has some balance of masculine and feminine energy. On average, women have much more female energy and men much more male. But it depends on the individual and their characteristics, their personality. If I try to explain it more concretely, I see male energy as a sailboat holding its course. Narrow focus, speed, rationality, goal orientation. Female energy is the sea through which the boat sails, by which the boat is embraced and held afloat. Open, flowing, emotional, full energy. Sometimes wild... And one cannot move forward without the other. Samo and I get along perfectly following this analogy. The sailboat and the sea. The wind in the sails is our mission."

"Ah, sea and sails." Danny reflected on his childhood memories of sailing with his uncle through the California bays. "A nice analogy. How does it transfer to the business world?"

"You've probably heard leadership gurus talk about how global companies are run in too 'masculine' a manner, and that the age is upon us when feminine energy should lead the way? This is true. The corporate world needs more emotion, understanding, and even love. Love for yourself and for others. I don't think the organizations of the future will be able to function at all without this. But not too much of it. It has to be the right balance. If you look at us here, we try to lead with the right relationship of the two forces. If you compare us to others, we'll probably have more feminine energy in the air than most. Even though the majority of our staff are men. I don't mean to say that our guys are 'pampered' in any way. Not at all. I just think that we've created a strong culture of empathy, compassion, acceptance, and genuine mutual collaboration. These are characteristics of female energy. And this isn't just needed in the business world. It applies to the whole world. Organizations and individuals. Private and public businesses. It's the same with me and Samo. It's all interwoven with us, anyway."

"What's all interwoven with you? Private life and business?"

"Yes. We don't believe in the idea of a 'work-life' balance. If it's really about balance, we might think of that as a scale. The more you work, the less you live, or vice-versa. That's nonsense. We both believe in the harmony of life. One cradles the other. Everyone is responsible for harmoniously fulfilling their life roles. When you find what your mission is, it's your work and it's your life, at the same time. Everyone should find their own correct path. Alone or in a company. Whichever feels right for you." She took a sip of water then turned her lightning eyes on Danny. "Have you found it yet?"

"Um...," Danny was caught unawares and felt embarrassed. "Well, yeah, um, I don't know. I thought I knew. Now that I'm listening to you, here, researching this unusual story...well, now I'm not so sure anymore."

Iza's eyes lit up. It was a moment she craved, a moment similar to when her workshops back at Kali Center had opened up a new world to eager clients. "And what did you think your path was? What is your mission in this life?"

Danny put down his fork and scratched the back of his neck. He didn't know exactly what to say. "I wanted to just publish some good stories and write a book or two that would sell reasonably well. Then maybe get in the circuit of giving talks at business events..."

"Okay. Why? To what end?"

"Uh, so I could earn money and be able to afford, well, life. So I'd be happy." As soon as he said those words, he could hardly believe what a cliche he sounded like. "Did I really just say that? Is that really my only goal? Damn," he thought.

"Don't you have enough money now and aren't you happy," Iza inquired.

"I have some. I'm kind of happy, too, at least I think I am. Just not quite the way I'd like."

Iza had transformed from interview subject to personal coach. Her colleagues had seen her do so many times, how deftly she could gently open people's eyes. Samo was used to it. Whenever he saw it happen, he'd step back and watch the master at work.

Her voice was now gentler. "And what is it that you'd like?"

Danny recited back his goals, a mantra he'd thought through many mornings. "I've always dreamt of a big house on Pacific Heights and a sailboat anchored in one of the San Francisco marinas. I'd definitely like that."

"And when you have it, you'll be happy?"

Danny again flushed with embarrassment. He thought of all the goals that sat written in a note on his smartphone. He'd go through them almost every morning, willing them to happen. They were all material goods in one way or another. He knew where Iza was leading him. "I don't know exactly. I would probably be happier than I am now. Not that I'm unhappy now. I want for nothing, really. But it would probably be better than it is now. I'd feel more...carefree."

"We load worry upon ourselves," Iza said quickly. "As you said yourself. At the moment you want for nothing, really. You have everything you need to be happy. All the material things you want are constructs in your mind that are limiting you. Most people in Western cultures think like this. But humans don't need much to survive. Everything else is just ballast. Worry is extra weight we pile onto our shoulders. Don't get me wrong, money can make your life more carefree. But you can meet your basic needs quickly with hard work. The rest is the weight of capitalism pressuring us all the time. Have more, more material things, constantly. But when we achieve basic stability with finances, enough to lead a normal life, then extra money isn't needed. It almost doesn't make sense, unless you want it to achieve a broader goal that transcends yourself."

Danny had heard similar words before. He recalled one of his afternoon debates with Clyde on the terrace of their office building. His boss had used almost the exact same words, but now Danny felt like he understood them differently. It was as if a new channel of understanding had switched on, one he hadn't known was available to him, to his head and to his heart. He instantly felt a strong desire to deepen this understanding within him. He didn't want Iza to see this switch, but it was too late. She knew what she was doing, having worked with people in similar eureka moments for so long, that little escaped her. Danny continued cautiously. "Uh, I don't know if I understand this quite right. Can you tell me more?"

"Sure. Making money for the sake of money itself, or being rich because our culture tells you to, will not make anyone happy. Happiness is found within us, not tapped from an external source. It all depends on your worldview. If we look only outwards, there is no way we can find inner satisfaction. We need to look inside ourselves and ask ourselves what we really want and what will make us happy. Money alone won't lead us there. Money has meaning only when we need it to fulfill our mission. Only then can advancing on that path indeed make us happy. In those terms, making money makes sense and is no longer an end unto itself but a means to a greater end. For me, that's the truest responsibility to myself and consequently to the whole world."

Danny silently chewed and stared vaguely at Iza's silver heart pendant. He thought about her words. With them, that list in his phone, his daily focus, suddenly seemed irrelevant. Iza left him to his thoughts for a few moments. Then she continued.

"Samo and I make money with Outfit7. A lot of money. Much more than we could ever need for ourselves alone. More of it will not make us happier or more fulfilled. But because we know that we will soon be spending this money to pursue broader goals, it fulfills us. So it's not the money that makes us happy but the fulfillment of the mission. Money is just the fuel. So what do you really want? What would fulfill you?"

Danny sat quietly looking at Iza. "I'm not even sure if I can answer that question right now..."

"You don't have to. It's not like it's something that just falls in your lap. But it's worth thinking about. Consider it. It's not easy to find the answer, but it is necessary if you want to be truly responsible to yourself. And to Nancy. And to everyone else. If you really want to own your shit. Only then can you start living a full life. A life in which you move forward to carry out your mission. If you have one, of course. Unfortunately, most people do not. And they're lost because they don't have the right compass. Because it's hard to navigate if you don't know what your destination is. Only when you find the answer to your 'why,' when you choose your destination, can you start on the right path to reach it. And that will make you happy."

"But how do I find my 'why'? I'm sure everyone would like to find it, but they can't..."

"As I said, it doesn't happen in an instant. It's a process that requires open eyes and an open heart. Look, I could talk about it all day, but I probably wouldn't reach a conclusion. But there are mountains of books written on this topic. I'm guessing that, in all of them, there's only one point on which they all agree. Money can't buy happiness."

"But a dollar more here and there can come in handy," Danny joked awkwardly, to relieve his own tension.

"Of course it would. But only to a certain extent. Then it's gratuitous. More money doesn't mean greater satisfaction. Samo once said it nicely: if you're already unhappy, it probably is better to be unhappy in a Ferrari than unhappy looking at one in a magazine. But having a Ferrari isn't the meaning of life, you know?"

Danny laughed. "I believe you're right..."

Iza turned her gaze to a neighboring table, where five coworkers waved to her as they chatted over their meal. "Just a sec," she said, as she turned toward them. "Hi Paul," said Iza in English.

"Hi Iza," one replied in native English. "How are you doing?"

"Great. And you?"

"Very well, thanks. We're just chatting with the team. Lunch Mix, you know."

"Well, enjoy," Iza replied. "I'm not going to bother you too much, because you'll obviously have a lot to say for yourself. Dober tek!" She smiled at the others and turned back toward Danny. "Look at them, in the midst of a Lunch Mix."

"Lunch Mix? What's that?"

"It's one of our practices to bring staff together, and it's been very effective. A while ago we wrote an algorithm that randomly selects five people from throughout the company each day, from any level or department. Those five have to have lunch together. This means that each employee takes a turn about once a month."

"Nice idea. What do they need to discuss?"

"Whatever they like. The point is just to get to know each other better and to connect. That's the only goal. It's really worked and it's been well-received by all. In addition to team-building programs, this has been one of the better networking campaigns organized as a staffing process. Connections are so important to us, as you've probably noticed."

"Indeed, I have. You're like a big family."

"We are a family. It's true, though, that the more we grow, the harder it is to maintain that spirit of connection. So we had to define solid processes and set clear rules at the start. That's what we did at the first big leadership meeting in Cyprus. Well, we'll continue there, where we left off, when Samo rejoins us."

CHAPTER TWENTY-TWO

Flashlight Leadership

Ljubljana, Slovenia, 8 December 2014

Lunchtime wound down and only a few others were seated at the vegan cafeteria. Iza and Danny had empty plates before them.

"I haven't asked you anything yet about how your management approach works," Danny resumed. "Is it very different from other companies? Do you have a special system?"

"Actually we really do. I don't know if you saw them earlier, but we have flashlights on the table in our meeting rooms to illustrate our system. I'll show you when we're back upstairs."

Danny flashed back to the flashlight he'd spotted on the table on the eighteenth floor. "I did see one, but couldn't imagine what it was for. You probably don't have such frequent blackouts as to need them at hand."

"No, you're right about that. At least we've not had them regularly for about thirty years," Iza replied with a smile. "It's a good illustration of what we're doing here. Hang on, maybe I have one with me." She rummaged through her small gold purse and pulled out a purple flashlight that was on her keychain. "Here it is." She switched it on and played the light around.

"You always carry a flashlight in your purse?"

"I do. To remind me, at all times, of the essence of our leadership. Ah you men, you will never know the secrets of women's handbags..."

Danny just smiled, recalling everything that Nancy kept in her purse. This really was a mystery to men.

"The flashlight symbolizes what we want to illuminate. Where do we invest our energy and how much of it do we use? You know, this might be good to mention in your story. It seems to me to be the key to understanding our success. And since we've already eaten, we won't be chewing anymore," she joked. "So I suggest you record this."

Danny was so engrossed in their conversation that he'd forgotten to record it. Well, they'd spoken about more personal topics, not for public consumption, so he shrugged it off.

"Of course," he said, "with pleasure." He rummaged through his bag and pulled out the dictaphone, switched it on and set it down on the table.

She handed him the flashlight. "What do you think is the most important part of this flashlight?"

He looked at it, turned it over in his hands. "Uh, I don't know. The battery?"

"Exactly. Well, all the parts are important. Each piece must work properly for the flashlight to work at all. But it's the battery that gives the whole system the energy it needs to operate. The battery symbolizes the purpose that drives us forward, the values that give us meaning. This is our corporate 'why'. Why we exist. Why we do what we do. And this energy of purpose and culture fills every one of us, every team, and consequently the whole organization. It gives us the strength to make big moves. The stronger the battery, the more energy in the organization. You've probably already noticed that our battery is pretty powerful. But that alone is not sufficient. The battery is not what provides light. What do you think is the second most important part of the lamp?"

"Maybe the lightbulb? If we want to light up something, we can't accomplish this without it."

"That's how we see it, too. The lightbulb symbolizes leaders and leadership. It shines forward the organization's purpose and culture. And it is the leaders who are the key to transferring that energy into the organization and beyond it. Without good leaders, there is no proper transfer of energy. But we need to know this: if the battery is too strong, the bulb will burn out. If the battery is too weak, the bulb won't be bright enough. Not every bulb works with every battery. Not every leader is right for every project and every corporate culture. And we're always on the lookout for an ideal match. Our leaders really need to fit snugly into our company. That's why we have such a thorough selection process and likewise rigorous performance reviews based on following our purpose and embracing our corporate culture. We work hard on their development. The better the leaders, the better the lightbulbs function. That covers competence, passion, influence, and even courage. We're looking for only the best light bulbs. Or at least those who, with good mentorship and training, can soon evolve into the best. So now we have the battery and bulb. What's next? Which part is still important?"

Danny looked at the small flashlight again. "The casing?"

"Also the casing. I'll explain that later. But before the casing, I'd say that the lens in front of the bulb is even more important." With a bright red-painted fingernail, she tapped on the flashlight's glass lens. "The lens amplifies the beam of light and determines its shape. The lens, in our analogy, symbolizes working teams. Without good teams, leaders cannot achieve anything. Like a lensless lamp. It might glow, but the light is completely diffused. When a good leader directs their team in a unified, planned manner, and their team has the right energy, then there are no limits. The leader orients, the team synergizes. The result is a true, strong, and properly directed beam of light."

"I get it. So you see the battery as the purpose, the leaders as the bulbs, the lens as the team. They all need to fit together properly. What about the casing, which holds all the parts together?"

"The casing represents processes, structure and rules in our little analogy. It takes the organization's component parts and makes them into a whole. It holds parts together and allows the system to run smoothly. The casing must be custom fit, to suit all the components. That's why we try to make our processes as streamlined and fluid as we can. We try to define the rules so we don't have any needless extra bureaucracy. They must be precise enough to guide us properly in our work and collaboration. What's allowed and what isn't. Where we have to follow procedures and where we can be free to decide as we see fit."

Danny had spent his young career analyzing business models. He had to admit that this was the easiest to follow. "This is really interesting. Above all, it's a simple, logical model. I'm sure that everyone here knows what each piece of the flashlight means."

"We try to help everyone understand, yes. That's not all, though. You can have the best flashlight in the world, one that shines brightest of all. But when darkness descends, it only lights up whatever it's pointed at. So the direction is very important. If we tried to make a flashlight shine everywhere, bouncing it around off of all corners of the market, we would derive almost no benefit from it. The direction in which we shine as an organization represents our vision, strategy, and goals. When we decide to illuminate our path, we swap out night for day there. That's why we're so successful in our chosen niches. For us, the surface that is brightened by our light represents success. This can mean the number of app downloads, web traffic, and ultimately the company's profitability. The more our light brightens a certain area, the more successful we are. The bigger and brighter the circle of light chasing away the darkness, the more profit we make."

"What if you determine that your direction is wrong?"

"Not a problem. Then we alter it. We shine elsewhere. As you know, when we first started out, Outfit7 was shining in some dark corners that proved to be dead ends. But now we've found the right direction and it is unlikely to change for a long time to come."

"If I understand correctly, the company is initially looking for the right niche in the dark with a flashlight. When it finds it, it amplifies the brightness and becomes ever more focused?"

"Something like that. That's how we did it. And another thing. If all the pieces of the flashlight are properly assembled, we just press the button and it turns on, on its own. The resulting light is a consequence of everything being in the right place. This means that the company is set up correctly. Light, in this case, represents synergy, team spirit, employee motivation. It's all just the end result of a well-assembled flashlight. Directors often ask themselves how to motivate employees, how to gain their commitment. The answer is simple. All they want to achieve is the result of a well-assembled flashlight. All the other intangibles fall into place on their own. Only in this way can the company achieve the right momentum and effect. This is the only way the flashlight can shine brightly."

"That is, if all the parts are placed as they should be, then the company's output, the result, is just a logical consequence? Financial success, too?"

"Precisely. In doing so, we need to make sure that all the pieces fit together properly. That they are compatible. If one part doesn't work as it should, then there will be no effective result."

"So how do we amplify the light? How do we make it brighter?" Danny asked.

"We have to constantly work on all segments at the same time. Never leave any one component out. We need to work on raising awareness about purpose and culture, educating managers and employees, building teams, updating processes... This takes a lot of time and effort, but it's worth it, as it exponentially amplifies the end result. That's what really matters. Companies spend too much time, far too much, dealing with urgent matters, putting out fires. They forget what really matters. Here at Outfit7, it's the flashlight that is important. Get the important things in order and then there are far fewer urgent episodes. The better you set yourself up, the fewer fires arise that need extinguishing. This leads to a lot of effort saved and energy redirected into what's useful, upgrading the flashlight's components. In practice it's not as easy as the theory, but it gives us focus and helps us direct our time and energy."

"Theoretically, this is really easy to grasp. But what does it look like in practice? Can you give me a specific example?"

"Sure. I'll leave it to your meeting tomorrow with our head of HR. Just to mention a few, in addition to culture and purpose, which we've already discussed, we have a really well-developed system for new employees and systems of mentoring and developing talent. We offer a boot camp for all new members and a mandatory training called 'The Core at Work,' which all staff attend. Not to mention our distinctive team-building events twice a year. They really move us forward and hold us together, at the same time. They're a way to set high goals and move towards them. In short, we use many approaches but with only one goal. To upgrade our corporate flashlight."

"Interesting. You've managed to package a very complex management system into a simple analogy that anyone can grasp. Sometimes it's most effective to simplify."

"There's an art to that. To simplifying. Less is more." Iza looked at the empty plates in front of them. "Well, we've had a nice long lunch. I suggest we head back up to the meeting room. Samo's probably wondering where we've been."

CHAPTER TWENTY-THREE

Becoming an Omni-Media Corporation

Ljubljana, Slovenia, 8 December 2014

Danny switched on his dictaphone again and set it down on the table. "We left off at 'no more Talking apps'," said Danny, feeling ever more relaxed as Samo and Iza took seats opposite him in the meeting room. Perhaps it was the scent of lavender in the room? He felt like he'd known these people for years. He had to pinch himself to recall who he was talking to, how important this interview was for his career. He quickly forgot the pressure and rose up once again on the breeze of energy that spun out of Iza and Samo.

"Could you describe that first leadership meeting in Cyprus?"

"Wait, wait," Iza jumped in. "We said earlier that Samo should explain about how he made money. Samo?"

He looked at his wife skeptically, over his glasses. "How I made money?"

"Yeah, how you earned your first income from projects, in the early days of your career."

Samo looked up and to the right. "Well, if you say so. I earned my first money back in middle school. That was when I programmed my first computer game and sold it, along with some other games, back in the days when games came on audio cassettes. That was even before floppy disks. And apparently they were popular. That started it all. Since it was successful, I programmed another one, then another. This wasn't serious money, of course. The first project worth mentioning in financial terms was a program I created for subtitling. Back then video rentals and collections at libraries were popular and foreign films needed Slovene subtitles. I created a more elaborate and more expensive software package than anything I'd made before. I think it cost the equivalent of around a thousand dollars per unit. I only sold two, but that was a lot of money for me. I was a freshman in high school..."

"Better two than none," Iza teased.

"Better than nothing, of course, but it had value beyond the cash I got for it. I proved to myself that I knew how to put things together that people needed and were willing to pay for. I began devoting myself to more serious projects towards the end of high school and the beginning of college, when I started to work with my dad. We looked at the market together and saw the need for software for freight forwarders, logistics firms. At the time, filling out a customs declaration was an art form unto itself. It was cheaper for freight companies to buy software than to teach staff to do the import declarations paperwork and invest time in doing it by hand. This proved to be a great niche because there weren't many companies at the time who had programs at all, much less good ones. One of my professors had actually made a competitive program. He sold it to just one logistics company that wound up later buying ours. All other students passed his exam easily. Well, as you might imagine, he made it difficult for me and Iza... We had to work our butts off to pass."

"I can imagine. It's weird to think that you were in competition with your professor. He teaches you the basics, then you overtake him in the market."

"The sign of great teachers is that their students outpace him. Isn't that really the point of teaching? But this project of ours was short-lived. As Slovenia got closer to joining the EU, customs declarations were replaced by EU-compatible forms. Competition also increased dramatically, as the big software companies finally noticed the same niche we had. That's why we abandoned the project. Then I programmed a few more things for the automotive industry. Several different programs, but they didn't really work on the market, or maybe we just didn't know how to sell them," Samo continued.

"What was your first big success then?"

Samo felt good giving a walking tour of his history. He was more relaxed than he had been all day, as he spoke. "Two of our classmates began working on credit reports. They needed software for full text search. It was kind of like what online search engines do today. This wasn't yet available on the market at the time. So I approached them and did some research and began programming in this new field."

Iza raised her hand, as if she were back in school, and waited for Samo and Danny to notice. "And from that money we were finally able to finish up the little house we'd built."

"That's true. In the beginning, you have to understand, there was no full-time work available for me. I didn't know exactly what to do at the time. I knew we needed money to finish our house and support our family. I even considered moving to Australia to take a job as a programmer, as they had really good options available then. I even sent an application to Google in the US, but I never heard back from them. Of course, that disappointed me at the time, but in the long run it was good that I didn't. If they had taken me, I'm not sure what would've happened..."

Samo gave Iza a meaningful look, so Danny assumed that they had talked a lot about what would have happened had he been offered that job. Samo leaned forward, as if he were beginning a new chapter in his story. Now there was more pride in his voice.

"The world started placing increasing importance on full text search right around when we launched a Slovenian search engine at a new company I'd started working at, Delta Search. I was a stakeholder there. So I started working on that project full-time. Full text search became my life. Our engine was constantly growing. It became very popular and financially very successful. After a few years, we sold it to Slovenia's largest telecommunications operator. That had been our plan all along. And that's how I got the startup capital for Outfit7. From there on, you already know the story."

Danny finished the note he was writing. "Thank you, Samo, for that explanation. I'll definitely fit it into the story. Maybe even the opening. Super..."

Then Iza leaned towards the dictaphone on the table. "Earlier we left off at the first leadership meeting in Cyprus. As I said before, we set it up at the encouragement of our American adviser. He also brought a moderator with him who structured the whole meeting. At the time, we really did lack structure. From our side, Samo and I attended, as did product manager Luka, our lawyer, and our new development manager. That was all, I think. It was a sunny November day, and we spent the whole day working. We debated the structural values in depth and defined the basis of our corporate culture. Then we defined the company's mission and vision, and laid out its basic processes. For example, the structure of managerial meetings, which remains unchanged to this day. It was intense and we covered a lot. Towards the end, we set business goals for the following year. Which apps we'd work on, how many new ones we'd launch, total download target numbers, etc. The numbers we came up with were impressive and, given the situation at the time, felt unattainable, unbelievable. But we'd always set our goals sky high and Samo stood by them. That's why the whole team believed we could meet them."

"What were some of the numbers?"

"I don't remember exactly. I just know they were huge, if you were to look at them from the perspective of an average observer. If you took into account the ultimate goal, a profit of one hundred million dollars in seven years, then they maybe didn't seem as outrageous. To be honest, we spoke very little about money and finances. Even today. I know we talked about whether we were focusing our attention on profit or distribution. We opted for the latter. If distribution is effective, it means we're also successful and will, in turn, bring in money. So most of the time we talked about apps, the expected number of downloads, and how to capitalize. That was the standard we set and continue to maintain. Money has always been the result of efficient business operations and well-honed ideas, which are reflected in our apps."

Samo nodded. "It's otherwise probably hard for someone from the outside to believe that there was so little talk of money, but it's true. Each of the founders was able to calculate for himself where he stood, with his shares. Figures on sales and revenue growth have always been transparent here."

"Did you achieve the goals set at that meeting?"

"Indeed. Achieved and exceeded. But, to be fair, because of an incident with Apple, it didn't look like the success that it was."

Danny had been waiting for someone to bring up this incident, which was hinted at early that morning. "Can you tell me about the incident? The one you mentioned earlier?"

Iza's expression shifted from enthusiastic to bittersweet. "Yes, that's the one. When we set business goals for 2012 at the end of the meeting, we wrote them on the board with a red, felt-tipped pen. Then we decided to manifest them, after which we were to set off for dinner at a nearby restaurant, to celebrate a successful first 'real' management meeting. The moment we finished the manifestation, Luka's phone rang. He looked at the screen and said, amazed, 'Jonathan from Apple! It's as if he knew we'd mentioned him earlier. I have no idea what he wants. I have to take this...' He went out onto the terrace and we could see him speaking passionately. Meanwhile, we happily gazed at our big plans, talked about them with satisfaction, and indulged our feelings as if we'd already achieved them. Then Luka came back inside. His face was, how should I describe it? Green. We asked him what had happened. He just mumbled, 'No more Talking apps.' What? We were stunned. He repeated. 'No more Talking apps...' Jonathan just told me that we have flooded their app store with our Talking apps and that they've decided not to publish them anymore. Period."

Iza was visibly uncomfortable recalling the story. "The room turned deathly silent. I still remember the moment and my skin crawls just thinking about it. We felt like our business's rocket had abruptly gone cold and was falling down to Earth. The sight of the target numbers in red on the board beside us, cut by this news, was bizarre. We knew immediately that it would be impossible to reach our goals without new apps in the app store. We just looked at each other, no one able to understand what had happened. What did it mean? What to do next?"

Samo picked up, in all seriousness. "It was a disaster. Like someone had just died. Then Iza burst out laughing."

"Laughing," Danny wondered. "Why? Surely crying would've been more appropriate."

"Well, it was really more of a moment for crying, but she was laughing. Of course we asked what the heck was wrong with her. She said, quite cuttingly, that we'd lit the fire under the cauldron in which we sat ourselves."

"What did you mean by that?"

"Just that. By manifesting these outrageous goals that we couldn't possibly achieve through our established work processes. As soon as the Universe heard our goals, it was obvious that some change was required to meet them. That change was Jonathan's call. Now everything was different and we'd have to just sort it out. If not, there'd be no way to achieve the goals."

"Wowee, what a good way to look at a bad situation... That you managed to find a positive in it... So what did you do next?" Danny asked.

"First, we cancelled dinner and ordered delivery. Then we opened a bottle of tequila and some beers, and started to think. We calculated that we'd be financially viable until February. We left the goals roughly the same, making only minor adjustments in the business plan through February 2012. We planned all night. In the morning we held an emergency crisis meeting online with our developers back in Slovenia. It was good and sobering for us, a reminder of how quickly it could all end. It had a strong impact on our future business decisions, as well. On one hand, it was a nasty blow. On the other, it was a kick in the ass that made us work even better and faster, so we didn't rest on our laurels."

Danny knew that Outfit7 was still working with Apple, so the story confused him. "What happened after that? How did you achieve your goals for that year? Did you make some deal with Apple?"

Samo nodded. "We made some adjustments to the plans and further refined the structure. It forced us into a new way of thinking and walking. We needed different apps, that was the bottom line. That was the birth of My Talking Tom. From the Entertainment category we shifted to the Gaming category. Our characters were no longer just repeating after users, but the user now had to take care of them. It was a big change in the concept. At the same time, it opened up a new way for us to make and even increase our revenues. As Iza said at the time, if we wanted to produce and manifest such big numbers, we needed to make big changes. It's no wonder that a call from Apple happened within minutes of the manifestation. It led to our immediate redirection. We shifted onto the right path, allowing us to achieve our goals."

"Amazing," Danny gasped, shaking his head.

Samo scanned his memories of a few years back. It was only now that he realized how wild everything had been then, and how long it took for him to realize that everything had been for the greater good. It certainly hadn't felt like it back then. "A few weeks after that, everything settled down, and we were even more prepared. We started to work even harder. In January 2012, we opened an office in London, in February one in Seoul. That was to cover distribution in Asian markets. China, at the time, was not yet well-covered with smartphones. We had development in Slovenia, senior management in Cyprus, marketing and sales in LA, and now operations in London and Seoul. When we had our first meeting in Cyprus, there were still only twenty of us, but things started growing rapidly then. By the end of the year, we'd launched all the new Talking Friends characters. Iza and I spent a lot of time in the US, where I was constantly meeting with Apple, Google, Facebook, Disney, and more. It was intense."

"Speaking of which, how did your collaboration with Disney begin? You worked with them a lot, right?"

"We started talking to Disney in mid-2011 and shortly after that began collaborating. By May 2012, we had made 10 three-minute webisodes with Disney Interactive starring our characters, which

Disney posted on YouTube. They were very successful, so we recorded two music videos with Disney Records that year. The first one, in which our characters performed, including Tom's sweetheart, Angela, quickly racked up 100 million views. I should also tell you about the interesting story we had with Talking Angela...or with her creator."

"Hang on, what do you mean by 'her creator'? Didn't you make Talking Angela?"

"Yes and no," Iza replied. "The story begins earlier. When Samo bought Tom on TurboSquid and it became successful, we started buying other characters on the same portal. Quite a few of them were designed by the same creator. Samo felt that it would be great if we could get into contact with this creator directly and invite him to join us. That way, working directly together, we could accomplish even better things."

"So you called him and offered him a job?" Danny asked.

"Ha," Iza said. "That was the idea. But it didn't go that smoothly. There was no way we could access his data through TurboSquid. We only knew the guy's name and that he was somewhere in the east, probably Russia or one of the former Soviet republics. We worked for weeks to find anything about him. Nothing. Then Samo came up with one of his unusual ideas. He asked himself how can you find a man in Russia about whom you have almost no information? Whom do you hire? Well, Danny, what would you do?"

Danny thought for a moment. "Huh, I don't know. Maybe hire a private detective?"

Iza laughed. "That's what a normal person would do. Samo kicked it up a notch. He hired the KGB."

"The KGB? As in Russian spies? No way..."

"Yup. That's exactly who. The KGB or the FSB or whatever they are called today."

Danny couldn't tell if Iza was joking. She was laughing, but seemed to be serious. "How do you go about hiring the KGB? That sounds like a Cold War spy novel."

Samo got up and poured himself a glass of water. "If something is really important to you, you do everything in your power to get it," he said. "The unknown creator of our most successful 3D models was the only one who really knew how to breathe proper life into potential future characters. I wanted him to be part of our team. In reality, we knew nothing about him. Just his name. He was like a benevolent ghost. When we unsuccessfully pursued all channels to find him, we took it a step further. In America, we'd heard of a guy with good contacts in Russia, some of whom could locate anyone in the whole Eastern bloc, provided that person was still alive. That's what they'd said. We decided it was worth a shot. We didn't have anything to lose. It took them just three days to get all the info we wanted: address, phone, email, where he worked. Everything. Viktor Bachenko, an academically-trained sculptor from Kiev, Ukraine. I contacted him immediately."

"Then what? Did he answer?"

"That wasn't easy either. At first there was no response from him, either by email or phone. After a long wait, I finally got an answer. He was interested and we could arrange a video call. It took a good month to coordinate everything. He spoke a little bit of awkward English, but we managed to make it through a first chat. It was only later that we learned why so much time had passed before he'd replied and why the early days of the collaboration were so awkward. Viktor didn't speak a word of English when he first got my email. Nada, zilch. Between that first email and our first video call, he had been frantically learning English with a private teacher, every day, just so that we could communicate. He was really special... But you have to be special to make really good 3D models. It's a specific skill set. He had it all. He was a true artist in this field. Of course, it's not always easy to work with artists. We'd taken that into account."

"Then you started working together?"

"Yes, he soon joined the team, but long-distance. He wasn't exactly one for teamwork, so most of our interactions were via video call and email. I'd call him from Cyprus while he was in Ukraine. We worked quite well back then. As early as 2012, he'd designed three characters from the Talking Friends series: Ben the dog, Angela the cat, and Ginger the kitten. Of all of them, it was Talking Angela, first released in December 2012, who was the biggest hit."

"Are you still working with him?"

"Because of the difficulty in getting things done when you're working remotely and one of you isn't very responsive, we decided to conclude our regular collaboration this year, and shift to contract work. We're just developing a new character, which is being set up by our team here, and I'm thinking of finishing it with Bachenko. Dotting i's and crossing t's is something he handles really well, the finishing touches that bring a character to life. Take Talking Angela, for instance. See her on the wall over there? Doesn't she look adorable?"

Danny glanced over to the wall to his right, which was adorned with a decal of a cute, white cat in a pink dress with a blue heart upon it. "Yeah, she's a cutie." He'd read quite a bit about her before the interview, especially the technical, behind-the-screen stuff. "In addition to being a really nice app, Talking Angela has a lot of technical innovations. Isn't that right? And girls seem to love her."

Danny smiled and looked at Iza. She smiled back. "This is true. The app is beautiful and the technology really does permit a semi-intelligent conversation with Angela. We foresaw that users could connect with our characters even more than simply repeating their words. You should be able to just talk to them. That's why we put a complex chatbot in the new app's background. We got help from one of the world's leading specialists in this technology. The chatbot needs written content – Angela's answers – and topics that the user can talk about with her and produce a logical response. Half of it is the work of a writer. We recruited some outside help but wrote most of her responses ourselves. The point is that this is what made the new Angela a real hit. People would post their conversations with her on social media, some of which were really delightful. It went viral immediately. And since she and Tom were linked, her success really supported Talking Tom, as well. There was synergy in both content as well as sales. Along with the other Talking Friends characters, we built a solid, recognizable brand. By the middle of 2013, we'd already reached our first billion downloads. When that happened, I can tell you, we indulged the team in a really big cake. Since then, we've celebrated every new billion downloads with a new cake. Yum!" Iza licked her lips.

Danny nodded, but continued with a touch of skepticism. "A billion downloads sounds like an awful lot. But in the world of apps it's still not an extreme number."

"That's true," Samo responded eagerly. "That's why we took it as a point of departure, not a final victory, and continued to work hard. Above all we shifted our focus to games that we couldn't have afforded to develop previously. By the end of last year, 2013, the first real Outfit7 game was released. My Talking Tom. It had all the possible Tamagotchi features that we'd been constantly upgrading. Users cared about it. Not just like a digital pet, but as a real, miniature friend. The data shows us that they felt real love for it. The comments we've gotten from users are amazing. That's why we added My Talking Angela this year, to follow suit. We actually launched her just this month and you probably saw the official internal announcement at Friday's team building. We shot a trailer for Angela just before that and posted it on YouTube. Iza thinks it's our most beautiful video to date. Did you see it?"

"Not yet."

"Well, have a look. It's really well done. We collaborated with a well-known video production company in Vienna. The result is something we're really proud of," Iza said.

Samo continued, his voice tinged with pride. "We now have just over 3 billion downloads, and growing rapidly. This, of course, is also evident if you look at our revenue stream. Maybe I should add that a small percentage of the revenue, in addition to advertising, now also comes from licensing our physical products. As our brand became more widely recognized, it made sense for us to turn our products into physical forms, as well. Now we have a series of products based on our characters, like that towel you're going to take home. In the beginning, we had to hire an agent to broker such deals, but later we took it upon ourselves. Through this avenue, we've been appearing at various conventions around the world, organizing events. One of the recent ones was in Hollywood. We've given talks and, as you probably noticed, we recently opened our doors a fraction more when it comes to public relations. We didn't want to be in the media much before. Iza and I didn't give a lot of interviews. Well, now we're more open to doing so."

"Lucky me," Danny joked. But this didn't result in any reaction from Samo and Iza. Samo continued as if Danny hadn't said a thing.

"It's really unusual for a company like ours to handle so many things internally, when you consider how relatively small our team remains. This year, despite all its complexity, we shifted to handling all our accounting in-house. Of course, the fact that we cover almost everything ourselves, with so little outsourcing, increases the company's revenues and thus its value. All told, this year we're anticipating some $70 million in revenue. And I don't think our potential is even close to being realized. So we're always looking for new opportunities. Following the successful collaboration with Disney, we started to develop our own TV series. We wanted to expand the world of Talking Tom and Friends into video production. This will help us become an omni-media corporation. Then we'll be able to say that we truly capitalized on our intellectual property."

"Wow, that is a good bundle of new info," Danny thought. "Good thing I'm recording all these details." He decided to encourage Samo's evident enthusiasm and follow this line of questions. "Fascinating. Can you tell me more about this? What are you working on now?"

"At the moment, I'm afraid that we can't. It's still a trade secret for now. Maybe in the future, if we ever meet again," Iza joked.

"Fair enough. If we're already in the future, what are your business plans moving forward? In addition to working with Disney, can you share with me any specifics?"

Samo thought a bit about what he could say and what he couldn't. "At the moment, in addition to finishing and developing our characters and filming our animated series, we're also planning several apps in the Gaming category. We've already made quite a few and we want to develop this area further. Some will be tied to our characters, others will be completely independent. This requires significant investment, but the potential return on investment is significantly higher. Above all, we'll see what the ever-changing market will say. The other question is what type of team we'll need to make this happen. The animated series alone required a big ontake of more employees, which, as you know, is not something we wanted. We want to remain small, agile, highly profitable. But we will remain flexible and change as circumstances and goals require. Our goals remain sky high. Without constant development and adaptation, they will be hard to reach. At the moment it seems that all our goals will be met and surpassed in the coming years, but this can quickly change. It's a tough industry for predicting the future. Whatever comes, we'll be ready. To change whatever we need to in pursuit of our goals. Everything, of course, aside from our mission and culture and the company's foundational objectives. Those remain."

"It seems that, with this interview, I'm here for the moment of your greatest growth," said Danny, scratching his hair and looking at the questions he'd prepared, to be sure he hadn't missed any. "But obviously there's a lot more to it. Well, as it turns out, we're nearing the end. I think we've covered just about everything I'll need for this article. If I might ask you something now that's a bit provocative... Many feel that mobile content is addictive for children. This results in them being glued to their phones and tablets all the time, which can be unhealthy. Now this is especially true if you feel a deep emotional connection to the character in your app, which Talking Friends characters certainly encourage... Do you see where I'm going with this? I'd love to hear your thoughts."

Iza's reaction showed that she was not at all bothered by the question. She'd been asked it often enough. "We have our apps evaluated by psychologists multiple times. We're especially concerned about their role in upbringing and education. We want our products to positively address both areas. The psychologists gave us very good feedback. Above all, they emphasized that our apps encourage positive upbringing. For example, you have to take care of Talking Tom. Feed him, take him to the toilet, put him to bed. He's not happy if he eats too much candy, if he doesn't get enough sleep, and so on. We work hard to make all the content as educational as possible. We managed to cover just about everything aside from the issue of our users taking care of their own bodies. We wanted to make it so the user would have to move, themselves, in order to take care of Tom. But that's very hard to do in games, especially those on phones and tablets. It's also tricky because kids can sense when something is forced upon them, especially something educational. You can quickly lose them. Everything must feel natural, organic. We haven't been able to come up with a good solution to encouraging users to move around, to encouraging physical activity. But we never had anything that was deemed unhealthy, much less weapons or violence, in all of our apps."

"Violence?" Danny interrupted. "Don't some of your apps have a feature where you can tap on the character and they fall to the ground because of it? Then stars spin around their heads?"

"That's true. There's a thin line between what is healthy and what isn't. What is violence and what is fun. Whatever felt like it was approaching that line, we turned into something fun, like it would be in a cartoon. To be sure, for any action that was on the edge, we'd receive mountains of emails from parents the world over. A nice example is our Talking Ginger, a naughty cat designed for young children. In our app, the user can unroll a toilet paper roll as quickly as possible while the cat is sitting on the toilet. You'd hardly imagine the number of children who tried this at home... Of course, this resulted in a lot of grumpy messages from 'angry' parents who then had to re-roll their toilet paper."

Danny imagined how many miles of unrolled toilet paper the app had prompted in the states and around the world. He couldn't hold back his laughter. "Good thing you weren't sued for environmental pollution."

Samo laughed, too, then continued in a relaxed tone. "If I could go back to how many children use these phones. That's really their parents' responsibility. They decide how much time a day their kids spend on them. Our job is to give them good, fun, educational content. If you already have a kid on your phone, then it's probably best to have them engaged in taking care of a cat than in some violent military game where the goal is to kill as many people as possible, and be rewarded for doing so."

"That's true."

"Maybe just one more anecdote about what our apps can do, though we probably don't know about most cases. Iza and I were in Orlando, Florida once. Between meetings we jumped into an Apple store because she needed a new computer. I wanted to pay and to have the invoice made out to Outfit7. The salesman was intrigued and asked what sort of business we were in. I said mobile app development. He asked what kind of apps? I told him we made Talking Tom. He looked at me strangely and said, 'Don't bullshit me...' I said I wasn't. He began to thank me profusely. It turned out that his son has Down syndrome. That no one but him and his wife knew what their child was trying to say. But when he played with Talking Tom, Tom would repeat what he said, and he wouldn't understand his own words. He wanted to understand those words that Tom repeated back to him, so he practiced at it, struggled with it. Until he got it right. He practiced enough so that he could understand his own words when Tom repeated them. It was the first big step towards this guy's son speaking clearly. Today, he speaks in a way that everyone understands. It really warms my heart when you hear such an unexpected story. And that's probably not the only one."

A moment of emotional silence followed, as Samo scrolled through his memories.

"Well, that's the story," Danny said, breaking the quiet. "Who would've thought that a talking cat could change someone's life like that." He looked at Samo, then at Iza, then down at the questions he'd prepared, every one of them crossed out. He closed his green folder and exhaled. "What can I say? That's a wrap. I don't know how I can thank you for your time. Now I just have to put it all together into a beautiful story. And I will. I can anticipate that this will get a lot of readers. You really do have a special story. I have to say that it also touched me personally, and made me think. Can I ask one more thing? Why is it that, given your reserved attitude towards journalists and your limited time, that you've been so generous with your time for me?"

"We're happy that we gave you all you need," said Iza. "If you need anything else, just reach out. You have my contact details. Why did we give you so much time? Ask your editor, Clyde." She winked at him, smiled broadly, and shook his hand in farewell.

CHAPTER TWENTY-FOUR

Beneath the Green Dragon

Ljubljana, Slovenia, 8 December 2014

The sound of feet padding along metal stairs caromed around the thick medieval walls of the corner tower at Ljubljana Castle. He slowly climbed higher, his eyes fixed on the elongated dragons that had been forged into the endless staircase's iron steps. Each floor, ever narrower, ever higher, offered a view out the windows of Ljubljana's old town center, its houses shrinking as he rose. He was winded by the time he reached the top and held onto the vertical red metal railing for support. I should get into better shape, he chastised himself. How can I be tired after just a few stairs? But the frustration melted away as he stepped onto the ramparts at the top of the tower. The cold wind rushed through his hair and the late winter sun made him squint. A huge green and white flag fluttered atop a long flagpole above him. It bore the symbol of a green dragon crouched atop a white castle tower. The tower on which he now stood. His driver, Milan, had said that this was the city's symbol. The sound of the flag pummeling its metal pole rhythmically against the wind reminded Danny of the similar sound of the sails rattling in the small sailboat he and his uncle used to navigate around San Francisco Bay so many years ago. He loved the wind.

Over to the edge of the rampart he stepped and leaned against the cold stone crenellations. Like the green dragon on the flag, he surveyed the city below. The silhouette of mountain peaks glistened in the distance against the setting sun. Beneath him stood the narrow medieval city streets and squares. A little further out, the Middle Ages yielded to modernity, and a few larger skyscrapers pierced the sky. Beyond them, only forests rushing up to the high mountains. "What a charming city. Nancy would love it," he thought. He hadn't seen her in a long time, longer than they'd ever been apart. He pulled the phone from his pocket and, with a few taps on the screen, captured the harmonious marriage of city and nature. He browsed his gallery, selected the best photo, and added a caption: "Only 6073 miles away." Then he added a smiley face and a red heart, and sent it to Nancy.

He crossed to the other side of the tower and spotted Crystal Palace among the high-rises in the middle distance. He'd been there for most of the day. An amazing day. He'd learned so many new things that had shaken up his outlook on life. So many things he'd been sure of until yesterday no longer made sense. The path he saw for himself in the future was merely the path that his milieu expected of him. Not his own. He was confused. World turned upside down, one day to the next. But he felt it was now as it should be. It was time to think deeply about what he wanted and what really made him happy. To date, he'd been convinced that the only way forward was through business success, financial stability. Achieve that and happiness would magically follow. But now a voice inside him scolded and told him that he'd always known that this wasn't the case. But he'd pushed ahead blindly, stifling that voice in stubbornness. Now he'd decided. It was time to find his true mission. To follow his intuition. But the more he thought about it, the more he feared stepping into the unknown. But this fear was accompanied by a warmth in his heart. What an odd cocktail of feelings. Through this potion of thought and emotion, his phone rang from its place atop a stone crenellation, where he'd absentmindedly left it.

"Hey Nancy!"

"Hiya, honey. Are you trying to tempt me with these romantic photos of yours?"

"You're awake already? Great. Yeah, I've got to enchant you a little. It's so beautiful here, isn't it? We should come here on vacation sometime. And to think I didn't even know where this country was before. Slovenia is truly wonderful."

"I just called to say hi real quick before I'm off to work. I'm still not quite awake, just rolling around in bed. Well, I'm glad you like it in Slovenia. But I hear that Tahiti is also beautiful. Maybe we should go there for vacation, my dear Daniel-san? How did the interviews go?"

"The interviews were great. It's hard to describe everything about today. It was amazing. Above all not at all what I expected. The Logins gave me the whole day. These people really think differently."

Nancy yawned loudly and caught herself doing so. Not wanting to sound disinterested, she followed up: "How do they think differently? Differently from you or from everyone?"

He pondered how to explain something to her that he didn't fully grasp himself yet. "I can't even tell yet. I'm going to have to sleep on it and listen to the recordings of the interviews. But what I can say already is that, for them, rich as they are, this isn't about money. They've got mountains of it, but it's not their focus at all…"

"No? What's the point, then?"

"It's clear as day, the point is in what they do. The mission behind the company. They're accumulating wealth only to fulfill this great life mission of theirs. And every word they said and everything I've learned about them confirms that it's genuine."

"That's the best reason to make money. They must know what they want and are headed in the right direction. Well, we can talk about it more when you're back. Three more days, huh? I really miss you, my darling."

Danny couldn't stop the train of his thoughts and almost missed Nancy's last few words. "They really made me think, with all that they do and how they look at the world. I will have to change a lot of things... And I miss you, too."

Nancy registered that this conversation would take longer than expected. She slowly began to hurry towards work, heading for the bathroom while still on the phone. "What did they say that made you think along those lines?"

"You know that I've been visualizing my future achievements, like a mantra, every day for the last few years. That I want to be professionally successful, to be able to afford a house for us, a sailboat, a new car... Well, now I'm realizing that this checklist is all well and good, but it's not my ultimate goal."

The way he said the last few sentences was in a voice that was new to Nancy. A disappointed voice, but with an undertone of optimism. She could tell that something powerful was moving within him. She inquired, slowly and carefully. "It's really not? So what is your ultimate goal?"

"I don't know yet. But I do know that most people are blinded by desire to accumulate money but they wind up overlooking what would really make us happy. I'll deal with that in the future."

She tried to bite her tongue, but couldn't resist. "You know, I've been telling you this for years..."

Danny's lips had grown dry. "Yeah, I know. I guess I didn't hear you. But it's clearer now. Not what I want to do, but how I should go about it. The search for my 'Why.'"

Nancy smiled at the other end of the line. She was glad that her husband's stubbornness about money had softened and he was apparently now open to the possibility of another path. "I'm really happy for you. If you need any help, you know how to reach me."

"I know how to reach you. In a warm bed in our little house." He smiled, then continued seriously. "But the responsibility for all this, all that I'm saying, is on me. I take personal responsibility for my actions..."

On the other side of the planet, Nancy nodded, thinking to herself, "Of course, I've wanted to tell you this ever since we've been together. I just hope that these new convictions will remain when you return to real life." But she said nothing.

He continued. "It's up to me to decide what happens to me in the future. That's the main lesson I've come away with. If you walk this path with me, I'll be even happier."

They spoke for a few more minutes about everything that had happened and how it might affect the future. Danny enjoyed the view from the castle tower, while Nancy sorted her morning routine at their home in San Mateo. During the course of the conversation, the sun set behind the mountains, pulling an orange and red band of light across the December sky. Festive lighting sparkled in the city streets below. The houses and squares of the old town were being dressed in red, green, and white Christmas colors. In the midst of it all, in a larger square, thousands of tiny yellow bulbs burned, winding their way up a huge Christmas tree. Like in a fairytale.

Danny made his way down from the tower, slowly headed across the castle courtyard and to the exit. His head bubbled with thoughts and ideas, but he tried to shake them off, for now. He had to sleep on it, then make a move. There was no way he could sort out everything that was percolating in his mind. And what did Clyde have to do with all this? What deal did he make with Iza?

7 UNICORN DRIVE

Part Three

CHAPTER TWENTY-FIVE

Own Your S#it

San Francisco, California, 16 January 2015

"My dear fellow journalists," Clyde began excitedly. "It seems that print sales of this issue will break all previous records. And it's only been out for a few days. Our online edition, especially Danny's article, is already approaching record readership!" He picked up a hard copy of the magazine's latest issue and turned the front page towards his colleagues. The smiling gray cat looked back at them next to the title "Own Your S#it: Why Make Millions and How." Talking Tom held his sweetheart, Angela, paw to paw in a dance pose. The cartoon yellow dance floor beneath them was paved with green dollar signs. Clyde pointed to the small photo of the author in the lower-right corner of the cover. "Danny, you hit a home run this time. A phenomenal story. A perfect storm of serious business, IT, management, and ethics. Precisely what our world needs right now. All this is already reflected in the numbers. Well done and a hearty congratulations!"

Basking in his coworkers' applause, Danny beamed with excitement and satisfaction. He'd finally succeeded. A hit lead article! At the same time, he was the only one in the room aware of what else hid behind his story. "If they only knew," he thought. "This was just a summary..."

The journalists soon left the weekly editorial meeting and only two remained. One sat in a large leather chair behind an oversized wooden desk, the other sat on a black conference chair opposite.

"Well, what's the good word now?" Clyde said, half-jokingly.

"What can I say?" Danny replied. "I guess the story was of interest to our readers."

"Of interest?" Clyde mocked back. "That's the understatement of the century. My inbox is bursting with compliments and follow-up questions and ideas from readers. They would love more. More stories along these lines. And I've been thinking..." Clyde stood, ran his hand over the Navajo Indian statue on his table and approached the window. "Phillip Westmore will be retiring soon. What would you say to taking over his role?"

This unexpected question made Danny's eyes widen. "A senior position? But Phil has been our lead reporter from the start. Are you sure I could fill his shoes?"

"I have believed in you for a long time, son. Now you've proven that you're entirely worthy of my trust. And you don't have to step into his shoes. Put on your own shoes. They'll keep you more agile, more modern. You've shown that you know how with this article."

He looked up and raised his eyebrows, signaling toward the magazine on his desk.

"That would be an honor. It's just...are you sure..."

"Yep, I'm sure. I've already spoken to the board about it. Everyone is in favor. Phil, too. He'll be happy to hand you his office come March."

Clyde had known for some time that Phil was leaving and someone would have to take his place. Danny was one option. He didn't tell anyone, however, that his senior colleague, Jim, was another. He had weighed both options for a long time and hadn't been able to decide. Danny was far less experienced than Jim and hadn't yet proven his chops. It would've been hard to argue in his favor in front of the board. Jim, by contrast, was a mature journalist and a more logical successor to Phil. But Clyde wanted the freshness Danny offered. Jim would've been solid, but same old same old. When Danny published this hit story, a weight slaked off of Clyde's shoulders. Now he could push for his favorite without hesitation, and he snapped into action. But he didn't intend to leave anything to chance, so he continued, in a more official tone. "Of course everyone, from journalists to directors, expects you to continue working as you have been for the past month. Do you understand? You have a great opportunity, but now you'll have to prove that you really deserve it. This isn't a minor assignment to take on."

"I really can't believe it. I'm very happy to accept. The offer and the responsibility that comes with it. I will do my best."

"I don't doubt that," said Clyde. He hoped the boy really would know how to harness his potential and, at the same time, enjoy it. He was giving him the opportunity he'd craved for so long. Now it was up to him to take advantage of it. To own it.

"Clyde," Danny resumed in a quieter voice after some silence had passed. "I've got another question. I kinda thought you'd tell me yourself, but you haven't. What sort of agreement did you and Iza Login have before my interview with Outfit7? What changed their opinion of us so dramatically? About me?"

Clyde smiled to himself, stared out at the bay, then turned to the young reporter. "I'll explain it to you sometime. We're not quite there yet."

Only the flickering candlelight interrupted the constancy of their gaze into each other's eyes. This made Nancy move the candlestick to the edge of the table and pick up her glass of bubbly. "The chia seeds in that dessert got stuck in my teeth. Not yours? Best to gargle with some champagne. Come on! To your recent success! And to your, to our future. And to seed-free teeth!"

She smiled and held out her hand, which grasped a crystal flute, which she inclined slightly towards the man across the table. Danny picked up his champagne glass, too, bowed his head slightly, and clinked. "Thank you, my love. It's so much easier thanks to you. I'm so grateful that you stood by me through it all. I don't know what I'd do without you." He placed his left hand on his chest and stared playfully at the ceiling. "Ahhh."

Nancy gave him a funny look, realized he was teasing, and kicked him lightly in the shin under the table. They both laughed. "You doofus."

"Ah, I'm just teasing," Danny continued, but with a more serious tone. "But it's true. I'm so glad you're in this with me. That we know how to support each other. In fact, publishing a story and scoring a promotion at work doesn't mean as much to me as does the way it came about. And where it might take us."

"That odyssey really did change you, huh?"

"It's funny… Basically nothing major has changed. Just my view of the world. The horizons that await us. It's all so easy, but at the same time so difficult. What weird creatures we humans are. It's just opened my eyes, nothing else. I don't do anything much differently. It's just that I've changed my flow of thought and my interpretation of events around me. I'm not looking for external reasons to explain what happens to me. I'm looking within myself. Learning to be the owner of my own shit. So far it feels a great deal more fulfilling."

Nancy looked at her husband contentedly. "Of course. Everything that happens to us is just a reflection of ourselves. If only more people took on this view, as you have…" She slid her right foot out of her black heels beneath the table and stroked his ankle playfully. "And for us, it's really just beginning…"

Slowly they drank their champagne and headed towards Danny's blue Mazda Miata, which was parked precisely equidistant from the white lines around it, in front of a vegan restaurant on the outskirts of town.

CHAPTER TWENTY-SIX

A Billion Dollar Sale

Zurich, Switzerland and Limassol, Cyprus, 6 December 2016

"I will not sell for less than a billion," Samo said firmly, more or less to himself. He leaned back, supporting himself on his elbows on the bed, looking thoughtfully at the frescoed ceiling. His blue suede shoes dangled over the edge of the bed. Meanwhile, Iza leaned against the metal railing of their bedroom's balcony and watched a flock of gray birds fly low over the morning mist of Lake Zurich. They swooped upwards towards their window, then wove around the towers of the luxury hotel that looked like a fairytale mansion.

"If you manifested a billion, you will get a billion. You know that perfectly well. Your purpose is pure and you have worked very hard. We all have. So there's no possibility that you will not get it."

He inhaled and nodded. "Yup, I know. But it seems to me that our investment bankers were a little frightened. I don't think they believe that the Chinese are willing to pay that much..."

"They're paid a commission. It's in their interest to earn us as much as possible."

"Of course it's in their interest. But I made it clear to them that we're not dipping below one billion. My sense is that they're afraid the sale won't happen at all because of that restriction. Better to get their percentage from a few hundred million than from zero. Any percent of zero is zero."

Iza turned from the view to look into the room. "I think we can easily move forward, even if they're doubters. In any case, we also have several other parties from other countries interested. We're in a good negotiating position. The strategy of having customers in several countries is really benefiting us now."

"True. Especially after all the potential Chinese buyers vanished overnight leaving only one. I find it hard to believe that this was a coincidence."

"Anyway, today is D-Day. I believe in you and I will stand by your side at all times. Besides, you know that, in our industry, the selling price can easily be ten times the annual profit. And this year our profit hit one hundred million. One hundred million times ten is... See? No problem." With a smile on her face, Iza turned away from Samo and looked again towards the distant, snow-covered Swiss Alps, over which the sun already shone. "This reminds me of Slovenia," she thought...

Samo looked at the clock on his phone. He slowly got to his feet and walked to the balcony. He extended his right hand. "Well, time to go. Whatever happens happens."

Iza took a final sip of her matcha tea and set the cup down on the small table, next to the fruit. She straightened her black skirt and took her husband's hand. "Whatever happens happens? We know exactly what will happen. A billion is gonna happen."

Hand in hand, they pushed through the heavy hotel room door. It closed silently behind them. Click.

———————————————∞ ∞———————————————

In the lobby in front of the meeting room, two members of the Outfit7 financial and legal team awaited them, alongside the Englishmen: a trifecta of lawyers and a duet of bankers from a large investment bank that represented Outfit7 in the sale.

"Good morning. Are we ready, then?" asked one of the bankers.

"Always," Iza replied. Samo nodded.

Along a soft carpet they walked until they entered a large room in the center of which stood a huge mahogany table. A cleaning lady was just dusting the framed photographs of celebrities who had visited the hotel. A porter by the door switched on a huge crystal chandelier that softly illuminated the perfumed space from on high. They sat at the table and opened their laptops. As if in sync, the door opened on the far side of the meeting room and the Chinese delegation entered. They wore tidy, dark suits and ties, and moved silently in single file, strictly sorted by hierarchy, as they approached the sellers.

"Geez, there are three times as many of them as there are of us," Iza whispered in Samo's ear. "Now I see why there are so many chairs on the other side of the table..."

Everyone stood, official greetings were exchanged, pleasantries about flights and the like, about the Swiss cold, and the good choice of hotel. Then they sat down, the sellers on one side, the hopeful buyers on the other. The Chinese delegation sat in two rows, negotiators in the front, assistants in the rear.

"Well, we have presented you with all the details about the company that is the subject of our negotiations," said the head of the investment bankers on the Outfit7 side. "All the financial data, all the future plans, all the details about the business are known. Over the past month, you have also met all the members of the Board and spoken with each individually. In this way, you've come to know where the company is now and what development potential it has already in place for the future." The banker swallowed hard in an effort to sound relaxed. "Our client Samo Login is authorized to sell by all 205 shareholders of Outfit7. And he insists on the sale price of... one billion dollars."

When he'd spoken, only the words of the Chinese interpreters echoed through the room, followed by a tortuous silence. The head of the Chinese delegation leaned over to the adviser to his right and they exchanged a few sentences, then shook their heads. Outfit7's English banker, who was fluent in Chinese, grew pale. Iza watched him from the corner of her eye and couldn't believe that such an experienced banker, who'd already shepherded a huge number of major sales, was so obviously nervous and doubtful at this pivotal moment. It was true that these negotiations were unconventional, and Samo stubbornly insisted on his position, but still...

The Chinese delegation's head straightened up and spoke slowly, while his words were translated. "We still feel that the price is too high. We understand the potential and the options for synergy that your company presents to ours upon merger. We have carefully reviewed your financial data and, based on the final calculation of the current situation, we wish to negotiate a more favorable price."

The English banker looked at Samo with a hopeful glimmer in his eye, but Samo replied with absolute confidence and without hesitation. "The company, regardless of the numbers, is worth exactly as much as the buyer is willing to pay for it. And the buyer will pay as much as he sees its potential for development. Outfit7 is currently in its fastest growth phase. We have never been in such good shape before. A lot of people have asked me why I'm even selling a business at a time when it's so successful. Strictly in terms of business, it really doesn't make sense. But I have my personal reasons for doing so. I do not have to sell this company. But I am choosing to sell it so that I can continue my personal vision, which currently lies elsewhere. As for the company itself, we have other interested buyers at the moment. The sale will happen one way or another. As you know, the potential for development is enormous. Therefore, the price remains unchanged. One. Billion. Dollars."

A flurry of whispered words in Chinese. "We need fifteen minutes to consult in private," said one of the Chinese team's advisers in broken English.

Everyone stood and slowly filed out of the room, the Chinese through one end, the Slovenian and English contingent through the other. On either side of the meeting room were smaller rooms where each negotiating team could retreat to finalize their battle plans. The porter in front of the meeting room door nodded in greeting as the Outfit7 team walked past him into their smaller room. He was accustomed to moving teams left and right from the meeting room, as negotiations and big sales were fairly frequent at this hotel.

The smaller room was furnished in a far more modern style. A video conferencing system linked to a large plasma television hung on the wall, and an illuminated bar, stocked with snacks and drinks, stood in a corner. Samo took an apple, bit into it, and walked over to the banker.

"Why is this move necessary? And right at the start?"

"Not to worry. This is a standard step in negotiations. It will happen many more times before we're through. Their side will ask for a recess and so will we. And believe me, it'll take more than fifteen minutes. Even if they agree on everything, they'll leave us waiting. I'd say at least an hour. In the meantime, they'll watch some movie or something... This is a tactic to make your opponent nervous." As he spoke, confidence, along with a more normal flesh tone, flushed back into his face.

"And?" Samo joked sarcastically. "Are they succeeding?"

"I don't know, Samo. They'll be tough negotiators. What if we lowered the price all the same, just a bit? Ten percent doesn't sound like much, and you'd still walk away with nine hundred million. As you know, our investment bank previously valued your company at between six hundred and eight hundred million. If we were to lower the price to nine hundred, I'm sure we could wrap up negotiations this morning. What do you say?"

Samo stabbed him with a very serious stare from his deep brown eyes through the glasses on his nose. "I say no. The price remains. One billion. Period. You are here to get us that amount. We will not discuss the price again. We can talk about conditions and timelines, but not about price. And if you can't lead the negotiations with that in mind, I'll do it myself."

The banker took a step back, somewhat embarrassed. "No, no, it's okay. We'll manage."

He was not used to such insistence, supported by data and a clear vision. He shifted back to stand next to his banker colleague on the other side of the room, to discuss how to proceed.

Samo sat beside Iza, who was enthusiastically playing Talking Tom Gold Run on her phone, one of the newer Outfit7 games, in a comfortable armchair. She paused the game. "What did you two decide?"

"Nothing. I told him the price stands."

"Okay. I agree."

They exchanged a few more words, then Iza resumed her game. It helped drive away her nerves. Even Samo pulled out his phone and began to answer the mountain of emails that had been piling up all morning.

After about forty-five minutes, a knock came at the door and they were invited back into the meeting room. Negotiations dragged on through the day, including over lunch, with several shifts to consultations in the smaller rooms. With each retreat, both teams grew more impatient. Everyone knew that the pauses made no sense and it was just a psychological game at play.

The afternoon winter sun had almost touched the hilltops above the city skyline, and the discussions dragged on. On Outfit7's side, Samo more or less led the negotiations himself. The bankers and lawyers advised only when they had to agree on the legal and financial details of the planned contract. Samo insisted on his terms, always arguing them well, holding fast despite all the concerns from the Chinese side. Every once in a while Samo positively surprised even himself with his powerful reply to every question or dilemma that the Chinese pointed out as a reason to pay less. Despite their strong arguments and ample negotiation skills, the Chinese team began to soften. It was no use arguing when, for every point they raised, Samo had a perfectly weighted, reasonable reply that assuaged any concerns. After hours of back-and-forth, jousting to and fro, two stares met in silence. One was through thin, metal-framed glasses, the other through glasses with thick, dark frames. The leaders of the two group stared each other down, respectfully but firmly. The silence elevated the tension in the room more than debate had. Everyone knew something was about to happen. It was as if a silent but insistent drum roll were forecasting the climax to the day's exhausting activity. An invisible chain of lightning flashed from one side of the oversized mahogany table to the other, charging the ions in the atmosphere more as each moment passed. Then the leader of the Chinese group looked down calmly, placed his palms on the tabletop, and said "我们协商过的."

The members of the Chinese delegation all began to nod and their translator shouted, in a burst of energy that made clear his relief, "You have a deal!"

In that instant, a boulder of pressure rolled off of Samo's shoulders. He couldn't at first even process the fact that he had really done it. He looked at Iza, who just half-nodded at him. But he saw her lips move just a millimeter and he knew how satisfied she was with the outcome. No more affirmation was necessary. He'd read all he needed in her wide, smiling eyes and the twitch of the lips.

Only then did he turn to the bankers and lawyers, who were still in some shock themselves, trying to fully grasp what had happened. An agreement to sell Outfit7 for the full $1 billion had just been reached.

The conversation continued into the late afternoon, but it focused on small bureaucratic matters needed to complete the sale, and for the lawyers to write up. The conditions were laid out for the final contract that the lawyers would finalize later on. And with that, the official negotiations were concluded.

After the final thanks and customary farewells from both sides, the banker hinted that Samo and his team should meet with him again in the smaller room. They locked themselves inside and the banker said, "Samo, I just wanted to say that you were brilliant. Truly. You don't see such negotiations every day. A hearty congratulations."

"Thanks," Samo replied lukewarmly. He could practically read the banker calculating his percentage in his head. "But I'd say the Chinese got a good deal. The company is indeed worth the price. If they manage it properly moving forward, their purchase will be repaid and then some."

"Of course, I'm sure of it," the banker said, with a tone that expressed both cynicism and relief. "Well, now I'll ask that we leave the hotel as soon as possible and head out somewhere. It would be best if we could fly home today, but I know that's not possible. What's important is to get you away from here and not to return until late. Perhaps we'll go out in the old city center? Zurich is beautiful, especially in December."

Iza thought about the cold winter outside the hotel and shivered in anticipation. "Why do we have to go out? It doesn't sound so appealing in this cold."

"Because we know how these negotiations work," the banker replied. "Regardless of the fact that we have already agreed on everything, I'm sure they will call us back. They'll certainly want to touch up this or that, to renegotiate certain parts of the contract. It's like that every time. And if we are happy with the way it currently stands, then it's better if we're not physically here. You should also book the first available flight in the morning."

About two hours later, the Logins and their negotiating team were walking around downtown Zurich and admiring the heart of the old town. As they crossed Muehlesteg Bridge, covered in lovers' locks, the banker's phone rang. Iza, who was walking beside him, overheard snippets of the conversation. The banker spoke with far more confidence than before.

"No, unfortunately we're no longer in the hotel and won't be back today. We've all agreed, anyway. It will have to remain as agreed upon."

Several more such calls came in, but the banker did not respond to their invitations to return to the meeting room. They simply couldn't. After all, they weren't even at the hotel. They returned only very late at night. Or rather, in the wee hours of the morning. Then they set off very early for the airport and their flights home, one to London, the other to Cyprus.

∞ ∞

"Then there will be no sale!" Samo snapped into the receiver of his telephone as he stood behind the desk in his Cyprus office. "It's been more than three weeks since the negotiations and you have yet to keep your promise! As I said, if a billion dollars in one lump sum is paid to our law firm, no matter how good our relationship may be, it is going to make me nervous. Call it a caprice, but in this case, I'm afraid we don't want to put our faith in anyone but ourselves. We want the money transferred directly to our own personal accounts. At least to all of the founders, who are the primary shareholders. The rest can be arranged through a law firm. I cannot understand why this isn't possible. Above all, it's not clear to me how we have been talking about this since the beginning and you still haven't been able to address it and make anything happen."

"It is just not our practice," said the banker on the line. "Sellers always receive their money via their law firms."

Given all the time already spent discussing precisely this issue, Samo was at his wit's end and really didn't know what else to say. "Well, for us your practice will be different. If you don't find a solution, we won't sign the contract!"

The banker took a deep breath. "We will try a little harder, but I don't think we can do much about it at this point."

Samo hung up and looked at Iza and their colleagues in the office. He was seething. "I really cannot understand this. How can they not find another way? If you ask me, they thought they'd finished with us after the negotiations and wouldn't have to lift a finger further. We are well aware that most of their transactions are conducted through lawyers, but they knew that we wanted a different approach from day one. I think he just made it clear that they don't intend to do anything more to resolve this for us. They are probably sure that we'll drop it at this point. Well, we won't. We've already agreed to this with the founders. As far as I'm concerned, there is another solution. We can call China and tell them the deal is off unless the bank finds the solution we want. Or maybe the Chinese can come up with a different way forward. Otherwise we'll just end this ordeal. I don't know..."

It was a black night at eleven. Iza rotated her turquoise ring around her finger and watched the distant lights dance in the hills. "You'd call China now? What time is it there, anyway? Four, five in the morning?"

He threw himself into his desk chair. "I don't think we have another option. Given how we've been in friendly contact over the last few weeks, I'm sure our Chinese partners could find a solution for us. It seems to me that, at the moment, I trust the buyers more than our own bankers."

After a brief consultation with his colleagues, Samo picked up the phone and called their lead contact in China, even though it was still before dawn there. They spoke for a few minutes, then he hung up.

"They'll snap into action straight away. They just need to talk to Beijing first and settle a few things with their banks. They say they'll find a solution and it shouldn't be a problem. The sale is on!"

———∞ ∞———

Samo stood surrounded by lawyers in Outfit7's glass meeting room. A mountain range of papers loomed before him. A few days after the call to China, everything had been arranged regarding the payments, and the lawyers drafted the final sales contracts for him to sign. He was authorized to sign the sale of shares on behalf of all 205 shareholders, the employees of Outfit7, whose personal approval of the sale had been obtained over the past few days. Each contract included additional forms, so more than a thousand signatures awaited.

Iza leaned against the door jamb and laughed. "Well, that's what you wanted and now you've got it. After all these signatures your hand will fall off."

"Joke as much as you like. If this marks the end of our sales saga then I'm happy to even sacrifice a hand. I don't even know where to start. Look at all this paperwork. I hope I have enough ink in this fountain pen. And the lawyers are still printing and carrying in more. In this supposedly digital age, I have to sign everything by hand to sell a digital business... What a world."

"I'm less interested in how you're going to sign all this than in the reaction of all those tiny Slovenian banks when shareholders' accounts start receiving thousands and thousands of dollars. I'm guessing that nothing like this has ever happened in our country before..."

CHAPTER TWENTY-SEVEN

The Energy of Money

San Francisco, California, 7 January 2017

"Did you hear that they sold Outfit7?" Danny read the text message from his editor in astonishment.

He immediately wrote back: "Really? I heard it was in the air. But it's happened?"

"Yes. For a billion."

"What?"

"Yes. $1bil. Nuts, huh?"

Danny pressed the call button. If Clyde had texted, then he wasn't asleep. And you can't have a proper conversation over text, anyway. Clyde responded immediately.

"Hey."

"A billion dollars?" Danny cut to the chase, skipping the formalities.

"Yup. Iza Login phoned me to tell me the news. They sold it yesterday. Exactly seven years to the day that they first sat in an office together.

They did what they said they'd do all along. Sell the company at its moment of highest growth."

Danny just smiled. "Of course they did. What else? Even though the price was rising by a few million every month, they went ahead and sold it. They really do stick to their guns. Who bought it?"

"A Chinese corporation. I'll explain more when I see you in person. And I've got another surprise for you. Can we meet in Palo Alto at three?"

Danny checked his schedule. "That should work. I don't have any afternoon appointments. Where?"

"Coupa Cafe in Ramona."

"The place we once went to meet with the Login's advisor?"

"That's the place. See you at three. Plan on staying a while. Oh, and bring your dictaphone."

"Why?"

"All will be revealed. See you."

∞ ∞

When Danny entered the restaurant, he reveled in the intoxicating scent of roasted Venezuelan coffee. Clyde was already seated at a table in the rear, browsing on his laptop.

"Here I am."

Clyde looked up thoughtfully. "Well hello. Grab a seat."

Danny pulled up a wooden chair and sat with his back to the entrance, looking at his editor. "So are you going to tell me what's cooking?"

"A lot is cooking. A beautiful update to your first Outfit7 story of a few years ago is on the front burner."

"They really sold it, huh?" Danny asked rhetorically, with a hint of pride on behalf of the Logins.

"They really did. It's been the talk of the entire business mediasphere all morning."

"I noticed. But no one seems to know exactly what happened and why. Everyone's speculating. That's a classic Outfit7 move. They do something amazing and leave everyone scrambling for details." He happily flipped through some of his memories from speaking with Samo and Iza two years prior. "That's them, alright."

"Well, that's why we're here today. You have your dictaphone?"

"I do. But I still don't know why."

Clyde just smiled and nodded towards the entrance, so his best reporter would turn and see for himself.

"What?"

"Turn around."

Danny turned and looked towards the glass door. From the light filtering in, he couldn't tell exactly who was entering. But then his eyes caught hold of a familiar face and his eyes widened.

"Iza Login? What's she doing here?"

"You can ask her that yourself."

"Gentlemen," she began, "how are you?" She hugged them both warmly.

"Iza, what brings you to our part of the world?" Danny asked in surprise.

"A plane," she teased. "I came to see what you were up to."

Clyde leaned his elbows on the table and stared at his young reporter. "Iza phoned yesterday and said that she'd like to meet with us today. Outfit7 has been sold and media outlets all over the world are clamoring to know how and why. And she said that she wants you to write the exclusive sales story. In a way that people will really understand."

Danny looked up at Iza, amazed. "Seriously? What an honor! That's why you came all this way? And just two days after the sale?"

"Exactly. With your last story, you so beautifully summed up our essence. I would be very happy if you would be the one to write this story, too. About the sale. You managed to translate our purposes, our mission, and our culture into a language understood by the broader business world. It would be great if you would do it again. One of my rules is never to change a winning horse. In this case, I guess you're our champion. My only condition is that this story should be even better than the last one." She laughed and Danny smiled, knowing that there was some truth in her words.

"What can I say? I'm delighted to write another story. And I'll do my very best. It's a pity I didn't know ahead of time, as I would've prepared..."

"Clyde and I agreed that it should be a surprise, and more fun if you didn't have time to get ready. We don't want you to be infected by the suppositions floating around the media at the moment. Let the story be genuine, straight from the horse's mouth, so to speak, unburdened by rumor. I'll tell you everything you want to know and then you pick out what you need for the story."

"Of course, with pleasure," Danny replied happily. "Let me just say that all that's happened to you over the last few years is brilliant, and my hat's off to you. You wrote your own story and it ended just as you'd said it would from the start. And in the end it sells for a billion. You are officially a unicorn! Perfect for a fairytale."

"The key is that Samo and I followed our original purpose throughout. It is also important that, in the end, we truly believed in the billion-dollar sale itself. We believed that we could make a unicorn. Maybe it's good to know this for your article: we're the first husband and wife team in the world to have managed something like this. As you say, Danny, it really does sound like a fairytale. For seven years we lived at fairytale 7 Unicorn Drive," she joked. "Only this fairytale turns out to be entirely true. Too few people believe in such stories, and that's why so few come true. We firmly believed in ours and the result speaks for itself." She looked at Clyde and Danny with sparkling eyes and a mist of pride.

"The Tale of 7 Unicorn Drive. It has a nice ring to it," said Clyde. "And what's the next chapter? Is Part Two already mapped out?"

"Yeah, we already have an outline in place," she continued. "We've established a foundation through which we plan to support a variety of projects in support of our ideas. This way we can run several different projects at once. To give you an example, one of them is the LoginEKO project, in which we plan to purchase a large plot of very fertile land in Serbia, in the southeastern part of Europe, where we will develop advanced systems for sustainable crop production. Now is the time to move forward and begin to fulfill our core mission: Healthy food for everyone. But we can talk more about this some other time. Our time today isn't limitless. We've got to catch a plane this evening, so I suggest we focus on the first part of our story: the sale of Outfit7."

"You're already flying off?" Danny asked in surprise. "Where to? Is Samo here with you?"

"Yes, Samo has some meetings at Stanford. Then we'll meet at the airport and we go first to Argentina for a few days, then we're off to Antarctica."

"Antarctica? That's going to be quite a trip."

"It will. We've always wanted to go there and see the continent in person. While it's still white. Antarctica beautifully symbolizes what we do. The fight for a better world. If we manage to keep it white, we've won. If not, we lose. Changing people's eating habits is, in our view, the first step. This is now our basic mission. And there's more. We're going on vacation because, frankly, we need to get some rest. This last year has been truly exhausting. We need to unplug. From tomorrow on... So? Shall we begin?"

"With pleasure." Danny placed his trusty black Sony dictaphone on the table and pressed REC. He scratched his hair in thought and began. "As far as I know, at this moment Outfit7 is at its zenith in business terms. Why did you two decide to sell right now? For your average businessman, this probably seems like a surprising decision, timing-wise."

"You know that we said at the beginning that we would sell it after seven years and for one hundred million dollars in profit."

"Indeed."

"Well, it's been seven years. Exactly as we manifested with the founding team. So we sold. And we ended up profiting ten times what we set out to earn. But believe me, a lot of people have asked us this same question and a lot of people wanted to convince us not to sell yet. That we should enjoy our earnings for a few more years, at least. Samo had a good answer to this line of argument. 'If we don't sell now,' he'd say, 'then greed wins. We don't want that.' And he's right. Isn't that so? Now we have enough to meet our basic goals and ample resources to really do something positive for our planet."

The waiter arrived and took their orders. Iza and Clyde ordered black coffee, Danny ordered a latte macchiato.

"Okay, so you decided to sell. When? And can you tell me more about how this played out? How did you find a buyer for that kind of money?"

"We decided to sell in March of last year. At one of the management meetings in Cyprus. We worked with our team and with external consultants, using a special technique handed down by African shamans. I'll skip over the details. Suffice to say that it was intended to help solve strategic problems, when you make important decisions based on feelings, not rational, hard data. Anyway, after this workshop I woke the next morning overwhelmed by the feeling that we had to sell. It was interesting that Samo and I hadn't really spoken much about it before. That morning I turned to him and said, 'Samo, we've got to sell the company.' He calmly replied, 'Yes.' And that was that. The same day we steered our ship in the direction of a sale and it became our top priority."

Danny had learned a lot about Outfit7 and how it was run, but this was still a surprise to him. "You sold a billion-dollar company based on... a feeling? Intuition?"

"Yes. Samo and I both strongly believe in such feelings, in our inner voice. Like you said, intuition. Straight away we started the sales process and we didn't ask ourselves why anymore. Of course, we did this in secret, so as not to cause a general panic in the company. Only a handful of us knew about it."

"Okay. I might have expected something along the lines, knowing you," Danny playfully commented. "What next?"

"Then we phoned one of our advisors who connected us with the biggest investment banks, since deals of this scale always go through them. The bank's job was to locate prospective buyers and guide the entire sales process. Since we chose a large investment bank with an office in London, Samo and I spent more time there during that period than in Cyprus and Slovenia combined. This bank, as we knew it would, wound up plumbing our depths and checking our plumbing. They wanted to know everything about us. Even more than the potential buyers did later. This exploration took three months. Only then did they agree to represent us, and they started the search for an interested party. We began making presentations to promote the company's sale. In the end, we had more than twenty parties who showed meaningful interest. That's when our international road show began."

The waiter arrived with oversized, brightly-colored cups, setting them down on the wooden table. Danny continued. "Where did all the potential buyers come from? Is that a secret?"

"No, it's no secret. Our strategy was to look for buyers in several different countries, to have a better negotiating position. We had suitors from the US, Japan, Korea, England, and China. Samo and I traveled to each country, courting each, representing our company. Samo was amazing in that role. He showed off Outfit7 to everyone individually, each with such enthusiasm and compelling data that even I would've bought it if I'd had the money. He really devoted himself to each presentation one hundred percent. It was clear that each presentation was entirely new for that audience, and that each company we presented to might end up as the buyer. Maximum effort. Even our investment bankers had never seen anything like it. At our roadshows, especially in China, we had as many as three full presentations a day. You can imagine how exhausting that was. I don't know where Samo got the energy. He took everything in stride. The presentations were followed by non-binding offers from interested parties."

"What were the offers like? Were they in the ballpark of what you hoped to get?"

"In principle, yes. But the range was huge. From two hundred million to a billion. In the end, we had to choose the finalists. Once we'd selected them, they hired independent auditors to thoroughly run due diligence on our company and its operations. They reviewed everything, down to the last cent. That was another exhausting month. It's good that we had everything nicely organized and meticulously recorded when it came to finances. It saved us, and them, a lot of time and effort. When that formality was covered, our entire management team had to present its work and vision to potential buyers. We practiced and polished the presentations in Cyprus, then presented them in Vienna, where all three delegations arrived one by one. In the end, of course, the final negotiations followed, then the signing of the contracts."

"That sounds pretty quick. Can we analyze a bit? When you decided on the potential buyers, how did the conversations play out?"

"We can go into details, sure. You just stop me if I'm moving too quickly. You know what I'm like, once I get on a roll..."

Iza went on to explain all the details of the sale process, leaving out only what she was not permitted to say, from a trade secret or contractual perspective. Above all, she wanted him to understand their reason for the sale and what was different about this sale from the experience of other companies of comparable size. Occasionally Clyde would add his two cents and join the conversation, sharing his knowledge of IT company sales of the past. But this was infrequent, as he largely left Danny to it and enjoyed the show.

"Can you tell me why you think Outfit7 gained such value in the market?" Danny continued. "A billion is something to celebrate. If I compare you to competitors, at least as far as I can tell, they'd be nowhere near such a valuation. Would you agree, Clyde? Not even if they were to go for a public offering. What's your secret?"

"I'd say our big secret weapon was Samo's steadfast negotiating technique," Iza laughed. "Of course, it's not just that. In addition to being extremely efficient and able to operate in the market with the efficacy of a company ten times our size, we had a clear focus and solid vision that customers believed in. And one more thing. When the Chinese market started to open up, we made an important decision. I think we were the first in our industry to enter it without an intermediary. We created a very dedicated internal team that focused only on China. We handled our own distribution entirely by ourselves, and of course advertising, as well. This was risky in the early days, because we had no idea about the Chinese market and how it worked. In the end, however, it turned out to be our smartest move, as it greatly increased the company's value, particularly in the eyes of Chinese buyers. Other than that, if we're quite realistic, we could have sold the company even earlier. We were successful. We could have found a buyer a while back if we'd been looking for one."

This last statement made Clyde straighten up a bit. "Would you have sold earlier?"

"I'm speaking hypothetically. Any company that's firing on all cylinders can be sold. The day when Talking Tom became a hit, we could have sold it. But we didn't. We initially manifested that we'd sell after seven years. And I believe that selling before that would've been a bad move, if not a retrospective failure. Now was the perfect time. And the yield was higher. Obviously we needed more energy for our new projects."

When Iza started associating money with some other concept, Danny's interest was immediately piqued. It was like a flashback to the interview two years back. "What do you mean when you say 'more energy'? Energy for what? The energy of money?"

"Money itself has no energy. It's just a currency for energy. A kind of battery that stores energy produced so you can use it later, elsewhere, for other things. Money only saves effort. If someone feels energy in money itself, then they're suffering from a disillusion. Maybe even a collective belief. But we do need to feel the energy in what we would like to do with money. That passion to fulfill our desires. The money itself is empty. It has no...vibration. Those who just want money run headfirst into a wall that they cannot surmount. Money alone is passionless. That's why it doesn't make us happy. In financial terms, you can be very rich, but you won't necessarily be happy. Everyone knows that."

"How would you explain, then, that successful people have a lot of money? If you want to be successful, then you have to be wealthy? Isn't that the American dream?"

"Yes, it is the basis for it. But you could also say the opposite. If you don't have money, then you're not successful. However, I do not agree. Those who are successful aren't those with money, but those who have somehow achieved inner peace. This has been demonstrated in countless examples the world over. An individual who is at peace within themselves, flowing energetically and already experiencing a feeling of well-being and prosperity. That's happiness. Money doesn't enter the equation. If the world worked towards achieving that feeling, rather than constantly chasing money, then the world would be a very different place. People would work towards their dreams, manifesting them, and finding happiness in doing so. And, if I understand correctly, there is someone seated at this very table who has greatly changed his outlook on money. Am I right?"

Danny swallowed his coffee, embarrassed. "Yeah, there just may be something to that. I must admit that I really have changed my beliefs in recent years. And yes, your story had a big impact on that, too. Uh...how did you know that?" Danny's gaze shifted reproachfully to Clyde, who just smiled back at him.

"More secrets," Danny continued. "Can you finally tell me what you two agreed on back then? How did you wind up inviting me to Slovenia after my, uh, unfortunate interview in London? It's been so long now, have I earned an explanation?"

"Maybe it's really time to tell him," said Iza, winking at Clyde. "After your interview with my son in London, I wrote an email to Clyde and explained everything I saw as a problem, why it went sour. I'm not even sure why I wrote to him at all. Usually after something like that we just cut off contact. No offense, Danny."

"No, no, it's okay. I'm well aware that I screwed up..."

"Well, Clyde called me right after that and explained his side of the story to me. We immediately clicked. If I recall, we spoke for almost an hour, remember that, Clyde?"

"Of course," he replied. "A lovely chat."

"Clyde also told me about you and your life goals. He said that you were very capable and that he sees in you the possibility of advancing on a personal level, too. You embodied the young, driven American with the conviction that money and financial success are the only real goal in life. And Clyde saw in you the possibility of a shift in your perspective. He saw our story as one that could open your eyes. And with your article, maybe more young people around the world like you might also change their outlook for the better. By saying this, he somehow convinced me to invite you into our family for a time. I don't know exactly why I believed him as I did, but that's how it happened. As I've said many times, intuition should never be ignored. Sometimes it takes us to places we've never even dreamt of visiting."

Danny's eyes were misty as he looked at his editor, the closest person he had to a father. After a few moments of silence, made only slightly less atmospheric by the constant buzz of the coffee grinder behind the bar, he reached out a hand to Clyde.

"Thank you so much, Clyde. From the bottom of my heart."

Iza was likewise moved by the moment, her heart warmed. She took another sip of her coffee, already imagining herself admiring the penguins on the vast glaciers of Antarctica.

CHAPTER TWENTY-EIGHT

The Future Is Out There

Ljubljana, Slovenia and Zrenjanin, Serbia, July 2020

The bells in the nearby church tower tolled twelve times, as they sat at a small wooden table outside a restaurant in the center of old Ljubljana. Nancy admired the white castle tower on the hill above them, topped by a white and green flag bearing the image of a dragon that flapped in the wind.

"So this is the tower you sent me that message from way back when?"

"Yup, that's it. More than five years ago..."

Nancy nodded. "Time flies when we're having fun. I'm so glad you brought me on vacation here before we'll be happily stuck at home for a while." She stroked her bulging tummy. "It's a lovely place. And in the state I'm in, I'd rather be here than in Tahiti." She smiled lovingly at him. "Above all, I'm happy with how everything that happened to you here has changed you."

Danny placed his palm over her belly and rubbed it gently through her white linen dress. "Yeah, it really did affect me. But in reality, nothing has changed. Just my view of the world. Now I know what

I have and what really makes me happy. Most of all it's you and what I create every day. I know that sounds cheesy. I had all of this before, I just didn't realize that this was what it's all about. When I recognized my passion in what I was already doing and already had, I became more successful and, as a result, more money came our way. It's really so interesting. Before, I was convinced that it had to happen the other way around. Now it's all clear to me. I just hope I can pass this all on to our child. Just like Clyde gave it to me."

Nancy looked at him with warmth. "I'm sure you will. You'll be a great dad. What's the plan now? Should we go on up? While I can still walk?"

"Definitely. You have to see this view of the city and the mountains beyond."

He left a tip on the table, took his wife by the hand, and they walked slowly down the narrow cobbled street up towards the green castle hill.

Millions of golden stalks of wheat swayed in the warm, late afternoon wind. Like waves on a gilded sea, they broke the monotony of the field that seemed to stretch infinitely into the horizon. Iza and Samo sat nearby on the grass beneath an ancient oak.

"This land is really fertile," Iza said. "Look at the harvest we'll have from our fields. We must be grateful for that."

Samo nodded. "We'll harvest nearly three thousand tons of wheat this year alone. Without fertilizers, without herbicides, without pesticides. And that's only half the crop. We'll gather the rest of it in the coming weeks."

"It's just a drop in the ocean if we want to feed the whole world. But it's a good start and it's a step towards our future. We could never have done it without Outfit7 and our Talking Tom."

"That's exactly why we built them both. And sold them. But I have to say that it gives me great satisfaction that the company continues to be successful. They're up to thirteen billion downloads this year. Can you imagine? That means that the buyer paid the right price for the company and its success story goes on. It's a win-win. We can all continue to create and work successfully."

A green combine harvester rumbled past, reaping the ripe wheat. A driver in red overalls waved at them from the window. His shirt bore the logo LoginEKO. Right behind it came another combine. And another. Three huge, green beasts moved ahead, one after another, gathering the precious crop. Iza and Samo waved back.

"Look up there!" Samo said suddenly, pointing to the sky.

"What is it? A flock of birds?"

"A flock of birds, yes, but what kind of birds? Are those flamingos?"

"Flamingos? In Serbia?"

"That's certainly what it looks like. That's downright surreal. What does that mean?"

"I don't know." Iza turned to him and looked him in the eye. "It will reveal itself when the time is right. That's how it's been every time."

Gazing up at the majestic flock of birds, they leaned back against the trunk of the mighty oak. The elegant flamingoes flew west, shifting with a synchronous swing of their wings, as if chasing the setting sun. They watched in silence, feeling the power of the ancient tree emanate from the grip of its roots. Iza slowly inhaled the warm summer air and touched the turquoise stone on her ring.

It will reveal itself when the time is right.

∞

THE END

———∞ ∞———

"To beloved Mother Earth.
Thank you for life, your love, support,
patience and trust."

Afterword

"Organizations address to the real needs of time and space with their purpose and culture." – *The purpose of the book*

What is possible and what is impossible, and where is the line between possible and impossible?

Too quickly we evaluate the unthinkable and deem it impossible. By doing so, we impose limits upon ourselves, and then we wonder why we are unhappy and unsuccessful.

The boundaries of our conceivable are expanded by respect and attitude towards truth, love, other people, and to all living beings and to nature itself.

Much has been written about harmony and balance: the balance in nature, work-life balance, the harmony of female and male energy... But how much of this do we really live? We truly believe that respect, love, truth, equality, and harmony are the key to pure co-creation, because they push the boundaries of the conceivable and, thus, the boundaries of the possible.

Only when we are aware of our mission and understand our life roles do we cease to evaluate and compare our work to that of others, thus enabling "escalated co-creation."

It is important to be aware that every individual's contribution is important, although they are not all the same because, without such a contribution, the end result would differ.

Our first readers said that the book you are holding now is a love story between a husband and wife who created the inconceivable with their love. For us, such business success was conceivable. Perhaps not entirely at the outset, but as we learned how our power and effect can multiply through mutual support and respect, we easily extended the boundaries of conceivable. Too often, people forget that the greatest potential lies in collaborating and co-creating with your life partner. It is easiest to become aware of how to support one another as we know our partners better than anyone.

Therefore, healing and conscious relationship-building are crucial. And our relationship with our partner is, of course, the most important one.

The purpose of our project and evolving discovery of our life mission have always been a great help to us.

People often confuse the concepts of purpose, mission, and success. Success, in our society, is usually measured in numbers—money and victories—as a result of limiting beliefs and internal wounds. Pure success is linked to one's personal mission and to how many goals of personal mission we have achieved. This is difficult to measure objectively, as we are in a constant process of discovering our mission throughout our lives.

Realizing the purpose of the project and, through that, our personal mission, is what makes us happiest, fulfills us most. Not success measured in victories when we compare ourselves to others. And if "traditional" success is not the one that counts, how does one replace it with mission and purpose? We hope you were able to find the answer to this question in the book.

This book contains our personal story. It allows for the possibility that someone who lived it in parallel experienced a different version of reality—reality is in the eye of the beholder.

Our thanks go to the writer of the book in hand, a good friend and long-term business partner, Dani Polajnar. Dani, our endless conversations, interviews, and reflections have poured forth into this book, in which you masterfully extracted the message that we wish to convey to the world.

To our dear co-founders of Outfit7, all our co-workers and partners, Talking Tom and your friends, and all spirits who guided us: without each and every one of you, this story would not exist. It was not always easy. On the contrary, it was sometimes inconceivably difficult. Together as a team we created, wrote, read, drew, and repeated our values.

Make it happen. No limits. Have fun. Work as a team. Own your s#it. Through this, we brought joy and fun to children, young people, and even grownups the world over. We hope that you never forget all the "fun-o-meters" with which we measured how many minutes of fun we created and delivered each month.

Thank you to everyone who participated in the creation of this book. There were many of you and each of you contributed a necessary piece.

Thank you to all our teachers and guides, earthly and otherworldly, scientific and spiritual, for being and for still forgivingly lifting veils, as well as heavy curtains, on the path to fulfilling our mission.

We are all a pure-power team.

Iza Sia and Samo Login

Note
from the Author

———∞ ∞———

It all started ten years ago, when I received Iza's email, asking me for advice. We'd known each other before, but we'd never really worked together up to that point. In a short note, she told me that she was now working in a new startup and that she'd like to organize a December team-building program for all their employees. She stressed that, after a busy 12 months, they deserved an end of the year event to promote bonding and help them relax as a group. There were just over twenty Outfit7 employees at the time. I hadn't heard of them. Another client, I thought. Great, but nothing out of the ordinary.

At that moment, I had no idea that this would be the start of a collaboration that would leave such a strong impression on our lives and lead to intertwined paths, both in our professional and private lives. From that December event onwards, as external organizers of their team programs, we had a front-row view of the company's explosive development; we got to know their very special corporate culture and had the privilege of helping them build it. An incredible business story was unfolding before our eyes.

So we decided to put the story of the last ten years into a book, the one you are holding in your hands. This is the story of Iza and Samo Login, based on the true story of their company, Outfit7, from its inception to its sale. It is a true story with one fictional element intertwined: an American journalist who is assigned to interview the Logins. He plays the role of the reader, an external observer learning of the unusual path of the Logins and developing himself along the way, inspired by what he sees. The entire story of the journalist was added in order to shed light on specific segments of Outfit7's development and culture, from which we can learn much.

The story of the company's development is almost entirely true to life and factual. Publicly available numbers, dates, locations, products, events and management practices were used, almost unchanged, in the book. All the more spiritual practices described in the book are also true. What has been left out or altered were aspects that were, in one way or another, trade secrets. An example of this is in the location and specifics of the sales negotiation detailed at the end of the book. On the company side, the story features real people whose names were changed-all but Iza and Samo Login, for whom this is something of an authorized biography.

To better understand their distinctive leadership system, the Flashlight Leadership model, detailed in the book, was developed, shortly after the sale of the company. However, it is based directly on the business practices of Outfit7 in the period before the sale, and other successful companies.

I have many people to thank for bringing this book into being.

First of all, thank you to both Iza and Samo Login, for the path we've walked together, in friendship and business, over many years. Thanks for your positive outlook, your energy, and all the time you've given me over the last year and a half, while creating this book. Without our many in-depth interviews, conversations, and fond reflections, this book certainly wouldn't have come to be.

Thanks also to all the co-founders and (former) employees of Outfit7 who participated in the preparation of this book. Your information was crucial in helping me cover all the details and fold in the pieces of this complex puzzle, resulting in the full picture, entitled 7 Unicorn Drive.

Thanks go to Noah Charney for his expert writing mentorship and for the final translation of the text, which is now more than just a translation — with your help, it has become a work of art in itself. That this was the case was also ensured by the precise eye and fluent language of proofreader Josh Rocchio.

The first external readers, especially Barbara Babnik and Irena Cerar, dissected the final text and "polished" where it was needed. Thanks go to them and to all the others who contributed their information and views in preparing this special story. And who helped keep my months of research and writing together in an unforgettable, beautiful memory.

Above all, thanks to my partner, Špela. You have stood by my side all this time and supported me in moments both smooth and rough. Thank you for simply being you.

My hope is that this story will open as many eyes as possible and warm many hearts around the world. To provide a long view and to feel where we are, where we wish to be and, above all, why. That we will be able to answer the question of how to be happy and successful at the same time, while developing ourselves at all levels, coexisting harmoniously with others and preserving our entire planet, Mother Earth.

The future is in our hands.

Dani Polajnar

About Iza, Samo, and Dani

———∞ ∞———

ABOUT IZA SIA AND SAMO LOGIN

Iza Sia Login and Samo Login have been a couple since high school. They were born in Slovenia but currently live in Cyprus. They both have an MSc in computer science, but the paths their careers took were quite different. After enjoying working together on academic and commercial projects in their college years, Iza held project management positions at Microsoft and Novartis, and, before launching Outfit7, ran her own holistic center. Before Outfit7, Samo served as founding Chief Technology Officer at a popular Slovenian search engine portal Najdi.si, which was acquired by Telekom Slovenija in 2009. Along with a team, the two founded Outfit7 Limited – one of the fastest-growing media entertainment companies on the planet, where Samo served as CEO and Iza as Deputy CEO.

They established the Login5 Foundation in 2013 with the purpose of creating "A World with Pure Air, Pure Water, and Pure Consciousness". They have been actively working on Login5 Foundation projects since the sale of Outfit7 in 2017, and their primary focus is on providing a better future for humankind in the most sustainable way. Their endeavors mainly center around sustainable crop and food production, as this challenge alone is big enough to deprive our children of a bright future if not solved in time.

The book you are holding focuses on another aspect, namely how to build modern teams and organizations that can achieve extraordinary results, results that are unthinkable to most people. They are sharing this with a purpose: to give everyone in the word the opportunity and knowledge to build better teams and to build a better world.

More about Login5 Foundation: www.login5.org

———————————∞ ∞———————————

ABOUT DANI POLAJNAR

Dani Polajnar is an author, keynote speaker, trainer and coach, with decades of experience in leadership and teamwork. He works with corporations from several industries to support them in shaping their corporate culture with one objective in mind: making their employees happy, engaged, and productive. His main mission is connecting people through the large pallet of his keynote speeches, leadership training, and corporate events. Polajnar actively researches new ways of thinking and understanding, which helps him connect and translate knowledge, skills, and spiritual practices of various cultures into the working environments of modern western organizations.

Dani is also a founder of the Teambuilding Academy (TBA), an organization devoted to building teams and strengthening bonds through high-end corporate events, training, and consulting.

More about Dani: www.danipolajnar.com
More about TBA: www.tbaeurope.com

The Unicorn Drive Method

———∞ ∞———

So, where does Iza and Samo's exhilarating story leave you, the reader?

Will you start owning your s#it? If so, you'll inevitably start paving your very own Unicorn Drive, whatever that may be or is yet to become, towards a purposeful and fulfilling life.

What you do next will determine whether this tale has borne fruits towards its purpose. If each reader becomes a ripple, soon the entire planet will be spreading Unicorn Drive's purpose like a tsunami. The purpose of such inspiring organizations is to answer the real needs of time and space, to anchor their own "Why?" at the center of their undertakings and construct their corporate culture around it.

No one can take your personal or organizational Unicorn Drive journey for you. That's why we put together a crystal clear and immersive method, which will help you take a path of your own: the Unicorn Drive Method.

It is a blueprint for how to turn your organization into a brilliant flashlight, covering both its individual components and their orchestration as a perfect whole.

Close this book powerfully, with intent. Then, explore the Unicorn Drive Method by visiting its official website and taking the next solid step or giant leap on your Unicorn Drive journey. And have fun doing it!

visit unicorndrive.com